On Sea & Land
Small Wars, Minor Actions and
Naval Brigades

On Sea & Land
Small Wars, Minor Actions and Naval Brigades

A Military History of the Royal Navy
Volume 2
1856–1881

ILLUSTRATED

Sir William Laird Clowes

LEONAUR

On Sea & Land
Small Wars, Minor Actions and Naval Brigades
A Military History of the Royal Navy
Volume 2
1856-1881
by Sir William Laird Clowes

ILLUSTRATED

Leonaur is an imprint of Oakpast Ltd

Copyright in this form © 2018 Oakpast Ltd

ISBN: 978-1-78282-762-7 (hardcover)
ISBN: 978-1-78282-763-4 (softcover)

http://www.leonaur.com

Publisher's Notes

Contents

The Second Opium War China, 1856-1860

The first China War, 1839-42, had not taught the lessons which it was designed to teach; and within a few years of its conclusion new difficulties began to arise between the British and the local authorities in various parts of the huge invertebrate empire. For a time, these were arranged as they arose, without resort to war; but they were arranged, unfortunately, in a manner which too often allowed the Chinese to remain in the belief that they had won diplomatic triumphs. The result was that both locally and at the capitals, the governing classes became steadily more and more inattentive to British remonstrances concerning acts of aggression, until, in 1856, the affair of the *Arrow*, and the vigorous action of Rear-Admiral Sir Michael Seymour (2), Commander-in-Chief in the East Indies, brought about the second China War, which lasted, with intermissions, for nearly four years.

The causes of the fresh outbreak of hostilities, (perhaps the best account of the origin and early part of the Second Chinese War is in G. C. Cooke's *China*, which has been freely made use of), are set forth in a dispatch which was sent by Seymour to the Admiralty on November 14th, 1856; and they may be thus summarised.

On October 8th, 1856, the *lorcha Arrow*, with a colonial register from the governor of Hong Kong, was boarded, while at anchor at Canton, by a Chinese officer and a party of soldiers, who, notwithstanding the protest of the English master, seized twelve of the crew, bound them, carried them off, and hauled down the British flag. Mr. Parkes, Her Majesty's consul, brought the matter before the Imperial High Commissioner, Yeh, and demanded the return of the twelve men by the officer who had abducted them, together with an apology, and an assurance that the flag should be respected in the future. Ultimately the men were sent back, but not in the public manner required; nor was any apology or assurance offered.

On October 11th, the matter was reported to Seymour by Sir

John Bowring, British Plenipotentiary in China, who suggested that an Imperial *junk* should be seized by way of reprisals. The making of the seizure was entrusted to Commodore the Hon. Charles Gilbert John Brydone Elliot, C.B., of the *Sibylle*, 40, senior officer in the Canton River, who was reinforced for the purpose with the *Barracouta*, 6, paddle, Commander Thomas Dyke Acland Fortescue, (posted, Sept, 7th, 1857), and the *Coromandel*, steam tender. A *junk* was duly captured, but, as it proved to be private property, it had to be presently released. Seymour then, (Oct. 18th), sent the *Encounter*, 14, screw, Captain George William Douglas O'Callaghan, and *Samson*, 6, paddle. Captain George Sumner Hand, to join the commodore, hoping that the display of force in the river would bring the High Commissioner to reason. It soon, however, became clear that that official was bent upon resistance.

In the meantime, Mr. Parkes proceeded to consult with Seymour and Bowring at Hong Kong, where it was decided to seize the defences of Canton, it being evident that any more moderate measures would, as usual, be interpreted by the Chinese as symptoms of weakness. Seymour accordingly moved his flagship, the *Calcutta*, 84, Captain William King Hall, C.B., as high above the Bogue Forts as her draft would permit; and, on the morning of October 23rd, proceeded towards Canton in the *Coromandel*, accompanied by the *Samson* and *Barracouta*, with detachments of Royal Marines, and boats' crews, from the *Calcutta*, *Winchester*, 50, Captain Thomas Wilson, and *Bittern*, 12, (condemned, and for some time awaiting sale), and with the commodore and the boats of the *Sibylle*.

On approaching Blenheim reach, the *Samson* and part of the force diverged up the Macao passage to keep that channel open, and to capture Blenheim fort, while the rear-admiral, with the *Coromandel* and *Barracouta*, went on, and anchored above the four Barrier Forts, about five miles below the city. The boats, being sent in, took possession of the works, two of which fired ere they were taken, and consequently suffered a slight loss. In the forts "were about 150 guns, from one foot bore, (a brass gun; journal of Capt. J. S. Hand), to four pounders."

The *Barracouta* was ordered to follow the *Samson*; and the commander-in-chief, having dismantled and burnt the forts, continued his route to Canton, off which he arrived at 2 p.m., and where he learnt that boats from the *Samson* and *Barracouta* had quietly occupied the Blenheim Fort, and also the Macao Fort, a strong island position mounting 86 guns.

Mr. Parkes formally announced Seymour's arrival to the High Commissioner, and explained not only what had been done, but also that further measures of like nature would be adopted unless reparation should be forthcoming. The High Commissioner chose to remain obdurate.

On the morning of October 24th, Sir Michael landed additional marines to aid detachments which were already ashore in Canton from the *Sibylle* and *Encounter* for the protection of the factory; and he himself went in the *Coromandel* to join the *Barracouta* off Macao Fort. Upon a preconcerted signal, the Bird's Nest Fort, mounting 8.5 guns, and a small fort, which being opposite the city, might have annoyed the factory, were seized without resistance. The Shameen Forts, at the head of the Macao passage, were subsequently treated in the same way; and all the guns and ammunition in them were rendered unserviceable or were destroyed.

Detecting no signs whatsoever of submission on the part of the Chinese, but rather a more intractable disposition than ever, Seymour landed the rest of his marines and a body of small-arm men to secure the factory, and stationed boats to guard against the approach of fire rafts, and attacks by water. This necessary work was superintended by Captain William King Hall, and the marines on shore were placed under Captain Penrose Charles Penrose, R.M., of the *Winchester*, while Captain Cowper, R.E., who had been sent for the purpose from Hong Kong, advised as to the strengthening of the weak points of the position. For the protection of American interests, officers, seamen, and marines were landed at the same time from the U.S. corvette *Portsmouth*, Commander Andrew H. Foote, U.S.N.

On October 25th possession was taken of Dutch Folly, a 50-gun fort on a small island opposite Canton; and it was garrisoned by 140 officers and men under Commander William Rae Rolland, of the *Calcutta*. All the defences of the city were then in British hands; and the commander-in-chief desired Mr. Parkes to write to the high commissioner that operations would cease when his Excellency should be prepared satisfactorily to settle the points in dispute.

His Excellency did not reply as Seymour had anticipated. At 12.30 p.m., a body of Chinese troops, part of a much larger force in its rear, attacked the position at the factory, in spite of Mr. Parkes's warning; but Penrose, with his marines, drove back the enemy, killing and wounding about 14 of them. On the 26th, it being Sunday, the men were allowed to rest.

Early on the morning of the 27th, Seymour caused a new letter to be written to the high commissioner, informing him that, since satisfaction had not been offered for the *Arrow* outrage, operations would be continued. At Bowring's suggestion an additional demand was made to the effect that all foreign representatives should be allowed the same free access to the city, and to the authorities at Canton, as was enjoyed under treaty at the other four ports, and denied at Canton only.

No reply being vouchsafed, fire was opened at 1 p.m. on the high commissioner's compound from the 10-in. pivot gun of the *Encounter*, and kept up at intervals of from five to ten minutes until sunset. At the same time, the *Barracouta*, from a position which she had taken up at the head of Sulphur Creek, shelled some troops who were on the hills behind Gough's Fort. The high commissioner retaliated by publicly offering a reward of 30 dollars for the head of every Englishman. A few gunners of the Royal Artillery, who had joined under Captain Guy Rotton, R.A., were that day stationed in the Dutch Folly, where two 32-prs. from the *Encounter* had been mounted.

On the 28th, these guns opened with the object of clearing a passage to the city wall. In the course of the day, Captain the Hon. Keith Stewart (2), of the *Nankin*, 50, joined the rear-admiral, with 140 of his men, and a couple of field-pieces; and 65 officers and men from the U.S. corvette *Levant* reinforced the American guard ashore. During the following night, the enemy apparently mounted guns on the city wall; and, anxious to give them no further opportunity for improving their defences, Seymour reopened fire early on the 29th. In the course of the morning. Commander William Thornton Bate, late of the *Bittern*, and acting Master Charles George Johnston, at some personal risk, ascertained that the breach was practicable; and a body of marines and small-arm men, about 300 in number, was told off for the assault, under the command of Commodore Elliot.

The rear-admiral accompanied the advance from the boats, which landed the force, and two field-pieces at 2 p.m. The seamen were led by the Commodore, Captain the Hon. Keith Stewart (2), and Commanders Bate and Holland, (posted, Aug. 10th, 1857); the marines by Captains Penrose, and Robert Boyle, R.M.; and the gun-detachment by Lieutenants James Henry Bushnell and James Stevenson Twysden; Bate gallantly showing the way, and carrying an ensign to the summit of the breach, the wall on each side of which was quickly occupied. Penrose moved to the gate next on the right, and, having signalled his presence there, opened it to a further detachment which was instantly landed under Captain William King Hall, Commander Fortescue, and Flag-Lieutenant George Campbell Fowler. (Com., Aug. 10th, 1857.) The gate was then blown to pieces, (by Capt. Rotton, R.A.), and the archway above it partially destroyed.

In the meantime, the guns had been placed in the breach, and had opened on some Chinese who began a desultory fire from their gingals, by which three people were killed, and eleven (two mortally) wounded. The latter were sent to Dutch Folly, where they were attended to by Surgeon Charles Abercromby Anderson, M.D., and Assistant-Surgeon George Bruce Newton. The rear-admiral, with the commodore and Mr. Parkes, visited the house of the high commissioner, and, at sunset, re-embarked with all his force, his object being, as he said in his dispatch, to demonstrate his power to enter the city. It is right, however, to add, that in the squadron the retirement was attributed to the impossibility of making a lodgement. (Hand: *Journal*. See also officer's letter in *Naut. Mag.*, 1857.) At all events, its moral effect was bad: and it is scarcely astonishing that, in the night, the enemy filled up the breach with sandbags and timber. On the 30th and two following mornings it was cleared again by fire from the ships.

Seymour once more wrote to the high commissioner, sending him indeed two letters, neither of which produced a satisfactory reply. In the interval, in order to protect the factory from the dangers of incendiary fires, the houses between it and the city were pulled down; and copies of the rear-admiral's letters, with a *précis* of the whole affair by Mr. Parkes, were distributed among the people through the medium of the native boatmen, who, in spite of what was going on, continued to furnish supplies to the ships. On the 31st, Captain Thomas Wilson joined, with 90 officers and men from his ship, the *Winchester*.

On November 3rd, the *Encounter, Samson*, and Dutch Folly began a slow fire on the government buildings in the Tartar city, and on Gough's Fort, and continued it till 5 p.m. Seymour also addressed yet another letter to the High Commissioner. At night an attempt was made to blow up the English clubhouse, in which were some seamen and marines; and, in consequence, no native boats were thereafter allowed to approach the sea-wall of the factory.

On the 4th, fire was resumed for four hours, and on the 5th, one of the *Samson's* 68-prs. in Dutch Folly threw shells into a distant fort on a hill behind the city. That day information was received to the effect that an attack was intended upon the ships and the factory, and that twenty-three war *junks* were at anchor below Dutch Folly, protected by French Folly Fort, which mounted 26 guns.

Commodore Elliot was ordered to take the *Barracouta, Coromandel*, and ships' boats, and disperse or capture the *junks*; and, Commander Bate having buoyed the narrow channel, the force proceeded at daylight on the 6th, and Fortescue presently anchored the *Barracouta* 800 yards above French Folly, and within 200 yards of the nearest of the hostile vessels, which were all ready for action. The *Barracouta*, in order to prevent the Chinese from training their guns on her, fired her bow pivot gun as she approached, and so provoked the enemy, who, from more than 150 pieces, retaliated ere she could bring her broadside to bear. In about five-and-thirty minutes, however, her grape and canister, and the approaching boats, under Captain Thomas Wilson, drove the people from their vessels; and the sloop was then able to give her undivided attention to French Folly, which, being soon silenced, was taken possession of by a landing-party under Captain King Hall. Its guns and ammunition were destroyed.

Two 32-prs. in Dutch Folly rendered material help during the engagement. The *junks*, being aground, or sunk, were burnt, with the exception of the admiral's ship, which was brought off, and two more, which escaped for the time, though one of them was afterwards burnt by Captain King Hall. Seymour mentions with praise the conduct of Commander Fortescue, of his senior Lieutenant, William Kemptown Bush, and of Lieutenant Henry Hamilton Beamish, of the *Calcutta*, who, under a very heavy fire, carried out the anchor by means of which the *Barracouta* was enabled to spring her broadside. (Her hull was pierced by 28 large shot, besides smaller ones. *Naut. Mag.*, 1857.) The affair, very bloody to the enemy, cost the British a loss of but 1 killed and 4 wounded.

On November 7th, the *Niger*, 13, screw, Captain the Hon. Arthur Auckland Leopold Pedro Cochrane, C.B., arrived from England; and a detachment from the frigate *Virginie* landed to protect French interests at the factory.

At 4 a.m. on the 8th, the squadron was suddenly alarmed by a bold attempt on the part of the enemy to destroy it with fire-vessels. The Chinese sailed four large *junks* down the river, and anchored them when they were close to the *Barracouta, Samson*, and *Niger*; whereupon they instantly burst into a blaze. The *Barracouta* must infallibly have been burnt had she not slipped her cable with extraordinary promptitude. The *junks* were backed up by war-boats; but no damage was done, except to the Chinese. To prevent any similar occurrence Seymour caused lines of *junks* to be drawn across the river, above and below the shipping; nor was the precaution needless. On the 12th, one of the *junks* of the upper line was burnt by means of a stinkpot; and on the 18th, two small fireboats which had been sent from the shore, exploded alongside the *Niger*. Thenceforward no native boats whatsoever were allowed within the lines of *junks*.

In the meantime, at the advice of Sir John Bowring, the rear-admiral threatened the high commissioner with the destruction of the Bogue forts; but, failing, as before, to coerce him into submission, he left Commodore Elliot, with the *Samson* and *Niger*, to protect the factory, and on the afternoon of the 11th proceeded in the *Encounter* below the Bogue, where he found the *Calcutta*, in which he rehoisted his flag, *Nankin*, 50, *Barracouta*, *Hornet*, 17, screw. Commander Charles Codrington Forsyth, just arrived from Hong Kong, and *Coromandel*. On the 12th, the *mandarin* in charge was summoned to deliver up the forts, pending the Emperor of China's decision concerning the conduct of the viceroy and high commissioner; and the *Calcutta* and *Nankin* were placed in positions favourable for action.

As the demand was refused, the ships opened fire at 10.45 a.m. against the two Wantung Islands forts from the Bremer Channel side; and, after a considerable but ill-directed resistance for about an hour, (majority of the logs make the time to have been nearer two hours), sent ashore parties which took possession of them. In the *Nankin* a boy was killed, and 4 men were wounded; but fortunately, there were no other casualties. The forts were fully manned, and mounted upwards of 200 guns; and they were stronger than when taken in 1841. On the 13th, the Anunghoy forts, on the opposite side of the Bogue, were attacked and taken in a similar manner. They mounted 210 guns, but were captured without loss to the British. On the 14th, the commander-in-chief returned to the *Niger* off Canton. Concluding his report of these events, Seymour wrote:—

> The command of the river being now in our hands, I have no operation in immediate contemplation beyond the security and maintenance of our position; and it will remain with H.M. Government to determine whether the present opportunity shall be made available to enforce to their full extent the treaty stipulations which the. Canton government has hitherto been allowed to evade with impunity. . . . The original cause of dis-

pute, though comparatively trifling, has now, from the injurious policy pursued by the Imperial High Commissioner, assumed so very grave an aspect as to threaten the existence of amicable relations as regards Canton. Though I shall continue to take steps, in conjunction with H.M. Plenipotentiary, in the hope of being able to bring matters to a successful termination, I shall be most anxious to receive the instructions of H.M. Government on this important question. (Seymour to Adlty., Nov. 14th.)

The *Encounter* was stationed close off the factory as a guard; and the *Samson* was sent below the Barrier forts to join the *Comus*, 14, Commander Robert Jenkins, which was subsequently moved to below the Bogue to protect trade, and was relieved by the *Hornet*. On December 2nd, the *Samson* was ordered to the neighbourhood of Hong Kong, where petty piracy had become very troublesome. While, however, Seymour allowed the Chinese a short respite, the foolish conduct of the *mandarins*, and the intractableness of Yeh, provoked a conflict with the United States' ships in the river.

On December 6th, at the back of Stonecutters' Island, near Hong Kong, the *Samson*, after an exciting chase of a couple of hours, drove ashore several *junks* and destroyed five, besides liberating two market boats with passengers on board. These petty pirates flew the flag of the Ti-ping rebels; and it was consequently somewhat difficult for Captain Hand to make certain of their true status until he caught them, as it were, red-handed. (Hand to Seymour, Dec. 6th, 1856. Hand took two more piratical boats on Dec. 29th, off Tongboo, he having been sent in the interim to Amoy.)

In the Canton River little was done by the British during the winter months, beyond what was rendered necessary by the provocative action of the Chinese. On December 6th, it became advisable to capture French Folly Fort, which had been reoccupied; and the work was easily accomplished by the *Encounter* and *Barracouta*, and landing parties from the squadron. On January 4th, 1857, an attack on Macao Fort, which was garrisoned by marines of the squadron, was repulsed with no greater difficulty; and, later in the course of the same month, an attempt by war *junks* on the ships in the Macao channel was frustrated by the action of the *Hornet, Comus, Encounter, Niger,* and *Coromandel.* In returning to Canton with stores for the squadron, the *Samson* had an experience which brought much adverse criticism upon her gallant captain, who, as will be seen, did not in the least deserve it.

On the morning of January 17th, 1857, while passing above the second bar, she fell in with a large fleet of *mandarin junks*, (fast armed craft, otherwise called "snake boats"), which opened a heavy fire on her, and mortally wounded her pilot. Hand returned the fire as he approached, and, when abreast of the enemy, gave the order to stop the engines, with the object, no doubt, of doing as much damage as possible ere he went on. But although the Chinese shot had hulled the steamer in a dozen places, and wounded three people. Commodore Elliot, who happened to be taking passage, directed the *Samson* to proceed. Hand admits in his journal that he believes that he did no harm to the enemy, but chivalrously says nothing about the commodore's order. I have the fact, however, from an officer who heard the order given.

The harrying tactics of the Chinese, who seldom left the squadron alone for many hours together, annoying it almost every night with rockets, fire rafts, and all sorts of devilments, led Rear-Admiral Seymour to doubt the possibility of keeping the river communication open with the small force at his disposal; and, learning from India that no troops could be spared thence, he was disposed partially to withdraw from his position. The *Niger* left her station off the factory and anchored abreast of Macao Fort; the *Encounter* did likewise; and Dutch Folly was evacuated, and instantly reoccupied and burnt by the enemy. But it was finally determined to hold Macao Fort, and to keep at least the lower reaches of the river open.

The *mandarin junks* which had attacked the *Samson* on January 17th, and which generally lay in Escape Creek, had a brush with the Hornet in February, and lost one of their number, a vessel mounting sixteen guns, some of which were British Board of Ordnance 32-prs.; but they remained very troublesome, and, as they were about 120 in number, the *Hornet* and *Samson* were for a time stationed off the mouth of the creek to observe them. In March, in Sandy Bay, the *Hornet* destroyed 17 large *lorchas* and *junks*. On April 6th, the two vessels, with the tenders, *Hongkong* and *Sir Charles Forbes*, stood in to Deep Bay, as far as the depth of water would permit, in search of some *junks*, and, finding several, sent their boats, and those of the *Sibylle* and *Nankin*, up a creek, where 11 *junks* and 2 *lorchas* were taken and destroyed.

Numerous other craft were taken or burnt up and down the coast during the six or seven weeks following; and in the course of that period the British force in the river was reinforced; but the *Raleigh*, 50,

Commodore the Hon. Henry Keppel, C.B., one of the vessels which should have joined the flag, struck on an obstruction between Hong Kong and Macao on April 14th, and had to be beached between the Koko and Typa Islands, where she ultimately became a total loss. Keppel shifted his broad pennant to the *Alligator* (hospital ship), and managed to save all his stores, guns, etc.

At about the same time there arrived the good news that, although there was nothing like unanimity in England on the Chinese question, and although Seymour and Bowring were held to have acted imprudently, 5000 troops were to be sent out, and strong measures were to be adopted for the settlement of all difficulties, seeing that the action of those on the spot had put the credit of the country at stake, and that it must be supported.

Towards the end of May, therefore, active operations were resumed, the first blows being dealt at the troublesome *mandarin* fleet in Escape Creek, an eastward branch of the Canton River, (See Map following), by a flotilla under the orders of Commodore Elliot.

On May 25th, Elliot went on board the tender *Hongkong*, and, followed by the gunboats *Bustard*, Lieutenant Tathwell Benjamin Collinson, *Staunch*, (which seems to have subsequently fallen astern), Lieutenant Leveson Wildman, and *Starling*, Lieutenant Arthur Julian Villiers, and the tender *Sir Charles Forbes*, in the order named, towing boats manned from the *Sibylle, Raleigh, Tribune, Hornet, Inflexible,* and *Fury,* steamed into the creek, and soon sighted 41 *junks,* which were moored across the stream, and which opened a spirited fire from their guns—in each case a 24- or 32-pr. forward, and four or six 9-prs. The attacking craft then formed in line in as wide order as possible, and replied warmly, the Chinese sticking to their guns wonderfully well, but finally cutting their cables, hoisting their sails, getting out their sweeps, and fleeing further up. The steamers pursued until they grounded; and then their people abandoned them temporarily, and, jumping into the boats, pulled hard after the enemy.

One by one, several of the *junks* were overhauled. In most cases the Chinese, when a boat got alongside, fired a last broadside of grape and langridge at her, leapt overboard on the other side, and swam for shore. Thus, sixteen craft were disposed of in the main channel, by boats led by Captain Harry Edmund Edgell, of the *Tribune*, 31, screw. Ten more took refuge up a minor creek on the left, and were chased by a division of boats under Commander Charles Codrington Forsyth; whereupon their crews set them on fire and abandoned them.

THE MOUTH OF THE CANTON RIVER.

One vessel, which made for a creek on the right, was abandoned so hastily that her people had no time to fire her; and she was taken and towed out. The other *junks* got away by dint of hard pulling. The heat was terrible, and, although there were only two casualties from the enemy's shot, some damage was done by sunstroke.

In addition to some of the officers named above, the following were mentioned by the commodore with approval, in consequence of their share in that day's work: Commander John Corbett, (posted, Aug. 10th, 1857); Lieutenants Arthur Metivier Brock, (coms., Aug. 10th, 1857), and Edward Frederic Dent; acting-Mates Ralph Abercrombie Otto Brown, (actg. lieut., May 25th, 1857), and Thomas Keith Hudson, (actg. lieut. Aug. 10th, 1857), and Second-Master John Molloy.

On the following day, the outlets into the main stream of all the creeks communicating with Escape Creek were guarded: the Sawshee channel by the *Tribune*, Captain Harry Edmund Edgell; the Second Bar Creek by the *Inflexible*, Commander John Corbett; and Escape Creek itself by the *Hornet*, Commander Charles Codrington Forsyth, the idea being to scour the inland waters, and oblige all *junks* in them either to fight or to flee towards the guarded passages. At daybreak on the 27th, the commodore and the boats, towed for ten or twelve miles by the steamers, proceeded up the Sawshee channel. About ten miles above where the steamers had been left, the city of Touan-Kouan was sighted, and the mastheads of many war *junks* were observed over the land.

The boats, although threatened by a small battery, pulled on with such speed as to take the enemy completely by surprise. Both battery and *junks* were abandoned almost as soon as the boats opened fire on them; and orders were at *once* given to destroy all the vessels except one, the finest and heaviest armed war *junk* Elliot had ever seen in China. Owing, however, to the opposition of the enemy, who plied their *gingals* from among the houses on the banks of the narrow creek, all the *junks* had to be burnt. Even this could not be accomplished until landings had been effected to clear the neighbourhood. The force then withdrew. Elliot, in his letter to Seymour, says nothing about the number of people wounded; but it was much more considerable than on the 25th.

★★★★★★

No one was killed; but 31 people were wounded, including Lieuts. Francis Martin Norman (*Tribune*), and Henry Edmund Bacon (*Inflexible*); Mids. Arthur Edward Dupuis, and Edward

18

Pilkington (*Inflexible*); and Asst.-Surg. Miles Monk Magrath (*Inflexible:*).

★★★★★★

He mentions, however, with approval Captain Edgell; Commanders Forsyth, (posted, Aug. 10th, 1857), Corbett, (posted, Aug. 10th, 1857), and Edward Winterton Turnour, (posted, Aug. 10th, 1857), (late of the *Raleigh*); Lieutenants Edward Nares, and William Lowley Staniforth, (com., Aug. 10th, 1857); acting-Mate Thomas Keith Hudson; Chaplain and Naval Instructor the Rev. Samuel Beal, who was very useful as Chinese interpreter, and Lieutenant George Lascelles Blake, R.M. (Elliot to Seymour, May 29th.)

During all this time the Chinese force, consisting of the large fleet of war *junks* which had attacked Macao Fort on January 4th, and which had afterwards tried to block the Macao channel, lay in Fatshan Creek. The commander-in-chief had been for some days at Hong Kong, when, leaving Captain William King Hall there in the *Calcutta*, he embarked on May 29th in the paddle tender *Coromandel*, Lieutenant Sholto Douglas, and, accompanied by several gunboats, and by the boats of the flagship, under Commander William Rae Holland, (posted, Aug. 10th, 1857), entered the Canton River and proceeded as far as the second bar.

Actions at Fatshan Creek pic

His immediate object was to deal with the *junks* in Fatshan Creek, as those in Escape Creek had been already dealt with by Commodore Elliot. Some way up the creek, and nearly south of Canton, is Hyacinth Island, a flat expanse which very much narrows the channels. On the south side of the creek is a high hill, upon which the Chinese had built a 19-gun fort; opposite to it was a 6-gun battery; in the channel, moored so as to command the passage, were seventy *junks*; and the whole position was so strong as to be deemed impregnable by those who held it. Seymour caused his force to make rendezvous on May 31st, a short distance below the obstruction; and before dawn on June 1st he led to the attack in the *Coromandel*, with the *Haughty* following, each vessel having on board a detachment of seamen, under Commodore Elliot, and marines, under Captain Robert Boyle, R.M., and towing boats manned and armed.

19

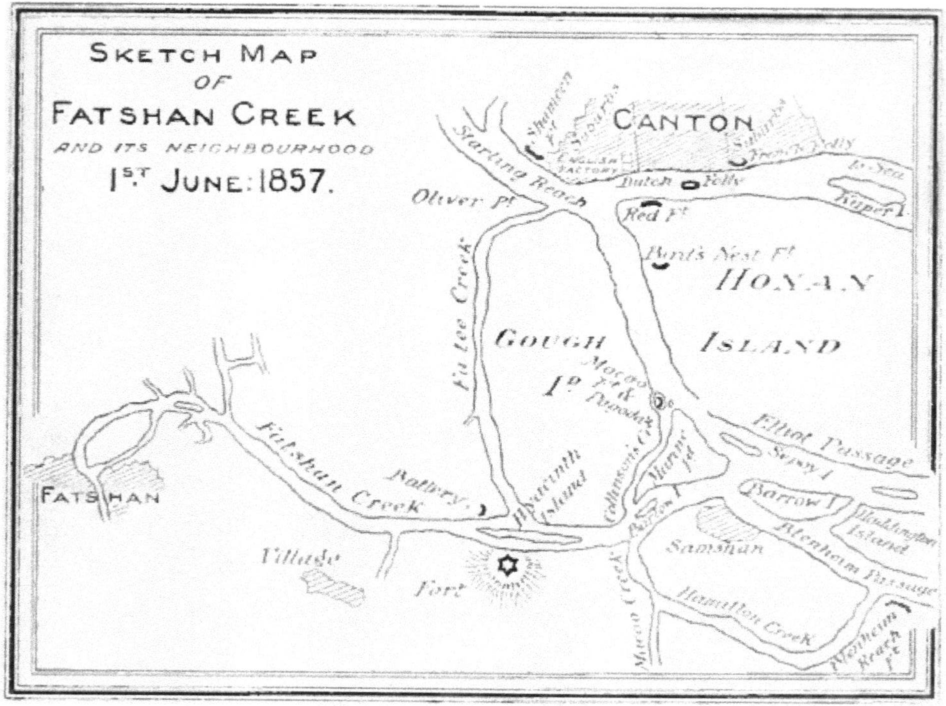

SKETCH MAP
OF
FATSHAN CREEK
AND ITS NEIGHBOURHOOD
1ST JUNE: 1857.

CANTON

HONAN ISLAND

GOUGH

Shameen Pt

Oliver Pt

Starling Reach

Fu lee Creek

Battery Creek

Fatshan Creek

FATSHAN

Village

Fort

Hyacinth Island

Macoa Pt
1st Torpedo

California Passage Mump

Missia Creek

1st Passage Mump

Asia Mump

Sinshan

Hamilton Creek

Elliot Passage

Sewy I

Barrow

Washington Island

Blenheim Passage

3rd Passage

To Sea

Rupert I

Hog's Nest I

Red Fort

Dutch Folly

Creek Folly
Fort

Shameen Creek

This force constituted the first division, the mission of which was to capture the 19-gun fort and its outworks. Commodore the Hon. Henry Keppel, in the *Hongkong*, Lieutenant James Graham Goodenough, with the second, third, and fourth divisions, was ordered, upon seeing the assaulting party mounting the hill, to advance up the channel on the other side of Hyacinth Island, and attack the *junks*.

Vessels employed in the action in Fatshan Creek :—

Coromandel, padd. tender	R.-Adm. Sir Michael Seymour (2), K.C.B.
	Lieut. Sholto Douglas (Com., Ap. 28th, 1858).
Hongkong, padd. tender .	Commod. Hon. Henry Keppel, C.B.
	Lieut. James Graham Goodenough (Com., Feb. 26th, 1858).
Haughty, scr. g.-b. .	Commod. Hon. Chas. Gilb. Jno. Brydone Elliot, C.B.
	Lieut. Richard Vesey Hamilton (Com., Aug. 10th, 1857).
Plover, scr. g.-b.	Lieut. Keith Stewart (3).
Opossum, scr. g.-b. . .	Lieut. Colin Andrew Campbell (Com., Feb. 26th, 1858).
Bustard, scr. g.-b. . .	Lieut. Tathwell Benj. Collinson.
Forester, scr. g.-b. . .	Lieut. Arthur John Innes.
Starling, scr. g.-b. . .	Lieut. Arthur Julian Villiers.
Staunch, scr. g.-b. . .	Lieut. Leveson Wildman.

and boats from the *Calcutta*, *Nankin*, *Raleigh*, *Tribune*, *Highflyer*, *Inflexible*, *Niger*, *Sibylle*, *Hornet*, *Fury*, *Elk*, *Acorn*, and *Cruiser*.

Sir Michael Seymour, in his dispatch, gives the following account of what occurred:—

The flight of several signal rockets showed that the Chinese were fully alive to our proceedings. When within about 1000 yards of the fort, the *Coromandel* grounded on a barrier of sunken *junks* filled with stones; and the enemy opened fire. The leading party of seamen and marines were immediately put in the boats, and sent ahead; and, under a very heavy fire of round and grape, in which the *junk* fleet joined, the fort was almost immediately in our possession, Commodore Elliot setting the good example of being one of the first in it. The landing was partially covered by the fire of the *Haughty*. One or two of the guns in the fort were immediately turned on the war *junks*. Happily, this important service was effected without loss.

The position was a remarkably strong one, and, defended by a body of resolute troops, might have bid defiance to any attack. The *Haughty*, having landed her party, went on, with Commodore Elliot and the boats of the first division, to co-operate with Commodore Keppel. I ordered a portion of the Royal Marines, under Lieutenant and Adjutant Burton, (Lieut. Cuthbert Ward Burton, R.M.), to remain as a garrison in the fort, and sent Captain (Robert) Boyle R.M., with the remainder, about 150 in number, to the scene of operations by land, to cut off the enemy retreating from the *junks*, and to prevent the advancing boats being annoyed by *gingals* or matchlocks from a large village adjoining—a favourite tactic with the Chinese. One half of this force was ultimately sent back to the fort, and the remainder rejoined the squadron up the creek.

As soon as Commodore the Hon. H. Keppel perceived the men of the first division ascending the heights, he advanced up the channel on the east side of Hyacinth Island, with the gun and other boats of the second, third, and fourth divisions, in the order stated in the programme. With the exception of the *Haughty* and *Plover*, the gunboats soon grounded, but, agreeably with my instructions, the boats were pushed ahead. The *junks*, which were admirably moored in position to enfilade the whole of the attacking force, soon opened a very heavy fire, keeping it up with great spirit, until our boats were close alongside, when the crews commenced to abandon their vessels, and to effect their escape across the paddy fields. The blowing up of one or two *junks* hastened this movement. In about twenty minutes we had possession of fifty *junks*.

Leaving the third and fourth divisions to secure the prizes, Commodore Keppel then proceeded about three miles further up the creek, where more mastheads were visible; and found twenty *junks* moored across the stream in a very strong position, which opened such a well-directed and destructive fire that he was obliged to retire, and wait for reinforcements. The launch of the *Calcutta* was sunk by a round shot; the commodore's galley had three round shot through her; and several other boats were much injured.

On additional boats coming up, the commodore shifted to the *Calcutta's* black barge, (in this he returned to the *Hongkong*, where he shifted into the late *Raleigh's* cutter), and again advanced; and, after a severe action, the enemy gave way. They were pursued as far as Fatshan, a distance of seven miles, and seventeen of them captured and burnt. In consequence of my orders not to molest this large and important city, the three *junks* which passed through the creek on which it is built effected their escape.

The result of this expedition was the capture of between seventy and eighty heavily-armed *junks*, mounting, on an average, from ten to fourteen guns (many of them long 32-pounders), nearly all of European manufacture. As no object would have been gained by removing the prizes, I caused them, with a few exceptions, to be burnt; and the flames and numerous heavy explosions must have been seen and heard far and wide.

This engagement opens a new era in Chinese naval warfare. Great judgment was shown in selecting the position for the fleet; and the Chinese, particularly the last division attacked by Commodore Keppel, defended their ships with skill, courage, and effect.

I enclose a list of casualties, which, I regret to say, is large, amounting to 3 officers, and 10 seamen and marines, killed, and 4 officers, and 40 seamen and marines wounded; but it is to me a matter of surprise that, under the circumstances of the case, the loss was not greater.

★★★★★★

Note:—The officers killed were Master's-Assistant E. C. Bryan (*Highflyer*), Mids. H. Barker (*Tribune*), and Major Kearney. The officers wounded were Capt. Hon. A. A. L. P. Cochrane; Lieut. John Stanley Graham; and Mids. Edward Pilkington, and Henry Nelson Hippisley. Master's-Assistant H. Staunch, who was slightly hurt, is not included.

★★★★★★

Declaring that all did their duty, the commander-in-chief recommended the Admiralty, in the bestowal of marks of its approval, to have regard to the seniority and services of those engaged. He mentioned by name only the two commodores, (Keppel, in consequence, was made a K.C.B., and Elliot a C.B. on Sept. 12th, 1857), and Master George Raymond, of the *Encounter*, (then lying off Macao), who had volunteered his services as pilot, and taken the *Hongkong* up Fatshan Creek—"a service of danger." Nor did Keppel, in his letter, dated from "the *Raleigh's* tender, *Sir Charles Forbes*," on July 2nd, single out individuals for special praise, beyond saying that Captain the Hon. Arthur Auckland Leopold Pedro Cochrane led the final seven miles' chase; but in a letter to his sister, the Hon. Mrs. H. F. Stephenson, the commodore gives some characteristic details. After describing the grounding of the *Hongkong*, Keppel goes on:—

Took with the Prince Victor of Hohenlohe, (H.S.H. Prince Victor F. F. E. A. C. F., of Hohenlohe-Langenberg, Count Gleichen, died a retired vice-admiral in 1891, he was a nephew of Queen Victoria), having previously been commanded by Her Majesty, through Sir Charles Phipps, to take every care of him, and left Victor Montagu, my proper gig's mid., on board; but the lifting tide soon put him in the midst. (Hon, Victor Alexander Montagu, retd. as a Capt., 1877.) The first division of the Chinese were attacked simultaneously by about 1900 men. I had not more than a quarter of that number to attack the second division, which was three miles higher up the river. . . . Boarding nets were dropped on our boats, but not until our men were alongside; and it enabled them all the quicker to sever the cables connecting the *junks*.

Raleigh's boats well up, and did not require cheering on. The Chinese fired occasional shots to ascertain exact distance, but did not open their heaviest fire until we were within 600 yards. Nearly the first fellow cut in two by a round shot was an amateur, Major Kearney, (D.A.Q.G. of China Exped. Force) . . . . We cheered, and were trying to get to the front when a shot struck our boat, killing the bow man. Another was cut in two. Prince Victor leant forward to bind up the man's arm with his neckcloth. While he was so doing, a shot passed through both sides of the boat, wounding two more of the crew: in short, the boat was sunk under us. . . .

The tide rising, boats disabled, our oars shot away, it was necessary to re-form. I was collared, and drawn from the water by young Michael Seymour, (later Adm. Sir Michael Culme-Seymour, G.C.B.), a mate of his uncle's flagship, the *Calcutta*. We were all picked up except the dead bow man. . . As we retired, I shook my fist at the *junks*, promising I would pay them off. We went to the *Hongkong*, and re-formed. I hailed Lieutenant Graham, (Lieut. James Stanley Graham, of the *Calcutta*, died a Capt., Feb. 3rd, 1873), to get his boat ready, as I would hoist the broad pennant for next attack in his boat. I had no sooner spoken than he was down, the same shot killing and wounding four others. Graham was one mass of blood: but it was from a marine who stood next to him, part of whose skull was forced three inches into another man's shoulder.

When we reached the *Hongkong*, the whole of the Chinese fire appeared to be centred on her. She was hulled twelve times in a few minutes. Her deck was covered with the wounded who had been brought on board from different boats. From the paddle-box we saw that the noise of guns was bringing up strong reinforcements. The account of our having been obliged to retire had reached them. They were pulling up like mad. The *Hongkong* had floated, but grounded again. A bit of blue bunting, (Keppel was then commod. of the Blue, or third class), was prepared to represent a broad pennant, and I called out, 'Let's try the row-boats once more, boys,' and went over the side into our cutter (*Raleigh's*), in which were Turnour, (Edward Winterton Turnour, late com. of the *Raleigh*), and the faithful coxswain, Spurrier, (wounded).

At this moment there arose from the boats, as if every man took it up at the same instant, one of those British cheers so full of meaning that I knew at once it was all up with John Chinaman. They might sink twenty boats, but there were thirty others which would go ahead all the faster. It was indeed an exciting sight. A move among the *junks!* They were breaking ground and moving off, the outermost first. This the Chinese performed in good order, without slacking fire. Then commenced an exciting chase for seven miles. As our shot told they ran mostly on to the mud banks, and their crews forsook them. Young Cochrane, (captain of the *Niger*, who was wounded, he was then 33, but his father, Adm. Lord Dundonald, was alive), in his light gig got the start of me. . . . Seventeen *junks* were overtaken and captured. Three only escaped. . . . (Keppel, iii. The letter was printed in the *Times*.)

These operations had a great moral effect upon the Chinese, and would, perhaps, have inclined them to listen to reason and to concede Seymour's demands, had it been found possible to follow them up promptly and with vigour. Unhappily, as will be seen, the sky was just then black for England, and she could not for the time concentrate her attention on the Chinese question, having to wrestle elsewhere for the very life of her Eastern Empire.

It may be mentioned here that, at the beginning of June, the *Samson*, being away on detached duty, learnt of the presence of some piratical *junks* in Mirs Bay, off which place Captain Hand accordingly presented himself early in the morning of June 8th. Getting out three of his boats, under Lieutenant George Henry Wale, (com. Feb. 26th,

1858), he sent them to cut off a craft which was seen standing into Double Haven, and himself went round in the frigate to Crooked Harbour, where he came upon a pirate mounting nine guns, and having 70 men, all of whom leapt overboard and made for the shore, only to be massacred there by the villagers.

Wale, after some resistance had been offered, took two *lorchas* and a *junk*, mounting in all 22 guns, which were convoyed to Hong Kong, where owners were found, and salvage money paid for them. They had apparently been captured by the other vessel. (Hand to Seymour, June 9th.) Commander John Corbett, in the *Inflexible*, took a pirate at about the same time. It may be mentioned, too, that on June 18th, the most southern of the defences of the Canton River, near the Bogue, and known as Chuenpee, was occupied by the British without resistance, and found to have been not only abandoned, but also partly dismantled. It was entrusted to the command of Captain Edgell, of the *Tribune*. On July 6th, the *Samson* towed the *Alligator*, bearing Keppel's pennant, to Hong Kong. (Keppel soon afterwards went home, Sir Charles Wood disapproving of his hoisting a broad pennant, in view of the loss of the *Raleigh*.)

France, like Great Britain, had with China treaties which were not observed, and her squadron in Chinese waters would have made common cause with Seymour's at once, had it been a little stronger than it was. The French Government, however, unwilling to let slip so good an occasion for settling long-standing difficulties, decided to strengthen its forces, so as to enable it to act with effect, and to send out Baron Gros with instructions to co-operate with Lord Elgin, (James Bruce, 8th Earl of Elgin and Kincardine, Kt.), who was being despatched from England with special powers to treat concerning all pending questions. Rear-Admiral Rigault de Genouilly, who went out in the *Nemesis*, 50, arrived in Chinese waters on July 8th, 1857, and, on the 15th of the same month, superseded Rear-Admiral Guerin. Thenceforward he was reinforced from time to time. Baron Gros did not reach China until October. (Chevalier.)

In the meantime, large reinforcements, naval as well as military, had been sent out from England; and the *Shannon*, 51, screw, Captain William Peel, C.B., had conveyed Lord Elgin to the scene of action. But Elgin, on reaching Singapore, had learnt of the outbreak of the Mutiny in India, and, not underrating its character, had wisely taken upon himself to divert thither the troops intended for China. On July 14th, still graver news reached Seymour, who was then preparing for a trip with Lord Elgin to the gulf of Pechili; and he thereupon sent to Calcutta the *Shannon*, with 300 marines who had arrived in China in the *Sans Pareil*, 70, screw, Captain Astley Cooper Key, C.B., together with the *Pearl*, 21, screw, Captain Edward Southwell Sotheby. The two ships sailed on July 15th, and, as will be shown later, were able to render most valuable services.

The *Sans Pareil* herself also proceeded in August to Calcutta with artillery and stores, but did not, as the other ships did, land a Brigade for service with the troops in the interior of India. (She was towed 745 miles of the way by the *Samson*, which expended 245 tons of coal on the run. Hand's *Journal*.) A party from her garrisoned Fort William for a time, but she returned to the Canton River on December 17th, in time for the operations then pending. Lord Elgin, seeing that, until the major danger should be crushed, little could be done in China, retired to Calcutta, to await a better opportunity, and left Seymour to blockade the Canton River. The blockade was declared as from August 7th, and, in the opinion of naval officers on the spot, was established not so much to annoy the Chinese as to prevent foreign vessels from going up to load, and so getting the trade into their hands at a time when the British and French were unable to enjoy a share of it. (Hand's *Journal*.)

Lord Elgin returned to Hong Kong at the end of September, but for some time afterwards nothing could be done, owing to the slowness with which the French squadron was reinforced, and to the absence of troops. Although, however, the 5000 men originally intended for China had, as has been shown, been diverted from their destination to meet the pressing need in India, 1500 men under General Charles T. van Straubenzee, chiefly Royal Marines, Royal Artillery, the 59th Regiment, and the 38th Madras Native Infantry, were placed at Seymour's disposal.

On December 10th, the French squadron anchored at the Bogue; and Rear-Admiral Rigault de Genouilly issued a proclamation to the effect that from the 12th he should associate himself with his British colleague in the blockade of the river. On the 13th he took his force up to Whampoa; and on the day following, Seymour, transferring his flag to the *Coromandel*, also proceeded to the front with the British gunboats.

A bloody and lamentable affair occurred on December 14th. Lieutenant Bedford Clapperton Tryvellion Pim, commanding the gunboat *Banterer*, took his second gig, with fourteen people in her besides himself, up a winding creek opposite High Island to a point near the town of Sai-lau, where, leaving two men in charge, he landed with the rest of his party and entered the place. His object, according to the correspondent of the *Illustrated London News*, who accompanied him, was partly recreation and partly information. On his return, he found that a number of Chinamen were assailing the two boat-keepers with brickbats. He charged the mob, and so got the whole of his people to the boat; but no sooner were they onboard than a sharp fire was opened upon them with *gingals*, and later with a small gun.

Pim, who displayed extraordinary personal courage, conducted the retreat along the narrow creek, standing in the stern-sheets, and using his revolver with great effect; but the fire was so hot, and victory seemed so hopeless, that one by one the people who were in a condition to do so waded ashore, and bolted in the direction of the *Nankin*, whose hull was visible over the paddy fields. Pim stuck to the boat until every other living person had deserted her, and then, using his last cartridge to shoot the Chinese leader, also leapt to land and took to his heels. Of fifteen people in the boat, five were killed outright, one died afterwards, and five more, including Pim, who was hit in six places, were wounded.

On the15th, the *Nankin*, by way of reprisals, shelled Sai-lau, and landed 250 men, who, after a determined resistance, entered the place, part of which they burnt, not, however, without suffering a loss of four wounded. Pim's expedition was a most foolhardy one, and, seeing that little or no good could possibly have been derived from it, should never have been undertaken. (*Ill. Lond. News*, Feb. 27th, 1858. Cooke.) A court of inquiry, nevertheless, found that he was justified in all he had done. His gallantry gained him his promotion on April 19th, 1858. (Pim, Capt. Ap. 16th, 1868; retd. rear-adm. July 5th, 1885: died, 1886.)

On December 15th, the marines, and a French detachment intended for the attack on Canton, were landed without opposition on the island of Honan, where they found excellent quarters; and in the course of the next few days the lighter vessels of the combined fleet were all stationed in readiness for the projected attack upon Canton.

★★★★★★

The stations of the larger vessels of the allied fleets during the bombardment were, beginning at the eastward end of the line:—

Ships.	Guns.	Commanders.	Stations.
Fr. *Primauguet*, scr. . .	8	Com. Vriguaud	Outside east end of
Fr. *Durance*, scr. . . .	4	Lieut. Thoyon	Kuper Island.
Br. *Furious*, pad. . . .	16	Capt. Sherard Osborn, C.B.	
Fr. *Dragonne*, scr. g.-v. .	4	Lieut. Barry	Off French Folly.
Br. *Surprise*, scr. g.-v. .	4	Com. Saml. Gurney Cress- well	Off S.E. corner of wall.
Fr. *Marceau*, scr. disp. v.	4	Com. Lefer de La Motte	
Br. *Nimrod*, scr. g.-v. .	6	Com. Roderick Dew	Outside the island (with
Fr. *Avalanche*, scr. g.-v. .	4	Lieut. Lafond	gunboats).
Br. *Niger*, scr. . . .	13	Capt. Hon. A. A. L. P. Cochrane	
Br. *Hornet*, scr. . . .	17	Com. Wm. Montagu Dowell	Off Yeh's Yamen.
Br. *Cruiser*, scr. . .	17	Com. Chas. Fellowes	
Br. *Bittern*, sailg. . .	12	Lieut. Jas. Graham Good- enough	Outside Dutch Folly.
Fr. *Mitraille*, scr. g.-v. .	4	Lieut. Béranger	
Fr. *Fusée*, scr. g.-v. . .	4	Lieut. Gabrielli de Car- pégua	Inside Dutch Folly.
Br. *Actæon*, surv.. .	—	Capt. Wm. Thornton Bate	Off the Factories (with
Fr. *Phlégéton*, scr. . .	8	Com. Lévêque	gunboats).
Br. *Hesper*, scr. store-s. .	—	Mast. Jas. Stephen Hill	Off N.W. of Honan
Br. *Acorn*, sailg. . . .	12	Com. Arth. Wm. Acland Hood	Island.

★★★★★★

A final demand for satisfaction and concession had been sent to Commissioner Yeh on December 12th, and ten days had been assigned to him wherein to reply. In the interim, a battery for mortars was erected on Dutch Folly rock, and a conference of the allied chiefs was held on board the *Audacieuse*, the headquarters of Baron Gros.

Captain Chevalier explains very lucidly the situation, and the difficulties which confronted the allied admirals, he says:

The task to be performed with the feeble means at their disposal was to strike a blow worthy of the strength of France and England, and, at the same time, of such a nature as to destroy Commissioner Yeh's illusions on the subject of the possibility of resisting the allies. It was one thing to make a way into Canton by main force, and altogether another thing to maintain oneself, with a few thousand men, in a city of a million inhabitants. Nor was there any doubt that, if order should cease to reign there, part of the Chinese population would give itself up to pillage, and would commit acts of brigandage which would strike at the honour of the two nations. In order to avoid such misfortunes, the admirals and the general, after careful study, made the following dispositions. The gunboats and the lighter vessels, going in as close as their draught of water would permit, were to

SKETCH MAP OF CANTON AND NEIGHBOURHOOD
DEC. 1857

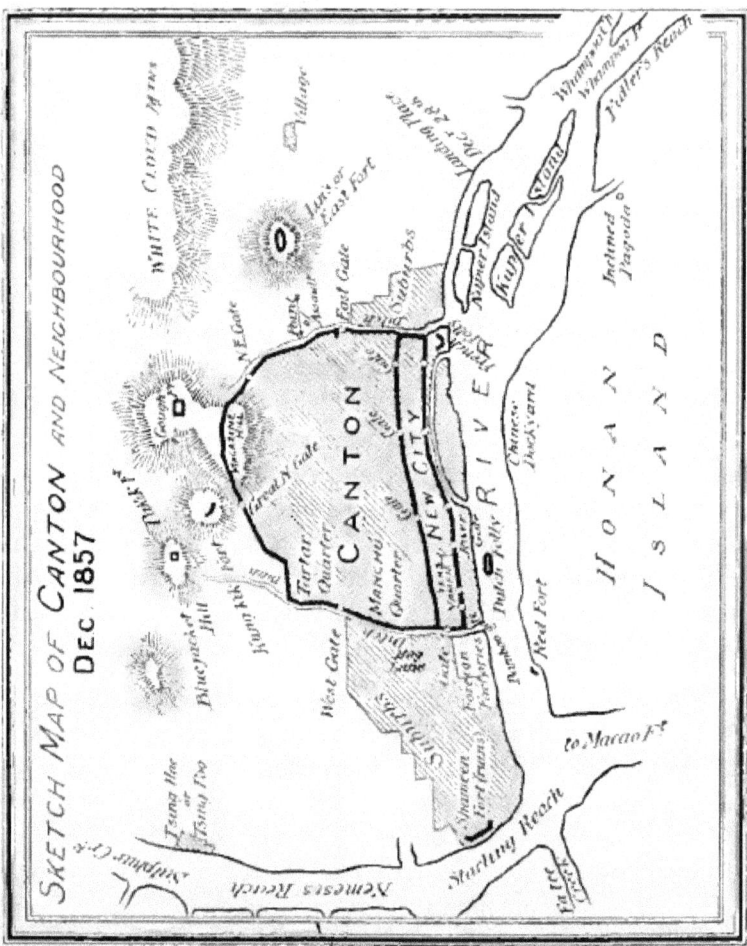

bombard the south face of the massive walls which surrounded Canton, so that the resulting breach would prevent the Chinese troops from communicating by way of the walls with the eastern portion. The expeditional corps, landed on that same side of the city, was to make its way along the walls, its aim being the capture of the positions which command Canton on the north. Supposing the double operation to succeed, the allies would hold Canton under the guns of the forts on the north, and under those of the squadron, which would still be ready to open on the south side; and it would then be seen whether the Imperial Commissioner would accept, without further delay, the terms offered to him.

Active hostilities were not resumed until daybreak on December 28th, when, it having become clear that the Chinese authorities would not give way an inch unless forced to do so, a general bombardment of the city was opened by the ships of the combined fleets, thirty-two in number, while the troops from Honan Island, and a French naval Brigade, were conveyed to the place of disembarkation, a point about two miles below French Folly.

After the army and the French had landed, the British Naval Brigade, of 1500 men, commanded by Commodore Elliot, and formed in three divisions under Captains the Hon. Keith Stewart (2) (*Nankin*), Astley Cooper Key (*Sans Pareil*), and Sir Robert John Le Mesurier M'Clure (*Esk*), also disembarked, and advanced to some rising ground to the eastward of the city.

★★★★★★

With the First Division were Capt. Geo. Sumner Hand (*Samson*), and Coms. Jno. Fane Chas. Hamilton (*Elk*), and Geo. Aug. Cooke Brooker (*Inflexible*), and parties from the *Nankin, Sibylle, Samson, Racehorse,* and *Inflexible*: with the Second Division were Coms. Arth. Wm. Acland Hood (*Acorn*), and Julian Foulston Slight (*Sans Pareil*), and parties from the *Calcutta, Sans Pareil,* and *Acorn,* and from Macao Fort: with the Third Division were Capts. Sherard Osborn, C.B., and Hon. A. A. L. P. Cochrane, C.B., and Coms. Wm. Montagu Dowell (*Hornet*), and Chas. Fellowes (*Cruiser*), and parties from the *Highflyer, Esk, Niger, Furious, Hornet,* and *Cruiser*. Genl. Order of Dec. 26th.

★★★★★★

Lin Fort, a work on the same side, was quickly seized by the French and the 59th; but the naval advance was checked; and the Brigade ultimately took up a position for the night in some buildings about 800 yards to the right of Gough's Fort, which annoyed it with a desultory fire during the hours of darkness. On the morning of the 29th the Brigade joined the rest of the force for the storm, and moved up behind a hillock, about 800 yards from the east gate, where the men had breakfast.

At about that time, while examining the ditch and wall, and pointing out to Seymour a good place for scaling, Captain William Thornton Bate, of the *Actaeon*, a most valuable officer, and a noted surveyor, was shot dead with a *gingal* ball. (Mids. Henry Thompson, of the *Sans Pareil*, was mortally wounded by a rocket at about the same time.) At 8.30, the scaling ladders were sent to the front, under Commander John Fane Charles Hamilton, (*Elk*), (posted, Feb. 26th, 1858); and at 8.45 the general advance was sounded, the point chosen for escalade being one which was sheltered by an angle of the wall from the fire of Gough's Fort. The French assaulted at a point 500 yards distant, and were the first up, but only by a minute or two. Commander Charles Fellowes, (posted, Feb. 26th, 1858), of the *Cruiser*, is generally credited with having topped the wall before any other officer or man of the Naval Brigade.

In an hour after the assault, the whole of the heights were in possession of the allies. The navy opened the north-east gate to the marines and artillery, and some of the *Samson's* and *Calcutta's* dragged up two or three field-pieces where the wall had been scaled, the guns being subsequently sent towards the heights under Lieutenant Henry Hamilton Beamish, (com., Feb. 26th, 1858.) In the course of a movement in the direction of Magazine Hill, where the enemy made a stand, some further casualties, which, however, were not very numerous took place, and Lieutenant Viscount Gilford, (later Adm. of the Fleet the Earl of Clanwilliam: Com. Feb. 26th, 1858), was badly wounded.

★★★★★★

In the whole operations, the Naval Brigade had 7 killed or mortally wounded, and 32 wounded. The officers killed were Capt. Wm. Thornton Bate, and Mids. Henry Thompson: those wounded were Com. Chas. Fellowes, and Lieuts. Visct. Gilford, and William Ormonde Butler. The Marine Battalion lost 4 killed and 32 wounded, among the latter being Lieut.-Col. Thos. Holloway, R.M.A., and Lieut. Wm. Fredk. Portlock Scott Dadson.

★★★★★★

After the city had been occupied, and Gough's Fort had been evacuated by the Chinese, resistance ceased, though there was some sniping till nightfall. On the 30th, flags of truce appeared in various places, and a message arrived from the Tartar general to the effect that he was willing to discuss matters. As, however, he did not appear upon the expiration of the time assigned to him, a party went the round of the ramparts of the old city, and spiked, or knocked the trunnions off, all the guns there. About 400 were thus dealt with; but most of them were already honeycombed, and almost useless.

The Chinese authorities were still obdurate. Every proposal made to the Imperial Commissioner was put aside by him; and although Canton was at the mercy of the allies, it was, or presently would be, still more at the mercy of the bands of robbers who were gathering round it from the country, unless, indeed, the Tartar troops, who were also assembling in the neighbourhood, should succeed, as no doubt Yeh hoped they would, in forcing the allies to quit both the city and the river.

A further step, therefore, had to be taken, and, on January 5th, 1858, at daybreak, three detachments, in pursuance of a pre-arranged plan, entered the city. One laid hands on, and carried off, the Tartar general, Muh; another, British, kidnapped the governor of the city, Peh-Kwei; and the third, also British, abducted, and ultimately carried on board the *Inflexible*, Yeh himself. Captain Cooper Key, indeed, took the commissioner with his own hands. The general and the governor were afterwards sent back to carry out their duties and maintain order, under the supervision of an international commission. This arrangement worked well, and it was found possible to raise the blockade of the Canton River on February 10th.

But China remained defiant. After having waited in vain for plenipotentiaries from Peking, Lord Elgin and Baron Gros determined to go northward, hoping that a naval demonstration in the vicinity of the capital of the empire would tend to accelerate the course of events. In order, moreover, to allow the ministers of the United States and of Russia to associate themselves in the negotiations, it was formally declared that the war with China, so far as Great Britain and France were concerned, was confined to the city of Canton. The arrival of large military reinforcements in the river enabled the admirals to withdraw with a number of their ships. (Chevalier.)

The plenipotentiaries first invited representatives of the Emperor of China to meet them at Shanghai, whither they proceeded; but, no one appearing there, they went on to the mouth of the Peiho, where Lord Elgin anchored on April 14th, 1858. A commissioner named Tan was sent down to the town of Taku to negotiate, or rather, no doubt, to procrastinate.

Soon, however, it became apparent that the enemy had no serious intention of treating on such lines as would be agreeable to the allies. Seymour and Rigault de Genouilly reached the mouth of the river in April; but part of the naval force was slow in making the rendezvous, owing to bad weather, the lateness of the monsoon, and the small steam power of some of the gunboats; and the admirals were only just ready to act when, on May 19th, recognising the uselessness of further delay, the plenipotentiaries placed the matter in the hands of their fighting colleagues.

The British screw gun-vessels, *Nimrod*, 6, and *Cormorant*, 4, with the French gunboats *Dragonne, Fusée, Avalanche*, and *Mitraille*, had already lain for several days within the bar, and within easy shot of the forts, though a little below them.

On the evening of the 19th these craft were joined by the small gunboats *Slaney*, bearing during the attack the flags of both admirals, *Firm, Opossum, Leven, Staunch*, and *Bustard*; the *Slaney, Firm, Staunch*, and *Bustard* having British, and the *Leven* and *Opossum* French landing parties on board.

Seymour says:

> The Chinese have used every exertion to strengthen the forts at the entrance of the Peiho. Earthworks, sandbag batteries, and parapets for the heavy *gingals*, have been erected on both sides for a distance of nearly a mile in length, upon which eighty-seven guns in position were visible; and the whole shore had been piled (*i.e.*, lined with piles driven into the mud), to oppose a landing. As the channel is only about 200 yards wide, and runs within 400 yards of the shore, these defences presented a formidable appearance. Two strong mud batteries, mounting respectively thirty-three and sixteen guns, had been also constructed about 1000 yards up the river, in a position to command our advance. In the rear several intrenched camps were visible, defended by flanking bastions. (See plan following.)

At 8 a.m. on May 20th, Captain William King Hall and the French Flag-Captain Reynaud delivered to Commissioner Tan a summons to deliver up the forts within two hours. By 10 o'clock no reply had arrived; and a signal was hoisted for the attack to be made in the pre-scribed order. Commander Thomas Saumarez (2) (posted, July 27th, 1858), leading in the *Cormorant*, and being followed by the *Mitraille, Fusée, Avalanche, Dragonne, Nimrod,* and *Slaney*, successively, and by the five small gunboats. The vessels were directed not to fire until specifi-cally ordered to do so; and, while the *Slaney*, 2, Lieutenant Anthony Hiley Hoskins, (com., Feb. 26th, 1858), bearing the flags of both admi-rals, placed herself where she could be of most service, and could best direct operations, the other craft, having on board, or towing, landing parties, British and French, which numbered in all 1178 officers and men, were told off as follows:—

ATTACKING THE NORTH FORTS.			ATTACKING THE SOUTH FORTS.		
LEFT BANK.			RIGHT BANK.		
Ships.	Commanders.	Commanding Landing Party.	Ships.	Commanders.	Commanding Landing Party.
Br. *Cormorant,* 4 . . .	Com. Thomas Saumarez (2)	Capt. Sir F. W. E. Nicolson (*Pique*).	Fr. *Avalanche,* 4 . . .	Com. Lafond	Capt. W. K. Hall (*Calcutta*).
Fr. *Mitraille,* 4	Com. Béranger	Capt. Sherard Osborn, C.B. (*Furious*).	Fr. *Dragonne,* 4 . . .	Com. Barry	Com. Chas. T. Leckie (*Fury*).
„ *Fusée,* 4 .	Com. Gabrielli de Carpégna	Com. S. G. Cresswell (*Surprise*).	Br. *Nimrod,* 6	Com.	Com. Jas. G. Goodenough.
Br. *Staunch,* 2	Lieut. Leveson Wildman	Major Robt. Boyle, R.M.	„ *Opossum,* 2	Lieut. ——	Lieut. E. G. M'Callum, R.M.
„ *Bustard,* 2	Lieut Fred'k. Wm. Hallowes	Capt. Lévêque (*Phlégéton*).	„ *Leven,* 2	Lieut. Jos. S. Hudson	Capt. Reynaud (*Nemesis*).
			„ *Firm,* 2 .	Lieut. ——	

The *Cormorant* led off at full speed; and the Chinese opened fire almost immediately. Although Saumarez was somewhat checked by warps which the enemy had thrown across the river, and which he broke, his French consorts did not keep pace with him, and, in conse-quence, suffered more than he did. The signal to engage was quickly made from the *Slaney*; and, ere the vessels had anchored in their as-signed positions, the effect of the return fire was very apparent, the shells bursting well in the embrasures, and dispersing men, guns, and carriages. The smaller vessels passed beyond the forts, and landed their parties on both banks on the flanks of the Chinese positions, while the larger craft, opposite the forts, occupied their direct attention.

On the south side, the first fort was entirely dismantled and aban-doned, and the second one partially so; and on the north side, the *Cormorant* and her French consorts completely crushed opposition. At the end of an hour and a quarter, the Chinese fire almost ceased. The landing then took place, the admirals themselves joining Captain Hall's party; and the enemy ran. Fifty yards of mud, two feet deep, had, however, to be floundered through ere the works could be reached. In a few minutes they were covered with flags, for half the French officers had tricolours in their pockets. Soon afterwards, the French sustained severe losses by the accidental explosion of a magazine. During the operations the enemy sent down numerous *junks* full of flaming straw; but the *Bustard* drove off the people who were trying to guide them by means of ropes from the shore; and the craft burnt themselves out innocuously.

After the action, Nicolson and Leveque moved up against two other forts on the north side, the 33- and 16-gun forts described by Seymour; and, supported by the fire of the *Bustard, Staunch,* and *Opossum,* took them with but slight loss, and also destroyed some entrenched camps in their vicinity. Everything was over by 2 p.m. When the necessary arrangements had been made at the mouth of the river, the force advanced to the town of Taku, which was occupied by Captain King Hall, Flag-Lieutenant Michael Culme-Seymour, and a party. Eighteen field-pieces were found there; and opposite the place was a boom of *junks* filled with combustibles, which was burnt on the 21st.

The British loss in the fighting of the 20th was only 4 killed, including the Carpenter of the *Fury,* and 16 wounded, including Second-Master Charles Prickett, (Master, Sept. 17th, 1858), of the *Opossum.* The French, however, had 67 killed and wounded. (Seymour's disp. in *Gazette* of July 27th: Chevalier: Corr. of *Ill. Lond. News,* and *Times.*)

On May 23rd, Seymour, in the *Coromandel,* with two other British gunboats, and Rigault de Genouilly in the *Avalanche,* with the *Fusée,* moved slowly up the river, towing a number of manned boats, and burning all the stacks of straw and small timber which might have been used for loading incendiary vessels. Such *junks* as were met with were ordered out of the river; and those which did not promptly obey the order were destroyed, so that the enemy should not be left with vessels out of which he could improvise fireships. A few shells also were fired at bodies of troops; but otherwise no hostile acts were committed by the allies, who arrived on May 26th at Tientsin, where there was no resistance.

★★★★★★

There was, nevertheless, some friction ere the negotiations were completed. Seymour was hooted while walking in the town, and on the following day Capt. Roderick Dew and Com. Saumarez were pelted with stones; whereupon the com.-in-

The attack on Taku Forts

chief ordered the marines into the place. The Chinese endeavoured to keep them out by shutting the gates; but Capt. Sherard Osborn and Com. Saumarez, scaled the walls with their boats' crews, and admitted the marines, who marched through the town. Hand's *Journal*: L. Oliphant's *Earl of Elgin's Mission*.

★★★★★★

The Court of Pekin was at last seriously impressed, and sent down to the admirals a note announcing that a high official, armed with full powers, would instantly appear to treat. Lord Elgin and Baron Gros reached Tientsin in the *Slaney* on May 30th, and were followed, at an interval of twenty-four hours, by the ministers of the United States and of Russia. In the meantime, reinforcements had been sent to the mouth of the Peiho; and 1000 British troops, together with 500 French, were forwarded to Tientsin, which they garrisoned. There was no further dallying; and peace was signed on June 27th.

The treaty of Tientsin contained no fewer than 56 articles, its most important provisions stipulating for: the confirmation of the treaty of Nankin; the appointment of a British minister to Pekin; his right of access to the Secretary of State at Pekin on a footing of equality; toleration of Christianity; the opening to travellers of all parts of China; the opening, as ports, of Chinkiang, and three other ports on the Yang-tse-kiang, besides Niuchang, Tungchow, Taiwan, Swatow, and Kiungchow; a revised tariff; the visiting by British ships of war of any port in the Empire; the concerting of measures for the repression of piracy; and the arrangement of an indemnity.

It looked as if all difficulties were settled, and as if all possible causes of future difficulty were removed. The forts on the river were destroyed and evacuated; and presently the allies withdrew from the Gulf of Pechili. But appearances were deceptive. The authority of Pekin did not suffice to coerce immediately the *mandarins* in all other parts of the Empire; and in many districts there was at the time open rebellion. Canton was besieged, and repeatedly assaulted; on July 3rd men from the *Sans Pareil* had to be landed to reinforce the army of occupation; and on July 19th, a cutter belonging to the *Amethyst*, 26, Captain Sidney Grenfell, manned by eight seamen and a marine, under Master Richard Cossantine Dyer, while in chase of a junk in the Canton River, was attacked by a *mandarin* row-galley, with seventeen men armed with *gingals*, rockets, and stinkpots, and defended by iron plates in the vessel's bow. Dyer made an excellent fight of it for half an hour, and killed 18 of his assailants, while no one in his boat was hurt.

The British made every effort to disseminate the fact and terms of the treaty among the natives; but it was extremely dangerous to do so; and an outrage perpetrated on a party from the *Starling*, 2, Lieutenant Arthur Julian Villiers, and *Nankin*, involving the killing of one seaman, and the wounding of two more at Namtao, near Hong Kong, obliged Commodore the Hon. Keith Stewart (2), of the *Nankin*, 50, and General van Straubenzee to adopt severe punitive measures, and to occupy the town on August 11th.

In this affair, in addition to the troops, the Samson, and five gunboats with a Brigade from the *Sans Pareil, Cormorant*, and *Adventure*, were engaged. Among those who distinguished themselves in the action were Captain Julian Foulston Slight, (posted, Ap. 28th, 1858), (*Sans Pareil*), Commander Thomas Saumarez (2) (*Cormorant*), and Acting-Commander Edward Madden, (Com. Aug.11th, 1858), (*Sans Pareil*), the last of whom was severely wounded. Two brass guns, each weighing about 30 cwt., were brought off, and the place was pillaged and partially burnt. (Hand's Journal: *Ill. Lond. News*, Oct. 16th.)

Lord Elgin went on a diplomatic mission to Japan; and, on his return, started from Hong Kong on November 8th upon an expedition up the Yang-tse-kiang as far as Hankow, a city seven hundred miles from the sea. Nankin (*a.k.a. Nanjing*) and its neighbourhood was in the hands of the Ti-ping rebels. The Ti-pings were perfectly prepared to be friendly; but, on November 20th, misunderstanding the objects of the gunboat *Lee*, 2, Lieutenant William Henry Jones, which had been sent ahead of the squadron to communicate if possible, their batteries opened fire on her; whereupon the other vessels of the escort, the *Retribution*, 28, paddle. Captain Charles Barker, *Furious*, 16, paddle. Captain Sherard Osborn, *Cruiser*, 17, screw, Commander John Bythesea, and *Dove*, 2, Lieutenant Charles James Bullock, attacked them, causing considerable loss. (In the *Retribution* Mids. Geo. Anthony Wyrley Birch lost an arm, and a bluejacket a leg. There were no other casualties.)

There were one or two other collisions with the Ti-pings during this expedition, notably on the following day, when the ships returned and re-engaged the Nankin forts, and on November 26th at Nganking; and, although it is now known that the rebels were acting under misapprehension, they were reported not only as having fired upon the British flag, but also as having violated a flag of truce, which it is clear they did not know to be one. (Wade's Report. 'Ti-ping Tien-Kwoh,' I. *North China Herald*; acc. by an officer of the squadron. L.

Oliphant.)

These affairs, and the somewhat similar trouble with the *Hermes* in 1853, were largely responsible for the attitude taken later by Great Britain with regard to a movement which was one of the most extraordinary of the century, and which, if assisted instead of discouraged, might perhaps have effected the regeneration of China, and saved the powers of Europe from much subsequent perplexity.

In the interim various ships under the orders of the commander-in-chief had been active in repressing the piracy which had begun to flourish anew during the prolonged hostilities.

On August 4th, 1858, the gunboat *Staunch*, Lieutenant Leveson Wildman, (com., Oct. 15th, 1858), while on passage from Shanghai to Hong Kong, chased three pirate *junks* off Taon Pung, and endeavoured to lash herself alongside the largest of them, but was driven off by a shower of stinkpots, and lost a gallant seaman, Edward George, who had leapt on board the enemy in order to secure her to the *Staunch*. Wildman had only two 24-pr. howitzers on board; and they were quickly dismounted, owing to being fired rapidly; but he remounted them, renewed the engagement, boarded and captured another of the *junks*, and, leaving her in charge of Second-Master George Morice, chased the third in his gig, and took her also. The big *junk* got away.

On August 22nd, 1858, Commander Samuel Gurney Cresswell, (posted, Sept. 17th, 1858), with his screw gunboat the *Surprise*, 4, her boats, and the boats of the *Cambrian*, 40, attacked a number of heavily-armed piratical *junks* under Lingting Island, near Hong Kong. The enemy opened fire at 1600 yards as the *Surprise* approached; but she did not return it until within 1000 yards; when she steadily poured in shot and shell, and gradually closed under a storm of round shot and rockets, canister and grape.

In the meantime, the *Cambrian's* boom boats, under Lieutenant John Whitmarsh Webb, (com., Nov. 5th, 1858), went inshore of the gunboat, and took the enemy in flank. The action began at 8 a.m. By 8.35 the pirates' fire had slackened; and, at about 9, two of their largest *lorchas* blew up. Firing then ceased; whereupon Cresswell pushed in with his own boats, joined the boats of the *Cambrian*, and landed near the *junks*, just after the crews of the latter had deserted their vessels and fled to the hills.

Advancing to the top of a ridge, the British discovered some more piratical craft in a snug creek on the other side of it, and, from their commanding position, killed a number of the people with their rifles, and drove off the rest. The sun was so hot that Cresswell, determining to spare his men as much as possible, returned to the gunboat, which, with the boats in tow, he took round to the creek. Having fired a few shells, he sent in the boats. No serious resistance was offered, though there was a little sniping from the neighbouring hills; and the work of burning such *junks* as could not be moved, and of bringing out the remainder, was accomplished without difficulty. Of twenty-six piratical craft at the island, nineteen were destroyed, and seven were carried to Hong Kong.

A third operation of a similar kind was conducted by Captain Nicholas Vansittart, C.B., of the *Magicienne*, 16, paddle, who, with the *Inflexible*, 6, paddle. Commander George Augustus Cooke Brooker, *Plover*, 2, screw. Lieutenant Robert James Wynniatt, and *Algerine*, 2, Lieutenant William Arthur, between August 26th and September 3rd, 1858, destroyed Coulan, an old piratical headquarters, together with a 14-gun stockade, 26 armed *junks*, and 74 row-boats, mounting 236 guns; and killed 372 pirates. (Seymour's disps. *Gazette*, Nov. 2, 1858.)

In April, 1859, Rear-Admiral Sir Michael Seymour (2) returned to England, upon the expiration of his term of service, and his supersession by Rear-Admiral James Hope, C.B.; and on May 20th he was rewarded for his work in China with a G.C.B. Hope was soon confronted with difficulties, most of which arose out of the fact that the Chinese placed one construction upon the terms of the treaty of Tientsin, while the British and French placed another. Lord Elgin had also returned to England; and in his stead, as Plenipotentiary and Envoy Extraordinary, his brother, the Hon. Frederick W. A. Bruce, had been sent out to proceed to Pekin, with the new French envoy, M. de Bourboulon, who arrived in the corvette *Duchayla*, accompanied by the dispatch vessel *Norzagaray*.

Hope, with a squadron, (and the French vessels, arrived off the island of Sha-lui-tien, in the gulf of Pechili, on June 17th, 1859. (*Chesapeake*, 51, screw (flag), *Magicienne*; 16, padd., *Highflyer*, 21, screw, *Cruiser*, 17, screw, *Fury*, 6, padd., *Assistance*, screw store-ship, *Hesper*, screw store-ship, and the gun-vessels and gunboats named later in the text.)

On the following day, proceeded to the mouth of the Peiho in order, as he explains, to intimate to the local authorities the intended appearance of the ministers, and to reconnoitre "the existing state of the defences of the river." These last seemed to consist principally of the reconstruction, in earth, and in an improved form, of the works destroyed in 1858, with additional ditches and abattis. There were, moreover, stronger and better booms across the channel. Few guns were seen; but numerous embrasures were masked with matting, obviously in order to conceal what was behind them. (It was generally believed that the new defences were the work of Russian engineers.)

The officer who was sent on shore to communicate was met by a guard, and assured that there were no officials nearer than Tientsin. He was prevented from landing; but, on telling the people that the commander-in-chief desired that the obstructions in the river should be removed to enable the envoys to go up to Tientsin, he was promised that the necessary work of clearing should be begun within the next forty-eight hours. On June 19th, the whole squadron was moved to the anchorage off the mouth of the river; and the smaller craft were sent inside the bar. On the 20th, Hope again examined the channel; and, finding that nothing had been done towards carrying out the promise of the 18th, he addressed a letter to the Taotai at Tientsin, repeating the announcement of the arrival of the envoys, and the request for free passage. To this letter an evasive answer was returned on the 22nd.

In the meantime, Bruce and de Bourboulon had formally desired Hope to take the matter into his own hands, and to adopt such measures as he might deem expedient for opening the way up. Hope, in consequence, informed the Taotai that, if the obstructions were not removed, he should remove them, using force if needful. This communication received no answer; and on June 24th, the whole of the rest of the squadron was taken inside the bar; and intimation was sent in to the effect that unless a satisfactory answer were received by 8 p.m., the rear-admiral would feel at liberty to take his own course.

There were three booms or obstructions. The first, or lowest, was of upon piles; the second was of heavy spars of wood, apparently moored head and stern, and cross-lashed with cables; the third consisted of large timber baulks, well cross-lashed together, tied with irons, and forming a mass about 120 feet wide and 3 feet deep. It was made in two overlapping pieces, as indicated in the plan; and the opening between these might have just admitted the passage of a gunboat, though the strength of the current would have rendered it difficult and even dangerous for such a craft to attempt to get through.

That night three boats, under Captain George Ommanney Willes, of the *Chesapeake*, passing through or circumventing the first boom, pulled up to the second, and cut one, and blew away with powder two, of the cables forming part of it. The boats he had with him were one from the *Chesapeake*, under Lieutenant John Crawford Wilson, one from the *Magicienne*, under acting-Mate Frederick

Wilbraham Egerton, and one from the *Cruiser*, under Boatswain W. Hartland. Before the return of the party, Willes examined the third or inner boom; and, in consequence of his report on it, the rear-admiral concluded that he would not be able to pass the works and attack them from above, but must attack them, if at all, from the front, and, upon silencing them, endeavour to carry them by storm. By morning, the Chinese had repaired the damage done overnight to the second boom. Hope determined to try to carry out both plans, and to employ the following craft:—

Ships (all screw).	Guns.	Commanders.
Opossum, g.-b.	2	{(Capt. Geo. O. Willes.) Lieut. Chas. Jno. Balfour.
Starling, g.-b..	2	Lieut. Arth. Julian Villiers.
Janus, g.-b.	2	Lieut. Herbert Price Knevitt.
Plover, g.-b.	2	{(R.-Adm. James Hope, C.B.) Lieut. Wm Hector Rason.
Cormorant, g.-v.	4	Com. Armine Wodehouse.
Lee, g.-b.	2	Lieut. Wm. Hy. Jones.
Kestrel, g.-b.	2	Lieut. Geo. Dacres Bevan.
Banterer, g.-b	2	Lieut. John Jenkins.
Forester, g.-b.	2	Lieut. Arthur Jno. Innes.
Haughty, g.-b.	2	Lieut. Geo. Doherty Broad.
Nimrod, slp.	6	Lieut. Robt. Jas. Wynniatt (actg.-Com.).

The above nine gunboats varied from about 235 to about 270 tons (B.M.) and seem to have carried each one 68-pr. of 95 cwt., and one 32-pr. of 56 cwt., besides, in some cases at least, two howitzers. Their proper complements were about forty, all told, but extra officers and men were in most of them. The remaining two vessels (*Cormorant* and *Nimrod*) were considerably more powerful.

The morning of June 25th was occupied in putting these vessels into position. The *Starling, Janus, Plover, Cormorant, Lee, Kestrel*, and *Banterer* were stationed on a line parallel with the works on the south side, or right bank, of the river; and the *Nimrod* was put in rear of that line, with her guns bearing on the more distant north fort. The *Opossum* was stationed in advance, close up to the boom of piles; and the *Forester* and *Haughty* were in reserve in rear of the line, the former having orders to move up to the *Plover's* post, should that vessel advance to the support of the *Opossum*.

The vessels on the right were under the direction of Captain Charles Frederick Alexander Shadwell of the *Highflyer*, and those on the left, under Captain Nicholas Vansittart, of the *Magicienne*. The strength of the tide, and the narrowness of the channel (about 200 yards) had rendered it a matter of extreme difficulty to take up the positions above described; and the *Banterer* and *Starling*, the vessels on the

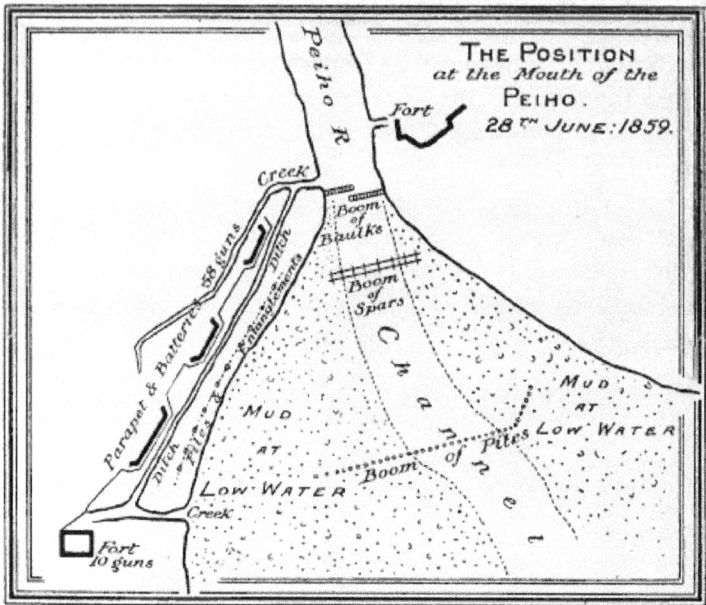

THE POSITION
at the Mouth of the
PEIHO.
28 TH JUNE: 1859.

extreme right and left of the line, both took the ground, the former in a good position, but the latter in one which, unfortunately, prevented her from taking much share in the action.

At 2 p.m. the *Opossum* was ordered to open a passage through the first barrier. She made fast a hawser to one of the iron piles, and, by 2.30, had pulled it out; whereupon, supported by the *Plover*, and closely followed by the *Lee* and *Haughty*, she moved up to the second boom. As she reached it, the forts opened a simultaneous fire from between thirty and forty guns, ranging from 32-prs. to 8-in. pieces. Hope at once ordered the ships to engage.

It was a hot day, with a clear blue sky; and the Chinese had the range to a nicety. The *Plover* posted herself close to the barrier, with the *Opossum, Lee*, and *Haughty*, in succession, astern of her. By 3 p.m., the four craft inside the outer barrier had suffered severely, and were rapidly becoming disabled. The *Plover* had lost her gallant young commander, Rason, who was cut in two by a round shot, and whose place was temporarily taken by George Amelius Douglas, Hope's flag-lieutenant. In her also fell Captain T. M'Kenna, of the 1st Royals, who was attached to the major-general commanding the forces in China; and among her wounded were the rear-admiral himself, and Second-Master John Phillips (acting). The four vessels were, consequently, dropped

44

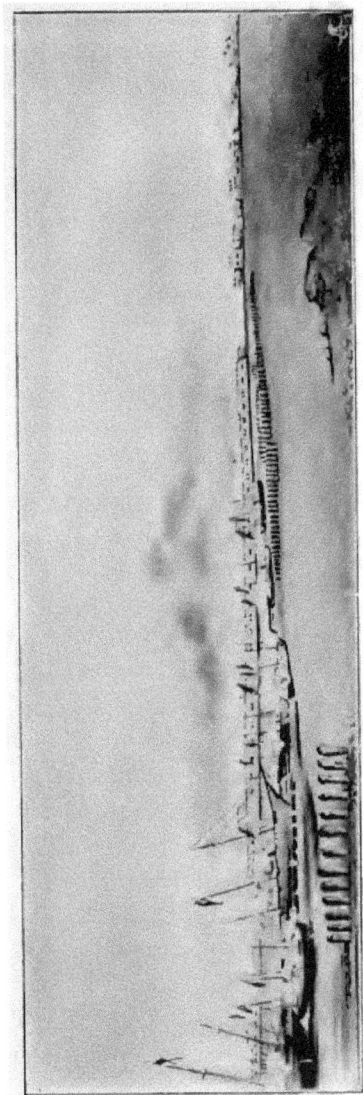

The attack on the Peiho Forts June 25th, 1859

down into fresh positions below the first barrier, where, having received fresh men, they renewed the action.

The *Plover* was so badly mauled that Hope shifted his flag from her to the *Cormorant*; and at 4.20, finding himself too weak for the work, he was obliged to summon Captain Shadwell, and to entrust him with the more immediate command of the squadron. (The *Plover* dropped down because her cables were cut by shot; and she drifted unmanageable until she grappled the *Cormorant*, and so brought herself up.)

It should be mentioned here that the French dispatch vessel *Norzagaray* was not armed in such a manner as to enable her to share in the attack; and that the *Duchayla* drew too much water for the purpose. Although, therefore, the French were as much concerned as the British in asserting the right of free passage for their representative to Tientsin, they bore no part in this naval attack; at which, indeed, they were represented only by Commander Tricault, of the *Duchayla*, who attached himself to the commander-in-chief, and remained with him until the landing. The Americans and Russians, less intimately concerned, were not represented at all; and, in fact, were professedly neutral.

At 5.40 the *Kestrel* sank in her position; and the *Lee* had to he put upon the mud to save her from the like fate. At about that time, or a little before, there occurred an incident which has ever since most happily affected the relations between the two great English-speaking nations. (It may have been as early as 4.40 p.m. Accounts of those present vary as to the exact time.)

The *Cormorant*, flying the rear-admiral's flag, lay with her port broadside facing, and engaging, the works on the right bank. Lashed on her starboard side was the almost disabled *Plover*, in such a manner that the latter's bow gun cleared the *Cormorant's* bows by a yard or so, and could be fired across them at the forts. The *Banterer* was aground on the *Plover's* starboard bow; the *Haughty* lay across the *Cormorant's* stern; and the *Lee* was aground on the *Haughty's* port quarter. The *Plover's* bow gun was almost silent, partly because many men had been killed or wounded while serving it, and partly because the survivors were almost worn out with fatigue.

The firing was still very hot on both sides, when up the river came a double-banked cutter, flying the Stars and Stripes in the stern. In her was Flag-Officer Josiah Tatnall, of the United States' Navy, senior American officer in Chinese waters, who had pulled up from his flagship below the bar, in spite of the storm of shot. He had fought against the British in the war of 1812. His coxswain took him alongside the *Plover's* starboard gangway; and, even as the bow-man was getting out his boat-hook, the coxswain was hit by a Chinese projectile.

Tatnall boarded the *Plover*, crossed her bloody deck, and went to visit Hope, who was lying wounded in the *Cormorant's* cabin. He expressed his sympathy; said that he trusted he might be of some use in removing and tending the numerous wounded; and remained for a short time with the British commander-in-chief. While he was in the *Cormorant's* cabin, his boat lay under the *Plover's* shelter; and her men watched the *Plover's* weary bluejackets working intermittently at the bow gun. At length, one of the Americans, and then others, climbed shyly on deck, and began to help, saying little or nothing, but gradually relieving the proper gun's crew, until the gun was wholly manned by Tatnall's men. They had fired it at least once when Tatnall reappeared.

"Hulloa there!" he cried, somewhat sharply, as he crossed the *Plover's* deck to the gangway; "don't you know that we are neutrals?"

"Beg pardon, sir," said one of the Americans, drawing off shame-facedly with his mates to the boat, "they were very shorthanded at the bow-gun; and so we thought we'd lend them a hand for fellowship's sake."

By 6.30 the fire from the north forts had ceased altogether; and by 7, that from the south ones was also silent, save that a single gun in the outer, another in the centre bastion, and a third in the detached fort on the south continued to ply the ships with shot.

A landing force, chiefly made up of about 350 marines and a few bluejackets, was brought from the vessels below the bar. There is strong evidence that Tatnall's steam boat, the *Toey-whan*, was allowed to assist in towing part of it up the river, though, no doubt, the nominal mission of the little craft was to fetch wounded from the gunboats below the barrier.

At 7.20 p.m. a landing was effected opposite the outer bastion of the south fort, the spot being selected because it seemed to have suffered most, and because an attack there could be best supported by the guns of the squadron. The force consisted of a detachment of sappers and miners, under Major Fisher, R.E., a Brigade of marines, under Lieutenant-Colonel Thomas Lemon, a division of seamen under Captain Vansittart, assisted by Commanders John Edmund Commerell, V.C., and William Andrew James Heath, and a small body of French seamen under Commander Tricault; the whole being under the orders of Captain Shadwell.

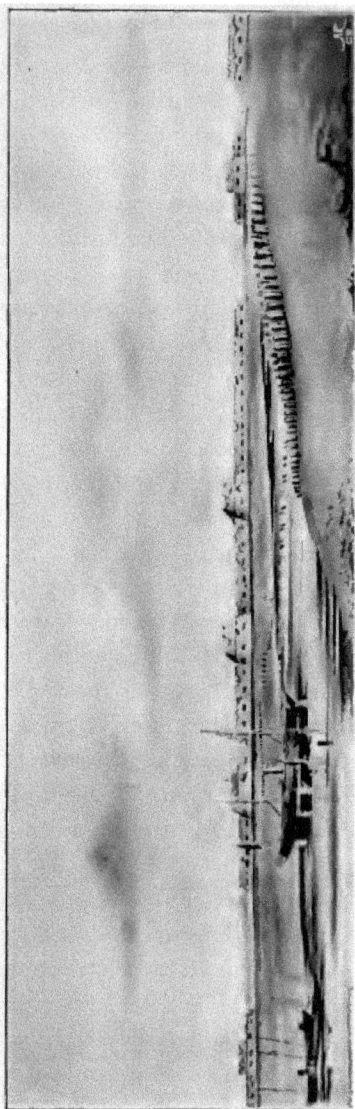

After the attack on the Peiho Forts

The party was met by a heavy fire from guns, *gingals*, and rifles, and, in addition, had terrible obstacles to contend with in the shape of stakes planted in the shallows and mud, and two, if not three, ditches. In the advance, Shadwell, Vansittart, and Lemon, with many others, were disabled, and the command devolved upon Commerell. About 150 officers and men struggled as far as the second ditch, and about 50 even got close under the wall of the fort; but, although those positions might have been held for a time, further advance, or a storm, was impossible without reinforcements.

Such was Commerell's unwilling conclusion after he had consulted with Fisher, Tricault, and Captain Richard Parke, R.M.; and he reported it to Shadwell, who ordered a retirement. This was effected in the darkness with the utmost deliberation and coolness, the force proceeding to the boats in detachments, and bringing off its wounded. It was accomplished by 1.30 a.m. on June 26th, the last to leave the shore being Commerell and Heath.

The *Kestrel, Starling*, and *Banterer* were raised or floated. The *Lee* became a total loss. After the action the *Plover* grounded within range of the forts, and, being necessarily abandoned, was also lost. The *Cormorant* went to her assistance, and grounded. She got off again on the night of the 27th, but piled up once more while endeavouring to move down, and on the 28th was swept by such a heavy fire that she presently sank.

This lamentable affair, therefore, cost the navy three vessels. The expenditure of human life was even more serious. No fewer than 25 officers and men were killed; 39 others were badly wounded; and 54 more received slighter injuries, during the preliminary attack; and the subsequent landing, and attempted capture of the south forts added to the total 64 officers and men killed; 162 badly wounded; and 90 slightly wounded. The whole British casualties, therefore, amounted to the appalling number of 89 killed, and 345 wounded—a much heavier loss than that suffered by the entire British fleet at the famous battle of Cape St. Vincent, in 1797. In addition, the French had 4 killed, and 10 wounded.

Among the officers killed were: Lieuts. William Hector Rason (comdg. *Plover*), Alfred Graves (*Assistance*), and Charles Henry Clutterbuck (*Chesapeake*); Lieuts. (R.M.) Hamilton Wolrige, and Henry Langton Tollemache Inglis; Capt. T. M'Kenna (1st Royals); and Mids. T. H. Herbert (*Chesapeake*).

Among the officers severely wounded were: Rear-Admiral James

Hope, C.B.: Capts. Charles Frederick Alexander Shadwell, C.B. (*Highflyer*), and Nicholas Vansittart, (he succumbed to his injuries), C.B. (*Magicienne*); actg.-Lieut. Claude Edward Buckle (*Magicienne*); Master Augustus John Burniston (*Banterer*); actg.-Mate Nathaniel Bowden Smith (*Chesapeake*); Midshipmen Armand Temple Powlett (*Fury*), and Gr. Armytage (*Cruiser*); Gunner W. Ryan (*Plover*); Lieut.-Col. Thomas Lemon, R.M.; Capt. William Godfrey Rayson Masters, R.M.; Lieut. John Chesterton Crawford, R.M.A.; Lieut. G. Longley, R.E.; and the Rev. H. Huleatt, Chaplain to the Forces.

Rear-Admiral Hope, in his dispatch, mentioned with commendation Capts. C. F. A. Shadwell, N. Vansittart, and George Ommanney Willes; Commanders John Edmund Commerell, William Andrew James Heath, and Armine Wodehouse; Lieuts. John Jenkins, Robert James Wynniatt, Arthur John Innes, George Dacres Bevan, William Henry Jones, Charles John Balfour, George Doherty Broad, Herbert Price Knevitt, George Parsons (2), and John Crawford Wilson; Master William Donaldson Strong; Mates Claude Edward Buckle, George Spotswood Peard, Frederick Edward Gould, and Visct. Kilcoursie; Mids. G. Armytage and Charles Lister Oxley; Paymaster and Secretary James William Murray Ashby; Asst.-Paymaster John St. John Wagstaffe; Second-Master Oscar Samson; Staff-Surg. Walter Dickson (2) M.D.; Surg. John Little, M.B.; Asst.-Surg. William James Baird, M.D.; Lieut.-Col. Thomas Lemon, R.M., Capts. (R.M.) Richard Parke, W. G. K. Masters, and Ponsonby May Carew Croker; Lieuts. (R.M) Langham Rokeby, John Frederick Hawkey, Harry Lewis Evans, and John Straghan; Sergt.-Maj. Wood, P.M., Q. M. Sergt. Halling, R.M.; Major Fisher, R.E., and Lieuts. R.E.) J. M. Maitland and G. Longley. (Hope's disp, of July 5th. The above account is the result also of conversation and correspondence with numerous officers who were present. See, too, Chevalier; and corr. in *Times*.)

As this hotly contested action resulted in a defeat, those who participated in it were never directly rewarded by the issue of medals or clasps, the granting of honours, or promotion; yet it must be admitted that, as, indeed, the exceedingly heavy loss indicates, officers and men behaved in a manner which added distinctly to the glories of the navy, and which could have been scarcely more creditable had victory rewarded their efforts. The attack failed, firstly, because the narrowness of the channel, and the artificial obstructions crippled the usefulness of the ships, and, secondly, because the assault, a frontal one, was made over most difficult ground against works which were supposed, but wrongly supposed, to have been silenced; and was attempted with insufficient force. It must also be admitted that, as usual, the British were very ignorant of the exact strength and dispositions of the enemy.

A distinguished officer who was present writes:

> After the retirement, the *Coromandel* received as many wounded as she could stow; and the rest were sent down by boats towed by the U.S. steamer *Toey-whan*, obligingly placed at our disposal by Flag-Officer Tatnall, in, as he put it, 'the cause of humanity.' This is when the expression, 'Blood is thicker than water,' was used by him to my chief, Sir James Hope. It was on the day after the action.

As the officer from whom I quote this was the rear-admiral's secretary, there can be no doubt that Tatnall used the expression on the occasion referred to; but there is some evidence that he also used it on the day of the action; and also, that his men used it when on board the *Plover*. I think, therefore, that, in all probability, it was an habitual expression with Tatnall at the time, and that it was imitated by his people.

Tatnall, it may be added, took the unfortunate side in the struggle which soon afterwards so nearly rent his country permanently in twain; and, in consequence of his action, he was obliged to withdraw to Halifax, Nova Scotia, where he lived in something approaching poverty. His attitude to the British in China in 1859 was not, I am pleased to say, forgotten by those whom he had befriended. As soon as his misfortunes were known in the navy, a number of officers who had served in China, and of others who remembered what had occurred there, subscribed a sum of money which, happily, saved the last days of Commodore Josiah Tatnall from absolute penury. (Letter to W.L.C. from the late Adm. Sir G. O. Willes.) His name can never be forgotten in the British service.

On July 3rd the British squadron repassed the Peiho bar, and proceeded to Shanghai, to allow the wounded opportunity to recover on shore, and to begin preparations for an attack on a more adequate scale, and so for repairing British prestige in China. Operations could not be resumed for twelve months. Both France and Great Britain decided to send out considerable bodies of troops from home, as well as large naval reinforcements; flat-bottomed boats, rafts, and stages for landing the armies had to be constructed; and not until June 25th, 1860, did the expedition begin to concentrate in Talienwan Bay, near Port Arthur, a spot which had been fixed upon for the purpose in consequence of representations made by Commander John Bythesea, of the *Cruiser*, who, in the interval, had thoroughly surveyed the Gulf of Pechili. (Other surveys, which were most useful as preparation for the operations of August, were made by Com. John Ward, 2, of the *Actaeon*. Hope to Admlty., Aug. 27th, 1860.)

The forces ultimately assembled included about 12,600 British and Indian troops, under Lieutenant-General Sir Hope Grant, and nearly 8000 French under General Cousin de Montauban. Rear-Admiral James Hope, (with temp, rank as vice-admiral), still commanded the British fleet on the station. Montauban left France with the title of "*Commandant en Chef des Forces de Terré et de Mer*"; but the French Government, preferring to imitate the arrangements of its ally, and to keep separate the naval and military commands, sent out after him Vice-Admiral Charner, who reached Shanghai on April 19th. Although, in the circumstances, such procedure was perhaps hardly necessary, war had been formally declared against China on April 8th, that power having previously refused reparation for its action in the Peiho in the summer of 1859.

One of the most troublesome questions to be settled by the admirals and generals was where best to disembark the army. It was necessary to find a spot or spots where the water should be deep enough to allow the transports to approach within reasonable distance of the shore, and spots, moreover, where the coast should be less muddy, and more healthy, than the major part of the coastline of the Gulf of Pechili. It was at length arranged that the French Army should land at a point to the south of the mouth of the Peiho, and should then proceed to attack the defences on the right bank of that river; and that the British should disembark at Pehtang, about nine miles to the northward of the river's mouth, and should devote their attention to the defences on the left, or north bank: but the French soon found that they could not carry out their part of the agreement without some risk, and without exposing their troops to the probability of being cut off from communication with their fleet.

The result was that both armies were ultimately taken to Pehtang. As had been the case at the time of the invasion of the Crimea, the French squadron was overcrowded with troops, while the British warships, the army being in hired transports, were fit for anything that might befall, and were free and unencumbered. Captain Chevalier expresses his strong sense of the advantages of this method, which, it may be hoped will be always followed when the British Navy and

Army co-operate on any expedition of the kind.

The main part of the work done on this occasion was done by the allied armies; and may, therefore, be passed over briefly here.

Pehtang stands at the mouth of the small river of the same name, and on the south bank of it. To the south of the town is a considerable extent of hard ground; and from Pehtang, south-westward to Sin-ho, about five miles distant, ran a raised causeway, flanked on each side by a ditch. From Sin-ho south-eastward to Tong-ku, a distance of little more than two miles, ran a somewhat similar causeway; and from Tong-ku, when taken, the Peiho forts on the north side of the river could be approached and attacked from the rear.

The transports stood in towards the mouth of the Pehtang on August 1st, 1860. Some gunboats had previously entered the river, and passed beyond two forts which overlooked the estuary, it being intended that if these forts should assume a hostile attitude, they should be shelled from above, a point from which no Chinese river forts of that day were capable of withstanding attack by water. The forts were found to have been abandoned; but one at least of them had been ingeniously mined in such a manner that any incautious entry by the troops would have caused an explosion.

The disembarkation began at once at a point below the tract of hard ground about half a mile south of the town; and the British, although by far the more numerous, completed the operation forty hours before the French, (Chevalier), chiefly in consequence of the foresight which had provided plenty of small craft capable of crossing the bar, on which, even at high tide, there were only ten feet of water. A battalion of Royal Marines under Lieutenant-Colonel John Hawkins Gascoigne, and a battalion of French seamen joined the army, which, on August 12th, marched to, and occupied Sin-ho, driving back a considerable body of the enemy, and taking two entrenched positions; and, on the 14th, attacked and captured Tong-ku, (a party from the Chesapeake being present), the Chinese then retiring into the northern forts, or across the river. On the right of the main force, during its advance, moved a smaller body under Brigadier-General Sir Robert Cornelius Napier, (afterwards Lord Napier of Magdala.) Grant advised Hope of his intention to attack the Taku northern forts on August 21st; and, in order to co-operate, Hope and Charner, on the previous day, sent the French and British gunboats, and the rocket-boats of the fleet into the Peiho.

When, at about daybreak on the 21st, the troops began to attack the inner fort on the north side, the vessels were prevented by the want of sufficient water from at once reaching the positions assigned to them; and, indeed, the gunboat *Dove*, Lieutenant Charles James Bullock, temporarily bearing the flag of Rear-Admiral Lewis Tobias Jones, who was in immediate command of the operations in the river, grounded in six and a half feet; and Jones had to transfer his flag to the *Clown*, Lieutenant William Frederick Lee. By six o'clock, however, the gunboats were able to open; at 6.15 a shell blew up a magazine in the inner north fort; and at 6.25 there was a similar explosion in the outer one. The Chinese fought well; but at about 9 a.m. the inner north fort was stormed; and although there was firing until near 11, the enemy then prudently relinquished further efforts, and, having lost terribly, hoisted white flags on all the works that remained in his hands.

In the afternoon, the outer north fort was taken possession of; and in the evening, the south fort, which had been evacuated, was occupied, and the booms across the river were removed. The iron piles, however, which formed the outermost barrier, were fixed with so much firmness that a passage could not be opened through them until noon on the 22nd. The gunboats then passed through, and anchored off Tong-ku. In this affair the ships employed had no casualties; but the marines who were with the army had 1 killed, and 29 wounded.

★★★★★★

Vessels employed in the Peiho, August 20th, and onwards: *Coromandel*, pad., temp, flag of V.-Ad. Hope, C.B.; *Dove*, scr., temp, flag of R.-Adm. Lewis Tobias Jones, C.B.; and (under Capt. Jas. Johnstone M'Cleverty, C.B.), *Havock*, scr., *Staunch*, scr., *Opossum*, scr., *Forester*, scr., and *Algerine*, scr.; with (under Capt. Lord John Hay (3), C.B.), *Clown*, scr., *Drake*, scr. *Woodcock*, scr., and *Janus*, scr.; besides rocket-boats contributed apparently by the *Chesapeake, Cambrian, Centaur, Encounter, Impérieuse, Magicienne, Odin, Pearl, Urgent,* etc. Hope's disp. is very meagre.

★★★★★★

On the 23rd, the *Coromandel*, bearing the flag of Vice-Admiral James Hope, together with a number of British gunboats, and subsequently of French ones, passed up to Tientsin, which, being destitute of troops and pacifically inclined, was occupied.

Lieut.-Colonel Gascoigne, in describing the work done by his battalion of Royal Marines, reported with approval the conduct of Lieut.-Colonel Joseph Oates Travers, Captains Jermyn Charles Symonds, John Charles Downie Morrison, and John Basset Prynne;

Lieutenant T. Herbert Alexander Brenan; Surgeon John Little, M.B.; Assistant-Surgeon Doyle Money Shaw: Sergeants Teacle, Knapp, and H. Trent; Corporal Kelly; and Privates Bray and Bowerman. (Gascoigne to Hope, Aug. 24th.)

On August 31st a *mandarin* of high rank reached Tientsin; and Lord Elgin and Baron Gros entered into negotiations with him; but on September 7th he was nowhere to be found. It therefore became necessary for the allied armies to advance upon Pekin. The Chinese attempted to cause further delay; and two battles had to be fought ere they were finally induced to submit. Not until Pekin had been taken, and the palace burnt, did the enemy agree to the terms demanded; and the Treaty of Pekin was concluded only on October 24th. During the advance up the river, the boats of the fleet, (especially those of the *Chesapeake, Cambrian, Impérieuse, Scout,* and *Simoon*), rendered immense assistance in transporting the siege train, and stores for the army.

The treaty provided for the opening of Tientsin to commerce; the occupation of that town, and of the Peiho Forts pending the payment of a certain proportion of an indemnity; an apology from the emperor; the cession of Kowloon to Great Britain; and the ratification of the previous treaty of Tientsin. In 1860, as at a later date, the Chinese distinguished themselves by their bad faith; and their barbarous treatment of Messrs. Parkes, Loch, de Normann, Bowlby, and other Europeans who fell into their hands, rendered them totally undeserving of the merciful light in which their long course of misconduct was viewed when the time came for the exaction of penalties. The evacuation of Pekin was concluded on November 9th.

In recognition of their services, Rear-Admiral Hope was at once made a K.C.B., (Nov. 9th, 1860), and a few officers were promoted, while a few others received honours at a somewhat later period. (*E.g.,* Rear-Adm. Lewis Tobias Jones, a K.C.B. June 28th, 1861; Col. Jno. Hawkins Gascoigne, and Lt.-Col. Joseph Oates Travers, C.B.'s, Feb. 28th, 1861; Capt. Geo. Ommanney Willes, a C.B., July 16th, 1861.) The work done was not, however, very lavishly rewarded. A monument to those of Hope's flagship, the *Chesapeake*, who perished during the commission, 1857-61, has been erected on Clarence Esplanade, Southsea.

Pirates & Small Operations, 1857-1861

While the China War was in progress, some of the small craft on the station were busily occupied in dealing with the pirates, who, taking advantage of the situation, were particularly active up and down the coasts. Lieutenant Henry Knox Leet, first commanding the *Firm*, and afterwards the *Slaney*, and Lieutenant Joseph Samuel Hudson, commanding the *Leven*, were among the officers who distinguished themselves in this branch of duty; but many others might also be named. On the east coast of Africa, where the slave trade then flourished exceedingly, the *Lynx*, 4, screw, Lieutenant Henry Berkeley, was one of the most active cruisers.

In the course of 1859 she also landed a small Brigade to co-operate with a force from the East India Company's steamer *Assaye* in an attack upon some rebellious subjects of the Sultan of Zanzibar and in the destruction of a small fort. In 1860, the *Torch*, 5, screw. Commander Frederick Harrison Smith, began on the west coast a useful commission, in the course of which she captured seven slavers; and some exploits of other vessels on that station will demand notice later. But the repression of piracy and slavery was by no means the only kind of minor service rendered by the navy.

In 1860, for example, Captain Thomas Miller, of the *Clio*, 22, screw, was instrumental in saving the city of Panama from capture by a mob, and in protecting some French subjects from infuriated negro rioters; and a party of seamen and marines from the *Satellite*, 21, screw, Captain James Charles Prevost, under Lieutenant Thomas Sherlock Gooch, was marched many miles up country in British Columbia in order to overawe certain miners who were causing anxiety to the government.

During the Persian War of 1856-57, a few officers of the Royal Navy were employed in those vessels of the East India Company which were engaged along the Persian coast, especially at the capture of Reshire fort on December 7th, and the occupation of the island of Karak, and of part of Bushire, on December 10th, 1856; but the navy itself did not share in the operations, which were under the maritime direction of Sir Henry John Leeke, Kt., (a capt., R.N., of 1826, who had become a rear-adm. on reserved half-pay in 1854, and who died in 1870), and Commodore Ethersey, of the H. E. I. Co.'s navy. In the years 1857-61, however, the repression of piracy in the Persian Gulf provided plenty of occupation for several of Her Majesty's cruisers, among which may be mentioned the *Ariel*, 9, screw. Commander Charles Bromley, and the *Lyra*, 9, screw. Commander Radulphus Bryce Oldfield. In the same years, in the West Indies, the *Styx*, 6, paddle. Commander Charles Vesey, rendered excellent service against the slavers in Cuban waters.

Early in 1857, Peru was in the throes of one of its too frequent revolutions. A politician named Vivanco, who was said to possess the sympathies of the richer classes, and especially of the ladies, was engaged in an attempt to depose the President, General Eamon Castilla, who was supported by the army, and by the mass of the people. Vivanco's chief power lay in the fact—an important one in a country having so large a sea-board as Peru—that he had with him the greater part of the small Peruvian Navy.

On March 24th, Vice-Admiral Henry William Bruce, commander-in-chief on the Pacific station, being then in the *Monarch*, 84, at Callao, received intelligence to the effect that two of Vivanco's war-steamers, the *Loa* and the *Tumbes*, had stopped the British mail-steamer *New Grenada*, while on her way to Panama, and, having boarded her, had taken from her 32,000 dollars, besides sundry goods, which, though shipped in the names of merchants at Valparaiso, had in reality been sent by Castilla to supply his troops in the northern part of the republic. (*Loa* and *Tumbes*, gunboats, built in England for Peru. The *Loa* had four long 32-prs., the *Tumbes* two, and a smaller brass gun.)

Bruce at once despatched the *Pearl*, 21, screw, Captain Edward Southwell Sotheby, in search of the delinquents; and she sailed at noon on the 25th. Early on the 28th, Captain Sotheby found the rebel craft off Lambeyaque, and, going to quarters, steamed alongside them, and sent to the *Loa*, the senior officer's ship, a boat under Lieutenant Nicholas Edward Brook Turnour, to demand the stolen money and goods, and the officers and men who had taken them. In default, the surrender of both craft was required within five minutes. As the money had been distributed, it could not be returned. The two Peruvian captains, therefore, wisely surrendered. The people who had not been implicated personally in the outrage were allowed the option of going ashore or of being carried to Callao; Lieutenant Seymour Walter Delmé Radcliffe was given charge of the *Loa*, and Lieutenant Henry Duncan Grant, of the *Tumbes*; and, with one prize on each quarter, the *Pearl* steamed back to Callao, arriving there on March 31st. One of the craft was quickly given back to her temporary owners; the other was detained for some time as security that similar depredations should not be committed again. (Williams: *Cruise of the Pearl*. Republished by Leonaur in *The Naval Brigades of the Indian Mutiny* along with *The Shannon's Brigade in India* by Edmund Hope Verney.)

H.M.S. Pearl

The Indian Mutiny, 1857-1858

It has been shown how, after their arrival at Hong Kong, in the summer of 1857, the *Sans Pareil, Shannon*, and *Pearl* were hastily despatched to Calcutta by Rear-Admiral Sir Michael Seymour (2), K.C.B., in order that they might assist in quelling the Mutiny in India.

The *Sans Pareil*, 70, screw, Captain Astley Cooper Key, C.B., landed a Brigade in August to garrison Fort William, Calcutta; but, after two or three months, returned, as has been seen, to Chinese waters, without having taken any active part in the suppression of the rebellion. The two other ships, however, sent their officers and men up country, and were able to render the most valuable assistance to the troops.

The *Shannon*, 51, screw, had been launched at Portsmouth in November, 1855, and, though other vessels exactly like her were launched in the years immediately following, she was for a time the largest steam frigate afloat. Her tonnage (B.M.) was 2667, or about one-fourth more than that of the *Victory*; and her nominal complement was 560 officers and men, though, on her arrival in India, she had more than that number on board.

The frigate had been commissioned at Portsmouth on September 13th, 1856, by Captain William Peel, C.B.,V.C., who has been already mentioned many times in these pages. On August 6th, 1857, she arrived in the mouth of the Ganges, and Peel at once offered the services of himself and his people to proceed to the front, and cooperate with the army. On the 14th, the captain, several officers, and about 390 seamen and marines, embarked in a flat, and were towed up the Hoogly to join the Lucknow relief force; and on the 18th they were followed by another party of 5 officers and 120 men, (some of these were recruited from merchant vessels at Calcutta), the frigate then being left with 140 people in her, under the command of Master George A. Waters. the officers with the Brigade were:—

Captain William Peel, C.B., (K.C.B., and died 1858); Lieutenants James William Vaughan, (com., Jan. 30th, 1858; C.B., June 29th, 1858), Thomas James Young, (com., March 22nd, 1858; V.C, Feb. 1st, 1859), William Charles Fahie Wilson, (com., March 22nd, 1858), Edward Hay, (com., March 22nd, 1858), Henry Rushworth Wratislaw, (com., March 22nd, 1858), and Nowell Salmon, (com., March 22nd, 1858; V.C, Dec. 24th. 1858): Brevet-Lieutenant Colonel Henry H. Maxwell (attached); Captain Thomas Carstairs Grey, R.M.; Second Lieutenant William Stirling, R.M.; Mates Henry P. Garvey, (killed in action), and Edward Hope Verney, (actg.-lieut., March 22nd, 1858); Midshipmen or Naval Cadets Edmund John Church, William Henry Richards, Martin Abbot Daniel, (killed in action), John Lewis Way, Edward St. John Daniel, Lord Walter Talbot Kerr, Lord Arthur Pelham Clinton, Edward S. Watson, and H. A. Lascelles; Chaplain Edward Lawson Bowman; Assist.-Surgeon James Flanagan (actg.), (surg., Aug. 3rd, 1859); Assist.-Paymaster William Thomas Comerford, (paym., March 22nd, 1858); Assist.-Clerk James Edward Stanton; Assist.-Engineers John W. Bone, Frederick William Brown, and Henry A. Henri; Gunner Robert Thompson; and Carpenter Henry Brice. Lieut. Lind af Hazeby, Swedish Navy, was also attached to the Brigade: and Captain Oliver John Jones, R.N. (half-pay), joined it as a volunteer.

As the Brigade took with it both guns and howitzers, as the towing vessels were of but small power and shallow draught, and as the current was strong, progress was slow; and Peel did not reach Allahabad, near the junction of the Jumna with the Ganges, until the second half of October. By the 20th the strength of the Brigade assembled there was 516 of all ranks. Of these about 240, under Lieutenants Wilson, Wratislaw, and af Hazeby, were left in garrison at Allahabad. On October 23rd 100 more, under Lieutenants Vaughan and Salmon, with four siege-train 24-prs., went to Cawnpur, and thence joined the army before Lucknow; and on the 27th and 28th the rest of the Brigade, with four 24-prs. and two 8-in. howitzers, followed, and was presently amalgamated with a small force which, under Lieutenant-Colonel Powell, of the 53rd regiment, was marching in the same direction.

Late on October 31st the column camped near Fatehpur, and, on the following day, marched twenty-four miles and defeated 4000 of the enemy at Kudjwa, capturing two guns. Powell fell, and Peel took command, and completed the rout of the mutineers, ultimately securing a third gun. The British lost 95 in killed and wounded, among the latter being Lieutenants Hay, R.N., and Stirling, R.M.; but the rebels lost 300 in killed alone. Peel then pressed on for Cawnpur. Writing to Sir Michael Seymour (2) on November 6th, from a camp between Cawnpur and Lucknow, he said:—

Since that battle was fought, with the exception of one day's rest for the footsore men who had marched seventy-two miles in three days, besides fighting a severe engagement, we have made daily marches. . . . At Cawnpur I was obliged to leave Lieutenant Hay with fifty men to serve as artillerymen for that important position. . . . I am much gratified with the conduct of all the Brigade; and there is no departure whatever from the ordinary rules and customs of the service.

Peel and Vaughan rejoined one another on November 12th before Lucknow, which had been relieved by Havelock and Outram, who, however, were so weak in force that they had been soon afterwards themselves besieged with the original defenders. On the 14th, when the Brigade's guns were in action, one of them burst, killing Francis Cassidey, captain of the main-top, and wounding several other men. On November 16th, during the successful attack on Secunderabagh, Midshipman Martin Abbot Daniel was killed by a round-shot, and Lieutenant Salmon was severely wounded. Salmon, however, won the Victoria Cross for that day climbing up a tree touching the angle of the Shah Nujjif, to reply to the fire of the enemy, for which dangerous service Peel had called for volunteers.

Boatswain's Mate John Harrison displayed similar gallantry, and was similarly rewarded. (On the same day Com. Thos. Jas. Young, and Wm. Hall, capt. of foretop, gained the Victoria Cross for gallant handling of a 24-pr. *Gazette*, Dec. 24th, 1858, and Feb. 1st, 1859.) The total loss of the Brigade on that occasion was 4 killed and 13 wounded. Fighting went on almost continuously until the 25th, when the relief was fully accomplished and the town evacuated. (Campbell to Gov.-Genl., Nov. 18th and 25th, 1857.) It was quickly occupied by the rebels, strongly fortified and heavily garrisoned.

Sir Colin Campbell, accompanied by the Naval Brigade, repaired to Cawnpur. On November 28th, on the way thither, a party of 36 bluejackets, with two 24-prs., under Lieutenant Hay, Mate Garvey, and Naval Cadet Lascelles, who was then acting as *A.-d.-C.* to Captain Peel, was engaged, in company with the 88th regiment, and did distinguished service. It was at about that time that Captain Oliver John Jones joined as a volunteer.

In the fighting near Cawnpur, between December 6th and December 9th, the Brigade had a share; and on January 2nd, 1858, it behaved with great gallantly at the action at Kallee-Nuddee. Lieutenant Vaughan was attacked while repairing a bridge across the river, which he then promptly crossed with three guns. On the further side he held in check a body of cavalry, and, himself aiming and firing one of his guns, made such good practice at the rebel gun which had originally annoyed him, that in five shots he dismounted the piece, destroyed its carnage, and blew up its ammunition waggon. Towards the end of the day Captains Peel and Jones, with three men of the 53rd regiment, while passing through a captured battery, were unexpectedly attacked by five *sepoys* who had lain in ambush. All the assailants were killed, the last falling to Jones's revolver.

During the subsequent marching, the Brigade excited the admiration of the army by the manner in which it moved its guns. If a weapon drawn by bullocks stuck in heavy ground, the seamen never failed to extricate it, manning both wheels and dragropes, and, if necessary, getting an elephant to push behind. The cheerfulness, too, of the Brigade was much remarked on; and, doubtless, it contributed to the keeping up of the spirits of all engaged throughout a terribly trying time.

In the fighting previous to the final capture of Lucknow in March, 1858, Peel and his men took a very active part, being present on the 3rd at the action at the Dilkoosha. On the 9th, while looking out for a suitable spot on which to post some guns for breaching the Martinière, the leader of the Brigade was severely wounded in the thigh by a musket-ball. His six 8-in. guns and two 24-prs. were chiefly employed in battering the *begum's* palace; and it was while riding to them with a message on March 12th that Mr. Garvey was killed by a shell from one of the rebel coehorns. Captain Jones, on the same day, most devotedly exposed himself on the parapet of a battery in order to direct the fire of the guns behind it.

On the 13th, when the guns had been placed in a somewhat more advanced battery, a coloured Canadian seaman named Edward Robinson betrayed extraordinary coolness in extinguishing a fire which had caught hold of some sandbags forming the face of the work. Under a storm of bullets from loopholes not forty yards away from him, he leapt out, and either quenched or tore away the burning canvas, being, however, severely wounded. He was awarded the Victoria Cross.

On the 14th, the Brigade, and especially a detachment under Commander Vaughan, Lieutenant Hay, Mate Verney, and Midshipman Lord Walter Kerr, took part in the blowing open of a gate leading to one of the courts of the Kaisarbagh; on the 16th the guns were advanced to the Residency; on the 22nd the rebels evacuated the town; and on March 29th the Brigade handed over the six 8-in. guns which it had brought up from the *Shannon*, and which were put into park in the small Imaumbarah, with the word "Shannon" deeply cut into each carriage.

SIR WILLIAM PEEL, AS A CAPTAIN R.N.,
DURING THE INDIAN MUTINY

The naval contingent from the *Shannon* saw no more fighting in India. The gallant Peel, slowly recovering from his wound, was to have been carried down from Lucknow in one of the King of Oude's carriages which had been specially prepared for him by the *Shannon's* Carpenter. When he saw the gorgeous equipage, he declared that he preferred to travel in a *doolie*, like an ordinary bluejacket. Unfortunately, the *doolie* selected for him must have been an infected one; for, soon afterwards, he was attacked with smallpox, to which, being already weakened by his wound, he succumbed at Cawnpur on April 27th, aged only thirty-four. He was, perhaps, the most brilliant naval officer of his day. (A monument to Peel and the officers and men of the *Shannon's* Brigade stands on Clarence Esplanade, Southsea.)

Sir Edward Lugard, with whose division the Brigade served in the advance to Lucknow, and during the operations there, bore the following high testimony to the behaviour of Peel and his men:—

The men were daily—I may say hourly—under my sight; and I considered their conduct in every respect an example to the troops. During the whole period I was associated with the *Shannon's* Brigade, I never once saw an irregularity among the men. They were sober, quiet, and respectful; and I often remarked to my staff the high state of discipline Sir W. Peel got them into. From the cessation of active operations until I was detached to Azimghur, I commanded all the troops in the city; and all measures for the repression of plundering were carried out through me, and, of course, every irregularity committed was reported to me. During that period not one irregularity was reported to me. Indeed, in the whole course of my life I never saw so well conducted a body of men. . . . Many a time I expressed to Peel the high opinion I had of his men, and my admiration of their cheerfulness and happy contented looks, under all circumstances of fatigue and difficulty. (Lugard to Vaughan.)

The Brigade returned slowly to Calcutta, and on August 12th and the following days, rejoined the ship, which, on September 15th, sailed for England. (Disps. of Peel and Vaughan; Journal of Lieut. E. H. Verney.)

On her way from China to Calcutta, the *Pearl* called at Singapore, and there picked up two companies of the 90th Regiment, which, on July 10th, 1857, had been wrecked in the Strait of Banca in the iron trooper *Transit*. Proceeding, the *Pearl* disembarked those troops

The Shannon Gunners

at Calcutta on August 12th. Captain Sotheby, like Captain Peel, offered his services to the government, and, on September 12th, he embarked some of the officers and part of the crew of his corvette in the paddle-steamer *Chunar*. This detachment, of 158 men, with one 12-pr. howitzer, one 24-pr. howitzer, and 24-pr. rockets, reached Dinapur on October 7th. There it was found that no carriage suitable for the 24-pr. howitzer could be procured.

The weapon was therefore left to be sent back to the ship. In lieu of it a 12-pr. howitzer and two 12-pr. mountain guns were supplied, and with them Sotheby landed at Buxar on October 10th, and took up his quarters in the fort. On the 23rd the detachment was summoned to Chupra, and the whole of it was in quarter there by the afternoon of the 26th. Thence it moved successively to Sewan and Myrwa. By that time another detachment, under Lieutenant Radcliffe, had joined from Calcutta, bringing up the force of the *Pearl's* Brigade to about 250 in all. A few had been raised from among volunteers from the merchant vessels at Calcutta; but the vast majority were seamen and marines belonging to the corvette. The officers of the Brigade were:—

Captain Edward Southwell Sotheby; Lieutenants Nicholas Edward Brook Turnour, Seymour Walter Delmé Radcliffe, Henry Duncan Grant, and Hawkesworth Fawkes; Mates Alexander Wighton Ingles, and Thomas Moore Maquay; Midshipmen Lord Charles Thomas Montagu Douglas Scott, Hon. Victor Alexander Montagu, Henry Frederick Stephenson, Charles Edward Foot, and Herbert Holden Edwards; Lieutenant (R.M.) Frederick George Pym; Second-Master (actg.) John Fowler; Chaplain and Naval Instructor, Rev. Edward Adams Williams, M.A.; Assistant-Surgeon William James Shone; Assistant-Engineer John George Shearman; Master's-Assistant T. R. Merewether; Clerk Thomas Henry Lovelace Bowring; Gunner Parkin; Boatswain Charles Band, (so says the Medal Roll at the Admiralty, Williams gives the boatswain's name as Cooley); and Carpenter John Burton.

The Brigade was attached to the Sarun Field Force, of which, on November 27th, Colonel Rowcroft took command at Myrwa. It first came into action with the mutineers on December 26th at Sohunpore, where an entrenched position was taken, and the enemy was dispersed. No one belonging to the Brigade was hurt.

By February 8th, 1858, the force arrived at Burhul, whence it moved up the Gogra in 150 boats, escorted by the small steamer *Jumna*, reaching Ghopalpur on the 10th; and on the 17th the strong fort of Chanderpur was captured by Captain Sotheby with 130 of the Brigade, 35 Sikhs, and 60 Gurkhas, acting in concert with the *Jumna*, which was under the orders of Second-Master John Fowler. Two guns were captured. The casualties on the side of the attack were insignificant, only about four people being wounded.

On the evening of February 19th, Nourainie Ghat was reached. That night a fort on the Oudh side of the river was seized; and, on the afternoon of the following day, an attack was made upon a body of rebels at Phoolpur. After a gallant and well-sustained action, the enemy was driven from the field, with a loss of three guns. Two days afterwards, the Brigade recrossed the river by a bridge of boats which it had constructed. There had been some friction with the native allies; and it was deemed advisable to keep a British force to guard the rear of the advance, large numbers of rebels being reported in the vicinity of Fyzabad.

The Brigade marched to Amorha on March 2nd. Colonel Rowcroft was there informed that the fort of Belwa, seven miles further on, was occupied by the mutineers. In the afternoon, 168 men of the Brigade, with four guns, some 24-pr. rockets, 35 Sikhs, and a regiment of Gurkhas, moved to Belwa, and, being there joined by the Bengal Yeomanry Cavalry, 250 strong, opened fired on the fort at 5 p.m. The place, however, proved stronger than had been anticipated; and, when darkness came on, the whole force withdrew to the Yeomanry camp, and, on the day following, returned to Amorha. That night and the succeeding day the rebels received very large reinforcements, chiefly from Fyzabad, but also from Nawabguuge, Gondah, and elsewhere.

The retirement from before Belwa had been interpreted as a British defeat; the Sarun Field Force, including the sick, was not then more than 1500 strong; and the mutineers, having collected many thousands of men and fourteen guns, were eager and confident. The little camp was, therefore, rendered as defensible as possible by means of an enclosing line of rifle-pits, and the clearing away of all jungle and houses which could shelter an advance.

On the morning of March 5th, it was reported that the rebels were about to attack. The force thereupon moved out, and took up a position about half a mile to the west of the village of Amorha, with the Naval Brigade and four guns under Captain Sotheby in the centre, astride of the road, a Gurkha regiment and the small detachment of Sikhs on the left, and another Gurkha regiment on the right. On each flank was a squadron of the Bengal Yeomanry Cavalry. The enemy was in such force as to overlap the British force by at least a mile in each direction; and he came on in excellent order in rear of a cloud of skirmishers. The naval guns, under Lieutenant Turnour, opened, and were replied to by ten pieces.

After an artillery duel which lasted for some time, Colonel Rowcroft threw out his skirmishers, and began a steady forward movement, which never ceased until the mutineers were driven from the field; for the cavalry, supported by the Gurkhas, cleared the foe from the flanks of the advance. As soon as it was evident that the enemy had been checked, Rowcroft reinforced his Royal Marines, who were in the skirmishing line, with a detachment of seamen, and pressed the foe all along his front. One of the first guns abandoned by the rebels was turned upon them, and worked by Lieutenant Grant, Assistant-Engineer Shearman, Midshipman Lord Charles Scott, and a seaman named Jesse Ward; and, as there was no port-fire wherewith to fire it, a rifle was discharged into the vent, and the retreating foe was plied with his own grape.

A brilliant cavalry charge threw the left wing of the mutineers into confusion; and soon the entire body fled, leaving behind it eight unspiked guns. The enemy was pursued for six miles, and, making a brief stand at one point, killed Second-Master John Fowler (actg.) and one Gurkha. Heat and fatigue at length put a stop to the action, which had lasted from 8.30 a.m. to 12.30 p.m. The rebels had attacked with about 14,000 men and ten guns, and had been completely defeated, with a loss of about 500, by 1261 men, with but four guns. The Naval Brigade had 1 officer killed and about 15 people wounded.

After the battle, in order to indicate to the enemy that the forces of the government were confident of being able to take care of themselves, the line of rifle-pits was filled up, and the camp at Amorha was pitched in the open plain. A small fort, however, was built to contain the sick, and the spare ammunition and baggage. There were many alarms until the end of April; and, during that period, the force was joined by the left wing of Her Majesty's 13th Light Infantry, while one of the Gurkha regiments was withdrawn from it and sent to Goruckpur.

On April 17th, a detachment went out and defeated a body of marauding rebels near the village of Tilga, capturing a gun; and, on April 25th, another body was met near Jamoulee. Owing to the intense heat, this affair was an unsatisfactory one, for the rebels would not stand and could not be followed far. On the next day, the force moved to Kuptangunge. The enemy was then all round it. With a view to freeing it somewhat, an attack was made on April 29th on the fort of Nuggur by a detachment which included 96 officers and men, two guns, and a rocket tube from the Naval Brigade.

The place was taken with but very trifling loss; and in the evening the detachment returned to camp. For some time afterwards, the Brigade remained at Bustee, where it went into huts on June 13th. From Bustee, several small expeditions were made against detached bodies of the enemy. One of these expeditions, on May 31st, turned a party of mutineers out of a position near Amorha; and on June 18th, another party of more formidable strength, was defeated at Hurreah, but withdrew in good order.

On August 29th, a section of the Brigade, 50 strong, under Lieutenant Fawkes, with two guns, took part in an engagement near Lumptee, and did good and steady service; and on the same day, another section, under Lieutenant Turnour, also with two guns, assisted in repelling an attack on an outpost at Hurreah, and, following the enemy, routed him on September 1st at Debreah. On the evening of September 6th, Commander Grant, (he and other officers had by that time been promoted), with 73 seamen and marines, two 12-pr. howitzers, a 24-pr. rocket-tube, and a detachment of the 13th Regiment, left Amorha, with a view to relieving a small garrison of Sikhs in the friendly town of Bansee.

At Gondah, Grant was joined by Captain Mulcaster, who arrived with a squadron of cavalry, and took command. Bansee was reached on the 8th, after a splendid march of 50 miles in 39 hours, the men being often up to their knees in mud, and sometimes up to their waists in water. Bansee was relieved only just in time, for the gallant Sikhs holding it had but three percussion caps per man remaining.

From Bansee, the expedition, which had been reinforced on the 10th by Brigadier Fischer, marched on the 12th, reaching Doomureah-gunge on the 13th, and driving back a body of the rebels. The howitzers, under Lieutenant Ingles, were most excellently handled. On the 14th, an effort was made to catch a body of mutineers at Intwa; but the roads were so bad that the attempt had to be abandoned; and on the 17th, the expedition returned to Bustee. Another naval force, under Lieutenant Ingles, formed part of an expedition which left Bustee on September 27th for Bansee, and which, having crossed the Raptee, got up with, and dispersed, some mutineers at Mowee on September 30th, after most exhausting marches.

69

On October 1st, the outpost at Amorha, which included 50 of the *Pearl's* people, with two howitzers, under Lieutenant Fawkes, was attacked by about 1200 mutineers, with two guns. The enemy was repulsed, after Lieutenant Maquay, who directed the howitzers, and four seamen, Lee, Williams, Rayfield, and Simmonds, had especially distinguished themselves.

On October 23rd, yet another expedition had to be despatched towards Bansee. On October 26th, when an insufficient British force was foiled in an attack on the jungle fort of Jugdespore, twenty-five miles north-west of Bustee, it was reported that the Brigade lost its guns in the retreat. There was no foundation for the story, which, however, gave rise to some amusing correspondence in the Indian papers.

In the middle of November, all the outlying parties were recalled, and the whole force left Bustee on the 24th for the northern jungle on the Nepal frontier, only a field hospital and guard remaining. A siege train had, in the meantime, arrived at Bustee, and had been handed over to the *Pearl's* people. On the 25th, Bhanpur was reached, and a Madras battery joined; and on the 25th, the force moved on to Doomureahgunge, where the rebels were very bloodily defeated, and a halt was made for some days, during which a bridge of boats was thrown across the Raptee, in face of a considerable army under Balla Rao, a near kinsman of Nana Sahib. On the evening of December 2nd, Brigadier Rowcroft learnt that another native force, under Nazim Mahomed Hossein, was six or eight miles up the river, intending to cross and join Balla Rao.

On the 3rd, therefore, a detachment, which included 2 guns and 50 men of the Naval Brigade, under Captain Sotheby, went out to the attack, and found the rebels at Bururiah in a strong position. The enemy stood with unusual steadiness, until his flank was threatened; whereupon he retired and scattered, carrying off his guns. The detachment then returned to camp; and on December 5th, the Naval Brigade crossed the Raptee, the rest of the force soon following.

The movement was part of a concerted plan to encircle the shattered armies of the *begum*, Lord Clyde being to the westward, Sir Hope Grant to the southward, and Brigadier Rowcroft drawing round from the eastward, while to the northward were the jungles of Nepal. A guard was left at the bridge at Doomureahgunge; and the remainder of the force marched to Intwa and camped there. The siege train, consisting of two 18-prs., one 8-in. howitzer, two 8-in. mortars, and two 5.5-in. mortars, arrived on the 18th and gave the Naval Brigade as much artillery as it could possibly manage. The mortars were entrusted to Lieutenant Pym, R.M.

On the 20th, the force advanced from Intwa to Biskohur, in Oudh, and, on the 22nd, to Goolereah Ghat, five miles from Toolseepur, where the remnants of the enemy were collected in great force. On the 23rd, in concert with the army of Sir Hope Grant, the force crossed the Boora Raptee, and attacked. Near the centre were the four naval guns and two 24-pr. rocket tubes, under Commander Turnour, Lieutenant Maquay, and Midshipman Foot. The rest of the Naval Brigade, and the siege train, under Captain Sotheby, was as close up as the nature of the ground would admit. In about an hour and a half, the rebels were completely routed, though they carried off most of their guns, and although the pursuit was somewhat ineffective, owing to lack of enough cavalry to undertake it properly. The mutineers numbered about 12,000; the attacking force, which had but 4 killed and about a dozen wounded, only 2500.

This was the last affair in which the *Pearl's* Brigade took part, and, indeed, the last general action of the Mutiny. The seamen and marines hoped to enjoy a quiet Christmas at Toolseepur, but were ordered on almost immediately with Brigadier Rowcroft, After a useless pursuit, nearly as far as the Nepal frontier, the force returned. On the last day of the year, the Brigade lay at Puchpurwah; and on January 1st, 1859, it was ordered back to the ship at Calcutta. Brigadier Rowcroft, on taking leave of it on the 2nd, said:

> The successes we have gained are mainly due to your courage and gallantry. I have also observed the excellent discipline and conduct of your Brigade, which reflects great credit on Captain Sotheby, and the officers, as well as on yourselves. I therefore regret to lose your services; but I am glad that, upon your departure, you are homeward bound, which you all so much desire.

On the 3rd, the Brigade departed, and, having embarked on the 17th in the steamer *Benares*, reached Calcutta on February 2nd. A *Gazette Extraordinary*, published at Allahabad on January 17th, when the Brigade passed through that city, expressed the high satisfaction of the Government of India with the great services of the *Pearl's* officers and men. The ship left Calcutta on February 13th, called at Madras, whence she sailed again on the 26th, and reached Spithead on June 6th, after having circumnavigated the globe, and been absent from home for three years and a week. She was paid off on June 16th, 1859; and a "paying-off" dinner on the evening of that day revived an old custom which had long been nearly extinct in the service, and brought officers and men all together for the last time. (Williams, *Cruise of the Pearl.* Disp. of Sotheby, Macgregor, and Rowcroft; Ind. *Gazettes* of Mar. 9th, 23rd; April 27th; May 11th; June 22nd; July 6th, 13th; Aug. 13th; Oct. 12th, 19th; Nov. 23rd, 26th, 1858; and Jan. 11th, 1859.)

The principal honours and promotions granted in respect of the services of the *Pearl's* Brigade were as follows:—

Captain E. S. Sotheby, to be C.B., June 29th, 1858.
To be Commanders: Lieut. N. E. B. Turnour, May 21st; Lieut. S. W. D. Radcliffe, and Lieut. H. D. Grant, June 18th, 1858.
To be (actg.) Lieutenants: Mate A. W. Ingles, May 21st; Mate T. M. Maquay, June 18th, 1858.

Cable Laying, 1857-1866

As in South Africa, forty years later, so in India during the Mutiny, the landed guns of the navy, and the indefatigable and resourceful manner in which they were moved and worked in difficult country, went far towards saving a very precarious situation. Yet it should not be forgotten that the navy does not exist for such work as had to be done by it on those occasions; and that it would scarcely have been called upon to do it had the British Empire been properly prepared to bear its immense responsibilities. It was only because the military administration failed at the pinch that the navy had to step in and adapt itself to duties which did not belong to it, and which, for the moment at least, diminished its efficiency for services more peculiarly its own.

The navy was intimately concerned in the laying of the first submarine telegraph cable across the Atlantic. An unsuccessful attempt was made in August, 1857, after the intended route, between Ireland and Newfoundland, had been surveyed by the *Cyclops*, 6, paddle, Lieutenant Joseph Dayman. (Com., Jan. 1st, 1858.) About half the cable was put into the U.S. screw frigate, *Niagara*, 40, Captain Hudson, U.S.N., and half into the screw battleship *Agamemnon*, 91, Master Cornelius Thomas Augustus Noddall; the programme being that the *Niagara* should lay the section between Valentia and mid-Atlantic, where a splice should be made, and that the *Agamemnon* should complete the laying to Newfoundland.

The two cable ships quitted Valentia on August 7th, accompanied by the *Leopard*, 18, paddle, Captain James Francis Ballard Wainwright, the *Cyclops*, and the U.S. paddle-vessel *Susquehanna*, 15. When 335 miles of the cable had been payed out, it parted.

In July, 1858, a more fortunate essay was made. It had been determined that the cable ships should proceed to a rendezvous in mid-Atlantic, there make the splice, and then steam away from one another in opposite directions. Again, the *Agamemnon* and the *Niagara* were employed, the former, however, being commanded by Captain George William Preedy, with, as navigators, Master Henry Augustus Moriarty, and Second-Master Samuel Libby. (Mast., Sept. 3rd, 1858.) The splice was effected on July 29th, and the *Agamemnon* then made for Kingstown Bay, Valentia, escorted by the *Valorous*, 16, paddle, Captain William Cornwallis Aldham, while the *Niagara* made for Trinity Bay, Newfoundland, escorted by the *Gorgon*, 6, paddle, Commander Joseph Dayman.

At the western terminus there waited the *Porcupine*, 3, paddle. Captain Henry Charles Otter, and, at the eastern one, the gunboat *Shamrock*, Master William Barnerd Calver; and, with the assistance of these, both shore ends were safely landed on August 6th. Unhappily, this cable worked only for a short time. It then became useless, and telegraphic communication beneath the Atlantic was not again effected until 1866.

The Sooso Expedition, 1857–1859

Towards the end of December, 1857, Commodore Charles Wise, of the *Vesuvius*, 6, paddle, senior officer on the west coast of Africa, was instructed by the Admiralty to proceed up the Great Scarcies River, about thirty miles to the northward of Sierra Leone, and to punish the Sooso tribe, which had gone to war with the Timmanees, allies of the British, burning several British factories, and even threatening Sierra Leone.

With his own vessel, and the *Pluto*, 4, paddle, Lieutenant William Swinburn, *Spitfire*, 5, paddle, Lieutenant James Carter Campbell, and *Ardent*, 5, paddle, Commander John Halliday Cave, and a party from the *Teazer*, 2, screw., Lieutenant William Henry Whyte, the commodore anchored off the mouth of the river on January 21st, 1858. The Soosos refused to evacuate the town of Kambia, which they had occupied, and which belonged to the Timmanees; and, in consequence, on January 31st, a force consisting of eight paddle-box boats carrying 24- and 12-

prs., a rocket cutter, a colonial gunboat having on board the governor and staff, and a detachment of about 250 seamen and marines, proceeded up the river, and anchored off Kambia on February 1st.

The town was strongly stockaded, and defended by an inner mud wall and flanking towers, while the plain between the place and the river's bank was studded with rifle-pits. Within a quarter of an hour, however, the town was set on fire by means of rockets; and a bombardment with shell killed, it was said, 200 of the enemy. Kambia being in ashes, the force descended the stream, destroying in succession Robelli, Makanka, Robaiyan, and Rokon, besides other villages. Although the people were exposed to a brisk fire from each place, the casualties among them were only 2 officers and 8 men wounded. Thanks to a liberal use of quinine, there was no fever in the force, which rejoined the ships on February 4th.

For this service Lieutenants Swinburn, Whyte, and Campbell were promoted, and three mates were made lieutenants.

The force had not landed to occupy the site of any of the destroyed towns; and the enemy, attributing the omission to weakness, presently became more aggressive than before; whereupon, in March, 1859, a fresh expedition, again under Commodore Wise, went up the river in 52 boats. The landing force consisted chiefly of marines, and the 1st West India Regiment. The stockade was stormed; the Soosos were driven out with heavy loss; and the Timmanees were put in possession of the town. The casualties wore trivial; and, as before, there was happily no fever.

At about the same time the vessels on the station were both active and successful in the repression of slavery. An armed slaver of considerable size and force was captured by the *Vesuvius's* cutter, under Mate Robert Henry More Molyneux, (actg.-lieut. in consequence, June 28th, 1859), assisted by the *Pluto's* gig.

The Bombardment of Jeddah, 1858

In the course of June, 1858, a dispute arose at Jeddah, the port of Mecca, concerning the ownership of a vessel which belonged to Indian subjects of Her Majesty. In consequence of this dispute, rioting took place; and on the evening of June 15th, the British vice-consul, the French consul, and several other Christian residents in the town were massacred. Several more only escaped massacre owing to the intervention of local officials, or to the opportune despatch to the shore of an armed boat from the *Cyclops*, 6, paddle, Captain William John

Samuel Pullen, which was lying off the town.

Pullen took the fugitives to Suez, and, having received orders, returned to Jeddah, where he arrived on July 23rd. He demanded satisfaction within thirty-six hours, and, getting no reply by the morning of the 25th, began a bombardment. At 11 a.m. an unsatisfactory answer from the local *pasha* was sent off to him; whereupon he resumed firing, and continued, with intermissions, until the evening of the 26th. On the 27th Turkish troops appeared in a transport, and were landed. Their commander seized the murderers, but professed that he had no power to execute them, although they had been found guilty by the native court.

Pullen insisted upon their execution; and, on the morning of August 5th reopened the bombardment in order to enforce his determination. More troops, and an officer of superior rank, arriving from Egypt, eleven of the murderers were executed in sight of the town and shipping on the morning of the 6th, and four more were sent to Constantinople. (Cons. Green to For. Off. Lord Malmesbury in House of Lords, July 19th, 1858.) The business was a natural result of the lamentable weakness of Turkish authority in Arabia; but, as proper satisfaction was given by the *Sultan*, the matter proceeded no further.

★★★★★★

The *Roebuck*, 6, screw, Lieutenant (actg.-Commander) Edwin Charles Symons, was also employed at Jeddah, during this year, in connection with the attacks on the local Christians, and subsequently at the Andaman Islands, on the occasion of a mutinous outbreak there.

★★★★★★

The Walker Incident, 1860

William Walker, the famous filibuster, who had been a thorn in the side of the Central American governments since 1853, had been driven out of Nicaragua in 1857 by the concerted action of the other states, and, making an effort to return in 1858, had been shipwrecked, and obliged to accept the hospitality of a British man-of-war. He, or his partisans, made yet another abortive attempt in 1859; and in 1860, after having written a curious history of his adventurous career, he set out from Mobile on what proved to be his last expedition. Previous to his departure, Great Britain had joined the United States in declaring that any further action by Walker against Nicaragua would be forcibly resisted.

Until a few years before, Ruatan, the principal of the Bay Islands, had been under British guardianship; but, under the Clayton-Bulwer Treaty, it had been ceded to Honduras; and the filibuster imagined that he might take advantage of this circumstance to make the island his base of operations against the republic of which he had been, for a short time, president. He therefore proceeded thither with a number of his old followers. Unfortunately for him, the British flag was still flying over Ruatan, the cession not having been actually carried out, owing to certain financial disputes between Great Britain and Honduras not having been settled.

While Walker was standing on and off, waiting for the British flag to be hauled down, the *Icarus*, 11, Commander Nowell Salmon, V.C., arrived at Ruatan from Belize, having on board the Superintendent of Belize, who, with Salmon, was to complete the cession of the islands. Seeing what was the state of affairs, and unwilling to do anything which might enable Walker to seize Ruatan ere Honduras could take possession of it, the British officials went to Jamaica for further orders. Upon returning, Salmon found Walker still in the neighbourhood, and learnt that he had endeavoured to utilise for his purposes the adjoining island of Bonacea. Chafing at being able to accomplish nothing in the islands, Walker and his people sailed over to Truxillo on the mainland, and captured it. Salmon followed him, and was informed that the filibuster had "annexed" the town, and made it a free port. The inhabitants, who had been maltreated, had taken to the forest.

With some little difficulty Salmon put himself in communication with the expelled Honduran governor, and discovered that the customs' receipts of the place had been mortgaged to the British Government in payment of a debt.

He therefore wrote to Walker, telling him that in the circumstances his acts could not be recognised, and that he must evacuate the town within twenty-four hours, and take shipping, which should be provided, for New Orleans. After some correspondence, in the course of which Walker magniloquently declared that he had come to introduce the code of Alfred into benighted lands, the filibuster agreed to the terms, and undertook to embark on the following morning. This was on August 20th. Pressed, however, by Honduran forces, he evacuated the town overnight, and retreated down the coast, with but seventy men.

On his way, he looted some mahogany-cutting settlements; and, upon hearing of this, the Honduran Government applied to Salmon for assistance. Salmon satisfied himself that there was precedent for giving it; and, taking in tow a *barque* with General Alvarez and 200 troops, went in chase down the coast. Off the Rio Negro, it was ascertained that Walker and his companions were making themselves at home on the mahogany-cutting station of an Englishman, near Lemas. Salmon proceeded up the river with his boats manned and armed; and, when within sight of the station, landed with General Alvarez, and walked to the building which Walker had made his headquarters.

To a demand for an unconditional surrender, and a threat that the guns in the boats would open fire on him if he refused, the filibuster asked for certain terms, which Salmon declined, alleging that, as Walker had already broken faith, he would not be allowed another opportunity for doing so. Walker then inquired whether he was surrendering to the Queen of England. The reply was that the surrender was to the commander of the *Icarus*; whereupon Walker fell his men in, and ordered them to lay down their arms. Both men and arms were taken on board the sloop and carried to Truxillo, where all but Walker, and Rudler, his chief of staff, were transferred to the *Gladiator*, 6, paddle, Commander Henry Dennis Hickley, and conveyed to New Orleans.

Walker declined to plead American nationality, and claimed to be president of the Nicaraguan Republic. Salmon, therefore, could not persuade the Honduran authorities to release the two leaders; nor, acting with and on behalf of them as he did, did he feel justified in taking up the position that the filibusters ought not to be punished. However, he appointed a Mr. Squire to watch the case on behalf of the United States Government. Walker was tried by court-martial on September 11th, and condemned to be shot on the following morning. Ere he died, he admitted the justice of his sentence. (J. J. Roche: *Story of the Filibusters*; Disp. of Salmon; Letter of Salmon to author, Oct. 12th, 1900; *A. and N. Gazette*, Oct. 6th, 1860.)

Walker's allusion to King Alfred indicates that he regarded himself as an enlightened law-giver. This singular man also regarded himself as a disinterested liberator; for, after his surrender, he sent for Salmon, and asked: "Would you have treated Garibaldi like this?" But Salmon, who seems to have had but little sympathy with liberators, even of Garibaldi's type, replied to the effect that, if it fell to his lot to be able to do so, he might possibly not hesitate. The "last of the filibusters" was little more than thirty-six at the time of his death.

Mexico, 1858–1861

Between 1821 and 1868 the form of government in Mexico was changed ten times; upwards of fifty persons became in succession rulers of the country as presidents, dictators, or emperors; and there are said to have been no fewer than three hundred *pronunciamientos*. It is hardly astonishing, therefore, that during that period Mexico got into occasional difficulties with foreign powers.

In 1857, what is known as the "Struggle of Reform" broke out. Ignacio Comonfort, who had been made provisional president of the republic by Alvarez, in 1855, had assumed a dictatorship, with the support of the clergy and the conservatives. Benito Pablo Juarez, the chief justice, and leader of the advanced liberals, or "*Puros*," headed the opposition. In 1858 Comonfort was deposed by Zuloaga, who resigned in favour of the conservative General Miramon, but was presently restored by him. Juarez claimed that, the president having been unconstitutionally displaced, the chief justice, as vice president, thereupon became legal president of the republic, and, accordingly, he ignored Zuloaga and Miramon, and himself acted as president.

Civil War resulted. An able, honest, and patriotic statesman, Juarez had the misfortune, throughout his active career, to be regarded with suspicion and intolerance by most of the Europeans with whom his energetic behaviour brought him into contact; and certainly, his methods were sometimes extremely highhanded. As early as the autumn of 1859, the *Amethyst*, 26, Captain Sidney Grenfell, which was then serving a commission during which she circumnavigated the globe, found occasion to interfere with the proceedings of his supporters at Mazatlan, and at San Bias, both on the Pacific coast. Trade was taken possession of; Mazatlan was blockaded; an American brig, which had been seized, and which lay under the batteries there, was pluckily cut out one October night by three of the frigate's boats, under Master Richard Cossantine Dyer; and Royal Marines, under Lieutenant Alfred Henry Pascoe, R.M., were disembarked at San Bias.

At length the Puros were triumphant, and Juarez was duly elected by congress to be president of the republic of Mexico. He readily agreed with Great Britain and France as to the payment of indemnities to persons of those nationalities who, residing in Mexico during the civil commotions, had suffered in consequence; and a convention to that effect was signed on March 16th, 1861. But the country, exhausted by the long strife, was in grave financial difficulties; and on

July 17th, following, congress was induced to pass a law, in virtue of which the payment of all public debts, including the indemnities, was to be postponed for two years. The representatives of Great Britain and France endeavoured, in vain, to procure the repeal of this measure, and then broke off relations with the Mexican Government. Spain, which also had claims, took parallel action, and, on October 31st, 1861, the three powers signed a convention providing for their co-operation with a view to obtaining satisfaction.

France dispatched a large naval and military force; Spain sent 6000 troops; Great Britain contributed only a battalion of marines, and a few vessels which happened to be on the station, including the *Challenger*, (bearing the broad pennant of Commodore Hugh Dunlop, from Jamaica), 22, screw, Captain John James Kennedy, C.B., the *Desperate*, 7, screw. Commander John Francis Ross, and the *Barracouta*, 6, paddle. Commander George John Malcolm. The British participated in the occupation of Vera Cruz in January, 1862, but on the following April 9th, wisely decided, in concert with Spain, to press matters no further, and to withdraw from Mexican territory. France, which had larger views than her allies, was left to prosecute alone an undertaking which became disastrous both to herself and Mexico, and to France's *protégée*, the Austrian Archduke, Ferdinand Maximilian Josef, who was made emperor in 1863.

The Royal Visit to Canada & U.S.A., 1860

In 1860, accompanied by a large suite, H.R.H. the Prince of Wales paid a visit to Canada and the United States. The screw battleship *Hero*, 91, Captain George Henry Seymour, C.B., was selected as the vessel in which he was to cross the Atlantic; and he embarked in her at Plymouth, and sailed on July 12th, escorted by the screw frigate *Ariadne*, 26, Captain Edward Westby Vansittart, and the screw sloop *Flying-Fish*, 6, Commander Charles Webley Hope. The outward voyage was made without incident. Returning, the prince embarked at Portland, Maine, on October 29th, and, encountering headwinds and bad weather nearly all the way home, did not reach Plymouth until November 16th, by which day the *Hero* had only about one week's ship's provisions left, and even the royal party was living on salt and preserved meat. The ships had plenty of coal, but, with the relatively low-powered engines of those days, had been unable to make head against the continuous gales. As Lord Palmerston said:

Our cousins in the United States, received the eldest son of our gracious sovereign, not as if he were a stranger belonging to another land, but as if he had been born in their own country.

Of the loyalty of the reception in Canada there is no need to speak.

The Ti-Ping Rebellion, 1860-1864

The history of the events which led up to Great Britain's active interference with the Ti-ping rebellion in China must be told at some little length. It affords an interesting study, and, I think, supplies examples rather of what to avoid than of what to emulate in dealing with great reform movements in Oriental lands.

After the collision with the Ti-ping rebels at Nankin, and elsewhere on the Yang-tse-kiang, in 1858, Great Britain, which had always recognised the Ti-pings as belligerents, (Bowring's Ordinance of 1855), re-adopted a professed policy, so far as they were concerned, of non-intervention. The rebels were, however, from time to time reminded that they must neither interfere with British trade nor imperil British interests. Thus, for example, a proclamation by the Hon. F. W. A. Bruce, dated Shanghai, May 26th, 1860, pointed out that, Shanghai being a port open to foreign trade, commerce would receive a severe blow, were the place to be attacked and to become the scene of civil war; and went on to declare that, without taking any part in the contest, or expressing any opinion as to the rights of the parties to it, the British might justifiably protect the city, and assist the Chinese authorities in preserving tranquillity within it.

★★★★★★

Yet, writing to Lord John Russell from Shanghai on June 10th, 1860, Mr. Bruce had said: "I am inclined to doubt the policy of attempting to restore, by force of arms, the power of the Imperial Government in cities and provinces occupied, or rather overrun, by the insurgents." And, after deprecating intervention, went on, "... . the Chinese, deprived of popular insurrection—their rude but efficacious remedy against local oppressors—would, with justice, throw on the foreigner the odium of excesses which his presence alone would render possible. No course could be so well calculated to lower our national reputation as to lend our material support to a government, the corruption of whose authorities is only checked by its weakness." See also Sykes' *Taeping Rebellion*.)

Mr. Bruce did not, unfortunately, wait for the rebels actually to attack Shanghai ere he began to make a distinction between them and the Imperial party, such as, apparently, he had no right to make so long as the Ti-pings were officially recognised as belligerents; for, a few months after his proclamation above alluded to, he refused to allow the consuls to hold any communication with certain insurgent authorities at Soo-chow, and ordered them to take no notice of a dispatch which had been received from one of the insurgent leaders. This attitude was inconsistent, and, as events proved, dangerous. Neutrality, such as Mr. Bruce professed, should not have allowed him to take more notice of Imperial than of Ti-ping dispatches; nor could he complain if, so long as he declined to notice communications from the Ti-pings, the Ti-pings paid little attention to communications from him. It was the anomalous and contradictory situation created by Mr. Bruce which, I believe, was originally responsible for the many bloody collisions which followed between the British forces and the rebels, who, it is notorious, were particularly anxious to gain European countenance, and most unwilling deliberately to provoke European hostility.

On August 18th, 1860, the rebel leader sent to the foreign ministers a notification of his intention to come to Shanghai, and of his determination to respect foreign churches and property, upon yellow flags being hoisted over them. (In response, he afterwards explained, to an invitation from the French. The *chung-wang* to the Consuls, Aug. 21st.) This was the dispatch which Mr. Bruce ordered his subordinates to take no notice of.

Instead of acknowledging it, and directly stating in reply that the rebels must on no account approach, he issued a "notification," based ostensibly on "reports" which had reached him, to the effect that, armed forces being understood to be in the neighbourhood, he thereby made known that the city of Shanghai, and the foreign settlement, were militarily occupied by the British and French, and that any armed force approaching would be treated as hostile. He sent a copy of this, not to the chief who had addressed him, but to a place out of the line of the march of the Ti-pings; and, in consequence, it was not delivered. Had he communicated with the *chung-wang*, (Ti-ping general-in-chief), who had written to him, what followed might have been avoided.

On August 18th, 1860, the Ti-ping Army, or rather, part of it, arrived before Shanghai, and drove in the Tartar outposts, subsequently advancing to the walls. They were met with shot, shell, and musketry from the European garrison of the settlement, and especially from Royal Marines, and Indian troops. Lieutenant John William Waller O'Grady, R.M., being particularly active, and Captain Frederick Edward Budd, R.M., keeping up a very hot fire from another position. It is said that, during the whole time, the rebels did not reply. (Corr. of Nonconformist, Nov. 14th, 1860; *Overland Register*, Sept. 10th, 1860; *Ti-ping Tien-Kwoh*, i.; *Times of India*, Oct. 24th, 1860.)

At any rate, about 300 of them fell, while there was not a single casualty on the part of the Europeans. When the Ti-pings had retired, parties were sent out to burn down such houses in the suburbs as might afford cover to the rebels. On Sunday, August 19th, the French burnt more houses, and, in the afternoon, the gunboats *Kestrel*, Lieutenant Henry Huxham, and *Hongkong*, together with Lieutenant O'Grady's marines, re-opened fire on any rebels who could be seen.

It is said that again the Ti-pings did not return a shot. It is certain, however, that, on the 20th they advanced in greater strength than before, determined, perhaps, to endeavour to avenge their comrades slaughtered, as they conceived it, in bad faith. Once more they were driven back; and during the following night, the *Pioneer*, 6, screw, Commander Hugh Arthur Reilly, added to their discomfiture by steaming up the river and dropping shells into their camp.

When, after the conclusion of peace with China, it became desirable that a British expedition should proceed up the Yang-tse-kiang to provide for the opening of the treaty ports there, it was necessary to make some preliminary agreement with the Ti-pings, who commanded many of the important points on the river.

Sir James Hope, therefore, communicated with the Ti-ping authorities at Nankin, and once more pledged British neutrality. He was instructed by Lord Elgin, (Parl. Corr., on Opening of Yang-tse-kiang), to say that the British did not appear as enemies, nor with the intention of taking part in the civil war. Mr. Parkes, who accompanied the vice-admiral on the subsequent expedition up the river, was instructed by Lord Elgin, (Jan 19th, 1861), to the same effect. But, when Hope, in the *Coromandel*, reached Nankin, he directed, (Hope to Aplin, Mar. 28th, 1861), Commander Elphinstone d'Oyley d'Auvergne Aplin, of the *Centaur*, 6, paddle, to tell the Ti-ping authorities that the British and French governments had ordered that any attempt to enter Shanghai or Woosung would be repelled by force, and that therefore the Ti-pings would do well not to go within two days' march of those cities.

If such orders had then been given, they were secret ones; but the Foreign Office approved, (Russell to Bruce, July 24th, 1861), of Hope's measures, and also of his having assured the Ti-pings that, if they obeyed him in this matter he would exert his influence to prevent any hostile expedition from leaving those places in order to attack Ti-ping troops. While expressing his approval, Lord John Russell added:

> You will understand, however, that Her Majesty's government do not wish force to be used against the rebels in any case, except for the actual protection of the lives and property of British subjects.

The upshot was that the Ti-pings ultimately promised not to attack Shanghai or Woosung that year (1861); and requested that, on the other hand, the Imperial troops might not be allowed into those places. Mr. Parkes accepted and reported this request as a condition. It was also arranged that if the Ti-pings should attack other treaty ports and not molest British subjects in their persons and property, commanders of British vessels, in accordance with instructions to be given them, would not interfere in the hostilities, except for the purpose of protecting their countrymen, if necessary.

The Ti-pings adhered to their undertaking relative to the year 1861, and refrained from advancing within 100 *li*, or about 30 miles, of Shanghai or Woosung. They might easily have taken both places had they wished, and had they had only the Imperial forces to contend with, for, during that year, they were extraordinarily successful, and made themselves masters of nearly the whole of the two rich provinces of Chekiang and Kiangsu.

That friction, nevertheless, occurred almost immediately was but natural, looking to the forward policy which Sir James Hope thought fit to adopt throughout. Mr. Bruce, writing to Lord John Russell on January 3rd, 1861, said that he had directed the British consul at Ningpo not to undertake the defence of that city, and, should it be attacked, to confine his efforts to a mediation, "which may save the place from being the scene of pillage and massacre"; and, in a letter to Hope, Bruce declared that he did not consider himself authorised to protect Ningpo. In his instructions to Mr. Sinclair, the local consul, he wrote:

> Your language should be that we take no part in this civil con-

test, but that we claim exemption from injury and annoyance at the hands of both parties.

All this was approved by Lord John Russell in a dispatch of March 28th, 1861. Yet, on May 8th, Sir James Hope, at Nagasaki, ordered Captain Roderick Dew, of the *Encounter*, 14, screw, to put himself into communication with the rebel leaders, and to require them to desist from all hostile proceedings against the town of Ningpo. At the same time, Dew was directed to communicate also with the Imperial authorities at Ningpo.

> . . . .for the purpose of ascertaining what their means of resistance are, and the probabilities of their proving successful; and, should you find them amenable to advice, you will point out to them such measures as circumstance may render expedient, and you will place every obstruction in the way of the capture of the town by the rebels.

This was not neutrality. Lord John Russell was being hurried on by Hope, but hurried on unwillingly; for, commenting on the "every obstruction" policy of the vice-admiral, Lord John, writing to Bruce, said:—

> I have caused the Admiralty to be informed, in reply, that I am of opinion that Vice-Admiral Hope's measures should be approved. . . . You will understand, however, that Her Majesty's government do not wish force to be used against the rebels in any case, except for the actual protection of the lives and property of British subjects.

Captain Dew, in pursuance of instructions, proceeded on May 24th in the gunboat *Flamer*, Lieutenant Henry Maynard Bingham, to convey Hope's ultimatum to the rebels in the vicinity of Ningpo. They were not to approach within two days' march of Ningpo upon penalty of coming into hostile contact with British forces. Dew, being unable to reach the rebel positions in the gunboat, put his little party into pulling boats. Upon reaching a town which was occupied by the Ti-pings, he noticed a discharge of gingals from the walls, though whether directed against him is doubtful: and he withdrew, after having left Hope's communication in a cleft bamboo stuck into the ground before the place.

If there was any firing at the party, it was probably the work of some ignorant underling or the result of mistake; for when, on June

11th, with the *Encounter* and *Flamer*, Dew took another copy of the ultimatum to Chapoo, which had been occupied by the Ti-pings, and landed with it under a flag of truce, he was not fired at; and the local commandant went out and received the letter in person. The document, dated "*Encounter*, June 11th," says nothing about any hostile act having been committed on May 24th; and therefore, it may be assumed that whatever occurred on that day was officially regarded as not calling for an apology.

The Ti-pings, be it remembered, were under no undertaking not to occupy Ningpo. The British, however, were under an undertaking to be neutral. Yet almost while Lord John Russell, writing on August 8th, (Blue Book on China), to Mr. Bruce, said that the desire of the government was to remain neutral as before, and to "abstain from all interference in the civil war," Captain Dew was assisting the Imperialists with plans for the defence of Ningpo, and fitting twelve heavy guns with carriages to mount on the walls. It is not astonishing that Mr. Bruce thought that:

> Captain Dew had gone farther than he was strictly warranted in doing in his desire to save the city of Ningpo. (Blue Book on China.)

In June, moreover, Captain Dew appeared in the *Flamer* off the Ti-ping town of Loochee, some distance up the Wong-poo River, and demanded the restitution of some boats and silk which had been detained for non-payment of duty at a time when duty was being paid as a matter of course at the same station by many European traders. It could not be contended that the Ti-ping occupation had injured the silk trade, duty or no duty; for Mr. Bruce himself, in a dispatch to Lord John Russell said that the export from June, 1860, to June, 1861, had been 85,000 bales; and that was, with one exception, the largest annual export ever then known.

By November, the only places in the Chekiaug and Kiangsu provinces south of the Yang-tse-kiang not held by the Ti-pings were the treaty ports of Shanghai, Chinkiang, and Ningpo. Those places were strongholds of the Imperialists; and the rebels were bound by all the principles of strategy either to complete their conquest of the provinces, or criminally to leave their cause in a position of great danger and peril. In spite, therefore, of Sir James Hope's communications, they approached Ningpo; whereupon the British and American Consuls, with Lieutenant Henry Huxham, commanding H.M.S. *Kestrel*,

H.M. SINGLE-SCREW, IRON, ARMOURED SHIP *AGINCOURT*.
(*Launched at Birkenhead, 1865.*)

Length, 400 ft.; beam, 59 ft. 4½ in.; mean draught, 27 ft. 9 in.; displ., 10,600 tons; I.H.P., 4600; speed, 13·3 kts.
Horizontal common return connecting-rod engines by Maudslay.
Armour: complete 5½ in. iron belt to upper deck, except at bows; 4½ in. forward bulkhead. Conning-tower, 5½ in.
Original armament: 10 12¾ ton M.; 16 6½ ton M. Complement, 710.

and a French naval officer, proceeded on November 28th to the Ti-ping headquarters, and verbally informed the leaders

That the undersigned take no part in this civil contest, but that they claim exemption from injury and annoyance at the hands of both parties.

Hwang, the Ti-ping general, agreed with the principle thus laid down, assured the Consuls of his desire to keep well with foreigners, and promised to behead any of his followers who should offer them annoyance. On December 2nd the Consuls visited another Ti-ping general, Fang, who was advancing from a different direction. They endeavoured to dissuade him from capturing the place, chiefly on the ground of the difficulty of keeping order afterwards. Fang replied that he could not allow Ningpo to remain in the hands of the Imperialists; but, at the wish of the Consuls, he consented to postpone the attack for a week. At the expiration of that period, the Ti-pings, on December 9th, 1861, took Ningpo, after it had offered a feeble resistance for about an hour, the Imperialists then fleeing. Hope, in his account of the affair, admits that—

Everything had been done to assist the Imperialists in the defence of the town, except the use of force in their favour; and their Lordships will not fail to observe how utterly useless such measures proved, in consequence of the cowardice and imbecility of the *mandarins*. . . . The behaviour of the rebels has been good hitherto; and they profess a strong desire to remain on good terms with foreigners.

The British Consul, writing to Lord John Russell, also said:—

Up to the present time there has been no slaughter, or massacre, or fires within the walls. . . . With the exception of a few men killed, and a certain amount of destruction of property, the rebels have, so tar, conducted themselves with wonderful moderation.

A few days afterwards. Sir James Hope proceeded to Nankin in order, if possible, to obtain from the Ti-ping leaders a renewal of their promise not to attack Shanghai for one year—that is, during the course of 1862. This they declined to give, partly because they considered that the British had not strictly interpreted their own promise to prevent the Imperialists from using Shanghai as a base for aggressive purposes; partly because Shanghai had become an Imperial arsenal and rallying place; and partly because they could not further forego their rights as recognised belligerents.

Upon that Sir James Hope, through Lieutenant Henry Maynard Bingham, of the *Renard*, on December 27th, 1861, put forward demands which, I think, can have been formulated only with an intention of finding a *casus belli*. He alleged that certain British subjects, by robberies committed in territories held by the Ti-pings, had suffered a loss amounting to 7563 *taels*, 1 mace, and 7 candareens, 4800 dollars, 20 bales of silk, and 2 muskets. The cash value of all this in British currency may have been as much as £3500. He further demanded that *junks* carrying British colours should be regarded as British vessels, no matter whether British or foreign built, and should be allowed to pass free on the river from examination or other molestation.

He went on to declare that the Ti-ping promise that troops should not approach within 100 *li* of Shanghai and Woosung had not been faithfully observed; and he ended by requiring that no Ti-ping troops should go within 100 *li* of Kiukiang and Hankow, and that Silver Island, the residence of the British Consul at Chinkiang-foo, should not be molested. The general tenor of the reply, (Jan. 1st, 1862), of the Ti-ping leaders was to the effect that compliance with the demands, some of which were new and of a distinctly unfriendly nature, would fetter the Ti-ping cause, and could not, therefore, be granted.

It was objected that no proofs had been advanced as to the alleged losses by British subjects, or that such losses had been caused by the Ti-pings; and that, if the losses had taken place, the British ought to have complained at once to the local officers, instead of waiting many months before complaining at all. It was also pointed out that, if the British flag were permitted to cover non-British vessels, the Ti-pings might see themselves deprived of nearly the whole of their customs revenue.

Bingham, by Hope's direction, at once answered with a threat to use force. It would occupy much more space than can be afforded here were I to follow out the arguments by which Sir James persuaded himself that it was his duty to prevent the Ti-pings from occupying Shanghai; but I cannot blind myself to the conclusion that, had not Hope desired hostilities, hostilities could very easily and honourably have been avoided. It was a case, and a case not altogether creditable, of the "prancing pro-consul" leading his countrymen into devious and dangerous paths ere they realised whither they were bound, or had time to inquire whether or not good reasons summoned them. There is a proverb that adversity makes us acquainted with strange bed-fellows. A forward policy did as much for Hope.

Not many months earlier. Commander Nowell Salmon, in Central America, had seized the filibuster William Walker, and handed him over for execution to the authorities of Honduras. Sir James Hope now associated himself with William Townsend Ward, who had been one of Walkers lieutenants, and who, still a filibuster, happened to be, in 1862, engaged on behalf of the Chinese Imperialists.

On February 21st, 1862, Hope began operations against the rebels by landing a Naval Brigade of 350 men and a 6-pr. rocket-tube, which, with about 600 disciplined Chinese under Ward, and 160 French seamen under the French Rear-Admiral Protêt, drove the small and ill-armed Ti-ping garrison from the village of Kaokiau, killing more than 100 of them, and suffering a loss of only 1 French seaman killed. A similarly one-sided engagement took place on February 28th at Seadong; and on March 1st, having been reinforced from Shanghai, the allies attacked the fortified village of Hsiautang, near Minghong, about twenty miles from Shanghai. About 100 rebels were killed and 300 taken prisoners, the assailants not losing a man.

On April 4th a stockaded camp at Wongkadzu, twelve miles from Shanghai, was shelled till the rebels quitted it. They were pursued, and about 600 of them were killed, while the allies, who had been again reinforced, had but 1 killed and 2 wounded. On April 5th 300 rebels were killed at the capture of Lukakong, the assailants once more having no casualties. They had, however, been repulsed on the previous day, and Hope himself had been slightly wounded. On April 17th, Chepoo, a village seven miles up a creek running into the Woosung river, twelve miles above Shanghai, was bombarded and rushed, the allies having but 1 killed and 2 wounded, but the Ti-pings suffering a loss estimated at 900. On May 1st, after four days' operations, the city of Kahding was taken, the European allies capturing 1000 prisoners and killing "some hundreds," while their Chinese colleague, General Lee, cut off the retreat of many others and "destroyed 2500 of the enemy." (Staveley's disp. of May 3rd.) These operations cost the allies not more than five or six people wounded.

On May 12th the walled city of Tsingpoo was escaladed. About 2500 Ti-pings were killed, and the whole of the rest of the garrison was taken prisoners. The allies here had but 2 killed and 10 wounded, though they also lost an artillery officer from exposure and over-exertion. The village of Najoor was taken on May 17th. This capture cost the life of the French Rear-Admiral Protêt and the wounding of 15 other British and French; but the Ti-pings had 500 killed. On May 20th the small town of Cholin, twenty-six miles S.S.W. of Shanghai and two miles from the sea, was bombarded and stormed. Here a most disgraceful and indiscriminate massacre took place, even women and children not being spared. (*Overland Trade Report*, June 10th. See also *North China Herald*. The French, announcing that they were avenging Protêt, were the worst offenders.) About 3000 Chinese perished. The allies had 1 killed and 4 wounded.

Up to that time Sir James Hope and General Staveley, in the neighbourhood of Shanghai, had met only ill-armed Ti-pings. Upon receipt of intelligence that the *chung-wang*, with a large and probably a more formidably-equipped army, had taken the field, and invested Kahding, and was threatening Tsingpoo, they returned to the treaty port. A half-hearted attempt to relieve Kahding was abandoned, owing to the immense numbers of rebels near it; but the only loss suffered by the British ere they retreated was 1 killed and 4 wounded. The Naval Brigade employed in these various affairs was drawn mainly from the *Impérieuse*, 51, screw (flag), Captain George Ommanney Willes, C.B.; *Pearl*, 21, screw, Captain John Borlase, C.B., who generally commanded; and *Vulcan*, 6, screw trooper. Commander Augustus Chetham Strode.

All this was done professedly in the interests of European commerce. It would hardly have been done had the merchants been first consulted. Messrs. Jardine, Matheson and Co., in their circular of February 27th, complained, not of what had been done by the Ti-pings, but of what was about to be done by the allies. They wrote:—

> The policy the allied commanders are adopting will, it is feared, lead to disastrous consequences. . . . Our interests call for a strict neutrality; but, so far from this course being pursued, our last advices report a combined expedition of English and French marines and sailors, in conjunction with a force of Imperialists, commanded in person by their respective admirals, against a body of some 6000 rebels which, of course, they defeated with great slaughter.

Nor, after he had begun hostilities, was Sir James Hope consistent. He grounded his action on the possibility that the advancing Ti-pings might destroy supplies. After describing his operations, he said:—

All these camps, which contained large quantities of rice collected from the surrounding country, were burnt, and the grain destroyed.

Moreover, only a few days before the attack on Wongkadzu, the *Flamer* destroyed a flotilla of 300 Ti-ping boats "deeply laden with rice and livestock."

In the meantime, Ningpo had been taken by the rebels. Mr. Consul Harvey reported that it was held with "wonderful moderation." On April 22nd, during certain rejoicings there, some shots were fired wildly in the direction of the foreign settlement, and, it was alleged, killed two or three Chinese. The true facts were never established; but when Commander Robert George Craigie, of the *Ringdove*, 4, screw, wrote to the local authorities on the subject, he received a civil reply and a promise that the offenders, when discovered, should be severely punished. On April 29th Captain Roderick Dew, in the *Encounter*, arrived off Ningpo from Shanghai. On the 27th he wrote to the local authorities, expressing his satisfaction at the replies and promises, and added that, in consequence of their nature—

> We shall not insist on the demolition of the battery at the point, but we still do that you remove the guns. . . . We again inform you that it is the earnest wish of our chiefs to remain neutral, and on good terms with you at Ningpo. . . . (These extracts are from the *Further Papers* issued in August.)

But on the very day after he had written so condolatory an epistle, he addressed the local authorities with a demand for the pulling down of the battery alluded to, and for the removal of all guns opposite the foreign settlement. After professing his unwillingness to be obliged to resort to force, and his desire to be neutral as between the rebels and the Imperialists, he threatened to destroy the battery' and capture Ningpo if his demands were not complied with within twenty-four hours. The rebel leaders protested that the battery was designed, not to injure foreigners but to defend the city, and that the guns had the same object; whereupon Captain Dew, who acted, no doubt in accordance with the private instructions of Sir James Hope, made further demands in a letter of May 2nd.

The rebels, on the 3rd, referred to the explanations which had been already tendered and accepted as satisfactory, and, while once more pointing out that the offending guns were absolutely necessary for the defence of the position against the Imperialists, went so far as to offer to block up the embrasures of certain pieces.

Thus, matters rested for a day or two. On the 5th Consul Harvey heard from the ex-governor of Ningpo that he was about to attack the city with a strong force, and that the support of the British and French admirals was solicited. Harvey communicated this to Captain Dew, who, going down the river, saw the ex-governor and the leader of the Imperial fleet which was to take part in the attack. A forward policy, as we have seen, had made Hope and Protêt the abettors of a filibuster. The same vicious system now made Dew the accomplice of a pirate; for the leader of the Imperial fleet was none other than Apak, a notorious freebooter, whom, like other criminals and scoundrels, the Chinese government did not hesitate to take into favour and to employ in its hour of need. Reporting on the 7th to Hope, Dew wrote:—

> I told them that, in consequence of the rebels refusing certain demands we had made, I should have no objection to their passing up, but that they were not to open fire until well clear of our men-of-war.

In consequence of Dew's permission, Apak and his *junks* passed up; and on May 9th Consul Harvey reported to Mr. Bruce that the Chinese fleet was "lying in front of our settlements," making preparations for an assault on Ningpo. Dew, on April 18th, had written to the Ti-ping chiefs that he would "not even allow the foreign settlement to harbour the Imperialists," provided that a battery (which on the 27th he had said might remain) were pulled down. He knew that the place could not be defended without the battery; and he knew that, if the Imperialists were allowed to place themselves opposite the foreign settlement, that settlement might be said to "harbour the Imperialists," since the Ti-pings could not then defend themselves at all without endangering the settlement, besides endangering the European men-of-war which were lying beyond it.

Early on May 10th the Imperialists, who had previously informed Captain Dew and Consul Harvey "in a private manner" (Harvey to Bruce, May 9th), of their intention, began to attack Ningpo, advancing from the direction of the foreign settlement, and then manoeuvring round and round the British and French vessels, and firing when in such positions as prevented the Ti-pings from replying without imperilling the Europeans. Dew never enforced his stipulation that the Imperialists should keep clear of his men-of-war; and, in his dispatch, (to Hope, May 10th), he was so disingenuous as to say nothing of the methods whereby, at length, the Ti-pings were unwillingly induced to fire in a direction of the settlement and ships. He does not say, as is perfectly true, that for some time the Ti-pings did not reply at all; and that, when they did at length fire in self-defence, they began by firing muskets only, deeming that they had less control over the projectiles from their heavy guns. What he does say in his letter to Hope is:—

You are aware, Sir, that the rebel chiefs had been informed that if they again fired either on our ships or in the direction of the settlement, we should deem it a *casus belli*. This morning at 10 a.m., the *Kestrel*, and French vessels *Etoile* and *Confucius* were fired on by the point battery. I cleared for action in this ship, when a volley of musketry was fired on us from the bastion abreast. The undermentioned vessels, *viz.*, *Encounter*, *Ringdove*, (Com. Robert George Craigie), *Kestrel*, (Lieut. Henry Huxham), and *Hardy*, (Lieut. Archibald George Bogle), with the *Etoile* and *Confucius*, French gunboats, now opened fire with shell on the walls and batteries, which was replied to with much spirit from guns and small-arms. . . .

It must be admitted that, on the 8th, in an ultimatum to the Ti-pings, he had written:—

We now inform you that we maintain a perfect neutrality; but if you fire the guns or muskets from the battery or walls opposite the settlement on the advancing Imperialists (thereby endangering the lives of our men and people in the foreign settlement), we shall then feel it our duty to return the fire and bombard the city.

It was equivalent to saying:

We are neutral, provided that you do not defend yourselves.

At 2 p.m., after a continuous bombardment, the city was stormed; and at 5, when all opposition had ceased, the ex-governor and his troops landed, and received charge of the city from Captain Dew, who re-embarked his Brigade. The rebels, on evacuating the place, left behind them 100 killed. The British loss was 3 killed and 23 wounded.

The rebels had at least behaved with moderation during their occupation of Ningpo. According to the correspondence of the *China Mail* of May 22nd, the pirates who supplanted them committed the most revolting atrocities on the 10th, 11th, and 12th. The *Hongkong Daily Press* began its comments on the affair by saying:

> There never was a falser, more unprovoked, or more unjustifiable act than the taking of Ningpo by the allies from the Taipings.

The *Overland Trade Report* said:

> So much mystery and double-dealing has been practised by the allies to wrest this port from the Taipings, and so little regard for veracity pervades the official dispatches regarding their doings, that the truth is most difficult to arrive at, and has certainly never yet been published. . . . The mode of accomplishing this design reflects indelible disgrace on British prestige. . . .

It has been mentioned that, upon learning that the *chung-wang* had collected a huge army for the recovery of his posts near Shanghai, Sir James Hope and General Staveley withdrew to that city. The only place of importance which they continued to hold beyond its immediate precincts was Soongkong, which they garrisoned in conjunction with some of Ward's disciplined Chinese. The rebels made a determined effort at daylight on May 30th, 1862, to carry Soongkong by storm, but were bloodily repulsed, mainly by the instrumentality of a detachment from the *Centaur*, 6, paddle, Commander John Eglinton Montgomerie.

On June 2nd, however, the Ti-pings won a small success outside the town, driving a body of Imperialists from a stockade, and capturing a gig belonging to the *Centaur*, and a number of Chinese gunboats in a neighbouring creek. By means of a sortie, the gig and some of the gunboats were retaken by the British and Ward's Chinese; and it is noteworthy that, in spite of what had happened at Ningpo and elsewhere, the gig's crew, and other Europeans who were taken in the gunboats, were not harmed during the time when they remained in Ti-ping hands. Other Europeans, including one Forrester, a filibuster friend of Ward, were liberated after the recapture of Tsingpoo by the Ti-pings on June 10th, although European advisers of the *chung-wang* advocated the wisdom of retaining the prisoners as hostages.

Sir James Hope raised the siege of Soongkong by despatching thither reinforcements under Captain John Borlase, C.B.; whereupon the *chung-wang*, with the bulk of his army, withdrew to Nankin.

At about that time the Imperial Government at Pekin was warned from London that Great Britain would "not go on protecting Shanghai for ever" and was encouraged to procure foreign ships and foreign officers for the purpose. (See China Blue Book, 1863; and Lay, *Our Interests in China*.) Captain Sherard Osborn, C.B., R.N., was induced to engage himself as admiral; and the British government, suspending the Foreign Enlistment Act, passed an Order in Council, (*Gazette*, Sept. 2nd, 1862), on August 30th, which authorised the fitting out and manning of vessels of war for the service of the Emperor of China. Vessels were accordingly fitted out in England, and they proceeded to China; but the entire arrangement, entered into by Prince Kung in an unofficial capacity, was disavowed by the emperor and his advisers when the flotilla reached what was to have been the scene of its operations.

★★★★★★

The vessels which went out from England to join this extraordinary force (others were procured, and armed and manned in China), and the officers of the Royal Navy who found employment in them, were as set forth below. Other officers were taken from the Indian Navy and from the mercantile marine:—

Keangsoo (flag), wooden, paddle, 1000 tons, 300 H.P. num. (built at Southampton, 1862-63, for the Chinese service):
Com. Charles Stuart Forbes (capt.); Sub-Lieut. Francis Charles Vincent (lieut.); Surg. John Elliott (surg.-in-chief).

Kwangtung, iron, paddle, 522 tons, 150 H.P. nom. (built by Messrs. Laird, 1862-63, for the Chinese service):
Lieut. William Allen Young, R.N.R. (com.); Lieut. Charles Edward Burlton (lieut.)

Tientsin, iron, screw, 445 tons, 80 H.P. nom. (built by Messrs. Laird, 1862, for the Chinese service):
ex-Com. Beville Granville Wyndham Nicolas (capt.).

Pekin (ex-H.M.S. *Mohawk*), screw sloop:
Capt. Hugh Talbot Burgoyne, V.C. (capt.); Lieut. Henry Mortlock Ommanney (lieut.); Asst.-Surg. Frederick Piercy (surg.).

Amoy (ex-H.M.S. *Jasper*), screw gun-vessel:
Lieut. Arthur Salwey (com.); Sec-Master Alfred Frederick Pearce (sub-lieut.)

China (ex-H.M.S. *Africa*), screw sloop:
Lieut. Noel Osborn (com.); Lieut. George Morice (lieut.); Asst.-Surg. Henry Fegan (surg.).

Thule, purchased screw schooner; tender to *Keangsoo*.

Ballarat, purchased steam store-ship:

Master Stephen J. W. Moriarty (com.).

★★★★★★

The Imperialists were willing even then to take over the flotilla, provided it should be placed under the control of the provincial authorities; but to such a course Captain Osborn refused to agree; and ultimately, he returned to England, the vessels also returning, or being sold. During the brief stay of the flotilla in Chinese waters, some of the officers and men belonging to it behaved in such a fashion that there was a general sense of relief among the European residents upon its departure. The disappearance of the "Vampires," as they were called, probably saved some of them from having to meet charges of piracy; for they had no commission whatsoever.

In the meantime. Captain Dew, (C.B., Aug. 26th, 1862), of the *Encounter*, being left a nearly free hand in the vicinity of Ningpo, associated himself with Ward, a Franco-Chinese force, and the Imperialists, and, aided by the British gunboat *Hardy*, and the French gunboat *Confucius*, conducted with varying fortunes a bloody campaign in the district comprising Tsekie, Yuyaou, Fungwha, and Shousing.

Shousing is more than a hundred miles from Ningpo—quite outside the radius, that is to say, of any operations ever contemplated by Hope and Bruce, when they determined to keep clear a certain region round the treaty ports; so that when, early in 1863, after the Imperialists, with their Anglo-Chinese and Franco-Chinese allies, had been badly defeated before that town, and Dew went to the spot with a 68-pr., in charge of Lieutenant Edward Charles Tinling, the Captain of the *Encounter* was at length checked by his superiors.

The fact that Tinling, a young officer who had been promoted for his gallantry at Ningpo, was mortally wounded in the course of another vain attempt to storm the city, called attention to the loose and semi-piratical manner in which the war was being conducted; and Rear-Admiral Augustus Leopold Kuper, C.B., (apptd. Feb. 8th, 1862), who, at the end of the previous October, had relieved Sir James Hope as Commander-in-Chief, was, perhaps, less tolerant of such excesses than his capable but too truculent predecessor had been.

There was at once an outcry in England as well as in China, in Parliament as well as in the street; and, by direction of the Admiralty, Captain Dew was at length informed officially that he had exceeded his instructions. It was high time. Not only in China had Great Brit-

96

ain been venturing upon paths which, with more honour, might have been avoided. The same newspapers which chronicled the doings of Dew, and the fitting out of the Anglo-Chinese flotilla under Captain Sherard Osborn, recorded the operations of the Confederate cruisers, which would have never harried the Federal trade at sea had Lord Palmerston, Lord John Bussell, and Mr. Gladstone been thoroughly scrupulous in their interpretation of the word "neutrality."

The navy was concerned in yet one more operation against the Tipings ere Sir James Hope handed over his command to Rear-Admiral Kuper. In October, 1862, the Imperialists informed General Staveley that if he would recapture Kahding for them, they would place a garrison in it. The town was accordingly bombarded for two hours on October 24th, and then taken by storm by a force made up of the disciplined Chinese, who, since Ward's death, were commanded by an American named Burgevine; some French troops, some more Chinese, under Lieutenant Kingsley, R.A., and Lieutenant Crane, R.A., and a Naval Brigade, composed of 570 officers and men from the *Impérieuse, Euryalus, Pearl, Vulcan, Starling*, and *Havock*, under Captain John Borlase, C.B. The Brigade lost 11 men wounded, one mortally.

General Staveley, in his dispatch, mentioned with approval the names of Commander Augustus Chetham Strode, of the *Vulcan*, and Lieutenant John Frederick George Grant, of the same ship; and among others who were employed on the occasion were Lieutenants Arthur Hart Gurney Richardson, Edward Hobart Seymour (who will be heard of again in connection with operations in China), Henry Holford Washington, Duncan George Davidson, Horace William Rochfort, John Hamilton Colt, James Edward Hunter, Robert Peel Dennistoun, John Gabriel Yarwood Holbrook, Herbert Price Knevitt, George Henry Barnard, and George Poole; together with Captains John Yate Holland, R.M., and Ebenezer Tristram Thomas Jones, R.M., and Lieutenant William Stewart, R.M.A.

The rebels are said to have had 1500 killed and wounded, while the Imperialists and allies had but 84 casualties in all. The place was at once handed over to Burgevine, who stained his success by ordering many of the 700 prisoners who fell into his hands to be blown from guns. It may be mentioned here that Burgevine was soon afterwards deposed from his command by his Chinese superiors, in consequence not of this but of other offences, and his place given to Captain Holland, R.M., aforesaid. In his hands the disciplined Chinese force did not prosper; and, upon his resignation, it was taken charge of by Major

Charles George Gordon, R.E., who, engaged in a less questionable cause, perished heroically at Khartoum in 1885.

From the time of Rear-Admiral Kuper's assumption of the command in Chinese waters, the active and systematic employment of the navy on behalf of the corrupt and unworthy government at Pekin, and against rebels who, according to their lights, were struggling for reformation, came to an end.

During the operations against the Ti-pings, the hunting down of Chinese pirates continued, among the officers most active and successful in the work being Commander John Moresby, of the *Snake*, 4, screw, who captured or destroyed fourteen craft belonging to these freebooters. The *Pearl*, 21, screw, Captain John Borlase, C.B., was conspicuous in the same kind of service, especially in May and June, 1861. The *Cockchafer*, 2, screw. Lieutenant Henry Lowe Holder, also distinguished herself. The scene of operations was, for the most part, off the coast of the province of Kwangtung.

The North Taranaki Maori War, 1860–1861

A renewal of the disputes over land-titles produced another native outbreak in the North Island of New Zealand early in 1860, the scene of hostilities being the neighbourhood of Taranaki, and the native leader being William King, the chief of the local tribe. A force, including two companies of the 65th Regiment, was sent to the spot, whither also the *Niger*, 13, screw, Captain Peter Cracroft, proceeded. A landing was effected at Waitara, on March 5th, no resistance being offered; and, on the following day, the ship was about to proceed to New Plymouth, when signals were made to her to the effect that the enemy, during the darkness, had built a stockade, which threatened to cut off the communication of the troops with their land base.

King, however, eventually abandoned this stockade without fighting. On the 17th he was discovered to have erected another *pah*, which he resolutely defended, until a bombardment obliged him to quit it also. In the meantime, the *Niger* had gone to Auckland for supplies, leaving only a few of her people to assist the troops. On the 26th William King murdered three men and two boys, and boasted that he would drive the Europeans into the sea. On the 28th, therefore, by which day the *Niger* had returned, the naval detachment on shore accompanied the troops into the country to bring into town some settlers who lived in exposed and outlying places; and Cracroft, at the desire of Governor Gore Browne, landed further officers and men to hold the town during the absence of the expedition. He disembarked in person, with sixty seamen and marines.

The rescuing force had not advanced more than four miles when it found itself warmly engaged with a strongly-posted body of the enemy. Word was sent back for reinforcements, and Cracroft went at once to the front with his men and a 24-pr. rocket-tube. King occupied a *pah* at Omata on the summit of a hill, and had severely handled the British force ere Cracroft's arrival; and of the small naval contingent, the leader, Lieutenant William Hans Blake, had been dangerously wounded, and a marine killed. Cracroft determined to storm the *pah*, and, addressing his men, pointed to the rebel flag, and promised £10 to the man who should haul it down.

He then moved to within 800 yards, and opened fire from his rocket-tube, which, however, made no impression. It was then nearly dark, and Colonel Murray, who led the military force, announced his intention of retreating to the town, whither he had been ordered to return by sunset, and advised Cracroft to do the same. "I purpose to take that *pah* first," said the captain. The visible withdrawal of the troops from the front of the position probably had the effect of rendering the enemy more careless than he might otherwise have been to

PART OF THE NORTH ISLAND of NEW ZEALAND to illustrate the operations of the War of 1860-1864.

what was going on on his flank. The result was that Cracroft managed to get close up to an outlying body of natives before his presence was detected. Within 60 yards of the enemy he gave the word to double. With a volley and a cheer, the men were instantly in the midst of the rebels, who, after a brave resistance, took refuge in the *pah* behind them, or escaped. The seamen and marines rushed onwards, met tomahawk with bayonet, and soon annihilated all resistance. Cracroft, who had not force enough to hold the position with, returned leisurely with his wounded, who were not numerous, and was not molested. On the following day, the enemy retired to the southward, having lost very heavily. (Corr. of *A. and N. Gazette*, July 14th, 1860: Fox, *War in New Zealand*.) It should be added that William Odgers, seaman, who was the first man inside the *pah*, and who pulled down the enemy's flag, was awarded the Victoria Cross. (*Gazette*, Aug. 2nd, 1860.)

Hostilities continued. On June 23rd a reconnoitring party of troops was fired at near Waitara; and, in consequence, an attack, with insufficient force, (347 in all, the natives were thrice as numerous), was made on a strong rebel *pah* in the immediate neighbourhood on June 26th, in the early morning. Part of the 40th Regiment, some Royal Engineers, and a small Naval Brigade under Commodore Frederick Beauchamp Paget Seymour, of the *Pelorus*, 21, screw, were engaged. After a hot fight, lasting for more than four hours, the British were obliged by overwhelming forces to retreat, after having lost 29 killed and 33 wounded, among the latter being Seymour, eight seamen, and one marine. Besides Seymour, the naval officers engaged were Lieutenant Albert Henry William Battiscombe, Midshipmen Ernest Bannister Wadlow, and —— Garnett, and Lieutenant John William Henry Chafyn Grove Morris, R.M.A. (*Taranaki Herald*, June 30th, 1860. Desps.)

The war was somewhat more actively prosecuted after the arrival on the scene of Major-General T. S. Pratt, who won an initial success, and then, on December 29th, with troops, guns, and 138 officers and men from the ships, (chiefly the *Cordelia* and *Niger*, and colonial steamer *Victoria*), under Commodore Seymour, entrenched himself at Kairau, opposite the strong position of Matarikoriko, which, during the two following days, he obliged the enemy to evacuate. He fought the action entirely with cannon, rifle, and spade, and, not unduly exposing his men, had but 3 killed and 21 wounded. After this success, Pratt adopted the practice of reducing the successive positions of his opponents by means of regular approaches. These tactics broke up the rebel combinations. A chief named William Thompson, whose tribe, the Waikato, had joined the Taranaki natives, finally proposed a suspension of hostilities, and on May 21st, 1861, a truce was arranged.

Governor Gore Browne had mismanaged matters; and he would, almost immediately, have provoked a new outbreak had not the home Government, realising that the position of the colony was becoming serious, recalled him by means of a dispatch which, while otherwise complimentary, informed him that he was superseded by Sir George Grey, who, as has been seen, had already been appointed governor in 1845, and who had since governed the Cape.

Grey seems to have used his best endeavours to pacify the natives. He even offered to submit the still unsettled land questions to arbitration by two Europeans and four Maoris, three to be appointed by him and three by the natives. This was refused. Grey then determined to abandon the disputed territory at Waitara, but to insist upon the restitution of the district of Tataraimaka, which had been seized by the rebels and held by them since 1861, in spite of the fact that there was no doubt whatsoever of the validity of the purchase of it in 1848 or 1849. Unfortunately, as it turned out, he sent a force to occupy Tataraimaka, without simultaneously proclaiming his intention of giving up Waitara. The resident natives made no opposition, but sent to William Thompson, of Waikato, for orders. He and the other leaders of the King party decided for war; and the Maoris at once began operations by falling upon a small escort party on May 4th, 1863, and murdering two officers and eight rank and file of Imperial troops.

The Waikato Maori War, 1863-1864

Grey then committed a worse mistake. He announced hurriedly that Waitara was to be abandoned, thereby encouraging his enemies, and sapping the attachment of his friends among the natives by unwittingly suggesting that he was influenced by fear and the consciousness of weakness. A few weeks earlier, Mr. John Eldon Gorst, (Sol.-Genl., 1885-86; Und.-Sec. for India, 1886-91, etc.), civil commissioner in the Waikato country, who had established a newspaper there to combat the teachings of Kingism, had had his press and material violently seized by the partisans of the King paper, *Hokioi*; and the timber ready for the erection of a court-house and barracks in lower Waikato had been forcibly taken and thrown into the river, while Mr. Gorst had been expelled soon afterwards. (Fox.)

Aware, after what they had done, that they were committed to

101

a serious struggle, the natives determined to invade Auckland; and Grey, getting early intelligence of their intention, decided to forestall matters by advancing into the Maori country. The senior military officer, Lieut.-General D. A. Cameron, C.B., who was at New Plymouth, endeavouring to punish the perpetrators of the massacre, was therefore recalled to Auckland, leaving behind him only enough troops to garrison New Plymouth; and the available British forces were soon afterwards concentrated along the Waikato River and the Maungatawhiri Creek, the boundary between the settled districts and the unsold Maori lands. The boundary was crossed on July 12th; on July 17th a small British detachment was defeated between Queen's Redoubt and Drury; and on the same day a body of rebels was driven back and scattered near Koheroa; but then there ensued a long and almost inexplicable period of comparative inaction, so far as the army was concerned.

In the meantime, however, the navy made itself useful. On June 4th, 1863, the *Eclipse*, 4, screw. Commander Richard Charles Mayne, co-operated in an attack which was made by the garrison of New Plymouth on a rebel position near the mouth of the Katikara; and on the night of August 1st, a detachment from the *Harrier*, 17, screw. Commander Francis William Sullivan, took part in a reconnaissance of Paparoa and Haurake. On August 3rd, Commander Sullivan, in the lightly-armoured colonial steamer *Avon*, also reconnoitred the Waikato River above Kohe-Hohe, and, for about half an hour, engaged a body of the enemy near Merimeri. On September 7th, the *Harrier's* boats, under Sullivan's direction, were employed to convey a force which was intended to support an unfortunate and costly raid made in the direction of Cameron Town.

While the army, under Lieut.-General Cameron, was getting ready for offensive operations, Commodore Sir William Saltonstall Wiseman, Bart., of the *Curaçoa*, 23, screw, who, in April, had been appointed senior officer on the Australian station, concentrated as large a proportion as possible of his available strength in New Zealand waters, and himself left Sydney, with troops on board, and one or two vessels in company, on September 22nd, arriving at Auckland on October 2nd. The *Curaçoa* herself at once landed 232 officers and men, who were sent up country to the support of the troops; and she remained as guardship at Auckland under Lieutenant Duke Doughton Yonge, with but three other officers and 90 men in her. She was kept ready for action in case of a sudden descent of the Maoris on the town. The other ships which then, or soon afterwards, co-operated with the senior officer in New Zealand waters were the:—

Miranda, 15, screw, Captain Robert Jenkins

Esk, 21, screw, Captain John Fane Charles Hamilton

Harrier, 17, screw. Commander Francis William Sullivan, (Capt. Nov. 9th, 1863. He was succeeded by Com. Edward Hay.)

Eclipse, 4, screw. Commander Richard Charles Mayne, (After Mayne's disablement, Lieut. Henry Joshua Coddington acted until the arrival of Coni. Edmund Robert Fremantle.)

Falcon, 17, screw. Commander George Henry Parkin

Besides the *Pioneer, Avon, Sandfly, Corio*, and other colonial vessels.

Late in October, General Cameron and Commodore Wiseman, in the colonial steamer *Pioneer*, made two reconnaissances up the Waikato, pushing, on the 31st, as far as Rangariri. On that occasion they passed the strong Maori position at Merimeri, and, having discovered a good landing-place about six miles above it, it was arranged with the commodore to embark a force from Queen's Redoubt. This force, in the colonial steamers *Pioneer* and *Avon*, with four lightly-plated gunboats in tow, got under way at 2.30 on the morning of November 1st, and reached the landing-place at about 6 a.m. (These gunboats, named *Flirt, Midge, Chub* and *Ant*, were originally cargo boats, and were thinly armed by Capt. Jenkins at Auckland, and then transported by him overland, *via* Manakau, to the Waikato.)

The troops disembarked unopposed, and began to construct a breastwork, pending the arrival of further forces. In the afternoon, however, the natives at Merimeri, seeing that their position had been turned, abandoned their works, and made off in canoes up the Maramarua and Whangamarino Creeks. Cameron at once proceeded to Merimeri, and occupied it with a force which included 250 seamen under Commander Mayne. The place was afterwards fortified.

Between November 16th and November 25th, an expedition, under Captain Jenkins and Colonel G. J. Carey, was engaged to the northward, and up the Firth of Thames, to the eastward of the country occupied by the enemy. It was made in the *Miranda, Esk, Sandfly*, and *Corio*. Although it took possession of some positions, and so accomplished part of its purpose, it did not come into actual collision with the enemy, and was therefore unable to deal any serious blow. The

Miranda remained for a time in the Firth of Thames. (Wiseman to Admlty., Nov. 30th.) During the absence of the expedition an important success was won on the Waikato.

After the abandonment of Merimeri, a strong force of rebels entrenched themselves at Rangariri, a village about twelve miles higher up the river. There, on November 20th, General Cameron, with troops, the four plated gunboats, and a Naval Brigade from the *Curaçoa, Miranda, Harrier,* and *Eclipse,* under Commodore Wiseman, numbering about 400 men, attacked them. He had in all about 1200 men, while the Maoris were but about 400; but the latter had the advantage of a strong position, though it was one from which there was no easy way of retreat, and one, too, which required a much larger force to hold it properly. The two divisions did not arrive simultaneously before the works. One, coming by land, threatened the front, while the other, brought in the steamers, was to have threatened the rear; but part of the latter was delayed by the strength of the current.

For an hour and a half, the position was bombarded, and then, at 4.30 p.m., an assault was ordered. The Maoris soon concentrated themselves in a very formidable redoubt in the centre of their lines, and bloodily repulsed four separate attempts to carry it—one by the 65th Regiment, one by a party of Royal Artillerymen, and two by 90 men of the Naval Brigade, gallantly led by Commander Mayne and Commander Henry Bourchier Phillimore.

It was then nearly dark. An attempt on the part of some of the brave defenders to get away across Lake Waikarei, and a swamp on their right flank, was partially prevented by the 40th Regiment, and a detachment of the marines, who, having by that time arrived by water, had moved round to the rear; but it was supposed that two of the most important leaders, King Matutaere, and William Thompson, escaped ere the way was blocked. The rest were trapped, and, although they kept up a desultory fire during the night, they surrendered unconditionally on the morning of November 21st.

Those who thus gave themselves up numbered 183 men and 2 women. The others had fallen or had escaped. It had been a magnificent defence; and the success was a very costly one; for, on the British side, 36 were killed and 98 wounded, many mortally.

★★★★★★

The British tactics at Rangiriri were adversely criticised at the time. The enemy was driven, without much trouble or loss, into the central redoubt, where he might have been either approached by sapping, or starved into surrender, if he had not previously succumbed to bombardment. Instead, he was stormed, at great expenditure of life. Fox thinks that he might have been reduced, with little or no loss, in a few hours, as he could not escape.

★★★★★★

The naval casualties were 5 killed, including Midshipman Thomas A. Watkins (*Curaçoa*), and 10 wounded, including Commander Mayne, (capt., Feb. 12th, 1864), (*Eclipse*), and Lieutenants Edward Downes Panter Downes, (coms., Feb. 12th, 1864), (*Miranda*), Henry M'Clintock Alexander, (coms., Feb. 12th, 1864), (*Curaçoa*), and Charles Frederick Hotham (*Curaçoa*). After the surrender, William Thompson, with a small party, approached the place with a white flag, but, having parleyed, withdrew again, not being able to make up his mind to submit. (Wiseman's disp. of Nov. 30th; Cameron's disp. of Nov. 24th; Fox.)

In addition to the naval officers already named, the following were mentioned in the dispatches: Captain Francis William Sullivan; Lieutenants Charles Hill, and William Fletcher Boughey; Acting-Lieutenant Robert Frederick Hammick, (lieut., Feb. 12th, 1864), commanding the small gunboats; Sub-Lieutenant Frederic John Easther, commanding the *Avon*; Midshipmen Sydney Augustus Rowan Hamilton, Frank Elrington Hudson, and Cecil George Foljambe; Assistant Surgeons Adam Brunton Messer, (surg., Feb. 12th, 1864), M.D., and Duncan Hilston, M.D.; and ordinary seaman William Fox (*Curaçoa*).

The prisoners were temporarily confined on board the *Curaçoa*, at Auckland.

For some days after the action, the flotilla was laboriously employed in bringing up supplies to Merimeri, Rangiriri, and Taupiri, to which last the general advanced on December 3rd. On the same day, Commodore Wiseman and Captain Sullivan, having lightened the *Pioneer* by removing the armoured turrets from her, pushed on in her to Kupa Kupa Island, about four miles ahead of the troops. Immense natural difficulties were encountered, but no enemy was seen.

There is no doubt that the Maoris were, for the moment, greatly disheartened; for, on December 8th, without further resistance. General Cameron was allowed to occupy Ngaruawahia, at the junction of the Hurutiu and Waipa Rivers, which together form the Waikato. Ngaruawahia was an important political centre, as it had been the headquarters of Kingism, the burial place of King Potatau, and the capital of his successor Matutaere. If Sir George Grey had seen his way to go thither to negotiate, as, at one time, he intended, terms might then have been arranged. Instead, he wrote to the natives that he would receive a deputation from them at Auckland. It is, however, not certain that William Thompson, the leading spirit, then really desired peace; for no reply to the governor's letter was ever received.

Cameron remained for some time at Ngaruawahia to collect supplies, but, at the end of January, moved up the Waipa, and arrived before Pikopiko and Paterangi, two posts which were very strongly fortified. While this movement was in progress, Lieutenant William Edward Mitchell, of the *Esk*, who was in command of the *Avon*, was fatally wounded by a chance shot from Maoris in ambush on the river bank. He was only two-and-twenty years of age. Acting-Lieutenant Frederic John Easther, of the *Harrier*, succeeded him in command of the *Avon*.

The Tauranga Maori War, 1864

Before the *Miranda* quitted the Firth of Thames, all the posts between that estuary and Queen's Redoubt, on the Waikato, were taken possession of, and held by detachments of the 12th and 70th Regiments, the Waikato militia, or the Auckland Naval Volunteers, which had been brought round with the expedition commanded by Captain Jenkins. On January 20th, 1864, with troops under Colonel Carey, of the 18th Royal Irish, Jenkins weighed, and proceeded down the coast to Tauranga, leaving the *Esk* in the Thames. The *Miranda*, which was accompanied by the *Corio*, encountered no resistance on the shores of the Bay of Plenty; and, when the troops had established themselves at Te Papa, the natives at first supplied them with provisions, though afterwards they became less willing to assist them.

At that time, the *Curaçoa* was at Auckland, while most of her people, under the commodore, were serving at the front; the *Harrier* was in the Thames or at Manakau, also with most of her people at the front; and the *Eclipse* was in the Waikato, with a detachment, under Lieutenant William Fletcher Boughey, co-operating with the troops. Sir Duncan Cameron lay for some weeks in the neighbourhood of the native strongholds of Pikopiko and Paterangi; but on the night of February 20th, he turned those positions by making a sudden flank march to Awamutu.

The formidable works on the Waikato were instantly evacuated by the Maoris, who concentrated at Rangioawhia, where, on the 22nd, they were defeated, with considerable loss in killed and prisoners. The majority of the rebels in what are now Waikato, Raglan, and Waipa counties then retired to Maungatautari, a stronghold on the Hurutiu. During these operations the navy appears to have suffered no loss; and in the few succeeding movements which terminated what has been called the Waikato campaign, the navy had practically no share.

In April, Sir Duncan Cameron had his headquarters at Pukerimu, on the Hurutiu, a place only about forty miles as the crow would fly from Tauranga, on the east coast. Most of the Tauranga people had been engaged in the actions in Waikato; and on April 1st, the *Miranda*, lying in the bay, had been obliged to disperse a number of them who had come down to the coast in a threatening manner. Lieut.-Colonel Greer, 68th Regiment, had by that time succeeded Colonel Carey in command at Te Papa; and, believing his position to be precarious, he asked Sir Duncan Cameron for reinforcements. Cameron not only sent them, but also went himself to Tauranga, and procured the assistance of some of the squadron in conveying thither a part of the troops.

The landing of these was completed on April 26th. The force then ashore numbered 1695 of all ranks, and included 429 officers and men from the *Curaçoa, Miranda, Esk, Eclipse,* and *Falcon.* In the bay were the *Miranda, Esk,* and *Falcon,* together with the colonial steamers *Sandfly, Alexander,* and *Tauranga.* The troops consisted mainly of the 43rd, 68th, and 70th Regiments, some Royal Engineers, and some Royal Artillery; and the guns landed were: one 110-pr. Armstrong, two 40-pr. Armstrongs, two 6-pr. Armstrongs, two 24-pr. field howitzers, two 8-in. mortars, and six coehorn mortars.

The South Taranaki Maori War, 1864–1869

A body of Maoris, said not to have exceeded 300 in number, and alleged by themselves not to have exceeded 150, had constructed a formidable work about three miles from Te Papa, on a neck of land which on each side fell off into a swamp. It is known in history as the Gate Pah. On the highest point of the neck was an oblong palisaded redoubt; and from the redoubt to the swamps were lines of rifle-pits. The rear of the position was accessible, though with difficulty; and across it Colonel Greer, with the 68th Regiment, succeeded in posting himself on the night of April 28th, while a feigned attack was being made on the enemy's front; and he stationed himself in such a manner as to cut off the supply of water to the work, and also, theoretically, to be able to intercept the retreat of the garrison. (On that day the *Falcon* had shelled the enemy out of a position at Maketu, and driven them along the beach to Otamarakau.) It is clear that the rebels, deprived of their water, and having no guns, might have been easily reduced without any resort on the part of Cameron to the costly and disastrous tactics which he chose to pursue.

The guns were planted in four positions at distances varying from 800 to 100 yards from the *pah*; and soon after 6.30 a.m. on April 29th, after the Maoris had fired a volley at the British skirmishers, the guns opened simultaneously. Sir Duncan Cameron reported that the practice was excellent, but other eye-witnesses have declared that it was extremely wild. The rebels lay low in their *schanzes*, and made but little reply. At about noon, a 6-pr. gun was taken across the swamp on the enemy's left, and hauled on to the high ground, whence it enfiladed the rifle-pits on that side and presently caused their abandonment.

The latter part of the bombardment having been directed chiefly against the left angle of the main work, the fence and palisades in that neighbourhood were destroyed, and a breach was effected by 4 p.m., when Cameron ordered an assault. For that purpose, 150 seamen and marines, under Commander Edward Hay of the *Harrier*, and an equal number of the 43rd Regiment, under Lieut.-Colonel Booth, had been told off. In addition, 170 men of the 70th Regiment had been directed to extend, keep down the enemy's fire until the last possible moment, and then follow the assaulting column into the breach; while the rest of the seamen and marines, and of the 43rd, were to bring up the rear as a reserve.

The assaulting column, favoured by the folds of the ground, gained the breach with but little loss, and entered the works, the 68th, from the rear of the position, closing up at the same moment and driving back the Maoris, who were already attempting to bolt. Inside the *pah* the rebels fought with desperation, both Hay and Booth being mortally wounded soon after they had got through the breach. But the place would have been carried had not a panic, which Cameron professed himself unable to explain, seized the assaulting column, or, rather, as would appear, the part of it belonging to the 43rd. The men turned round, communicated the contagion to their fellows, and rushed out pell-mell, shrieking, "There's thousands of them"; and in an instant they were flying madly back. Captain John Fane Charles Hamilton, of the *Esk*, with the reserve of the Naval Brigade, pushed up, but was shot dead on the top of the parapet. Nothing could be done to stop the disgraceful retreat; and the rebels, boldly showing themselves and firing into the backs of the fugitives, did terrible execution.

The force was at length rallied; but Cameron cared not to renew the assault. Instead, he ordered a line of entrenchments to be thrown up within a hundred yards of the *pah*, intending to conduct further operations on the following morning.

The night of the 29th was extremely dark. For a time, the rebels, as was their custom in such circumstances, howled and shouted. Suddenly the noises ceased, and the sound of firing was heard from the rear. The Maoris, with very little loss, had escaped through the lines of the 68th; and a British officer who crept into the *pah* at about midnight found it completely evacuated, save by a few British wounded, who had not been maltreated. Cameron, in his dispatch, says that the loss of the natives must have been very heavy, yet admits that only about 20 Maori killed and 6 wounded were found about the position. Natives afterwards estimated their total loss at no more than between thirty and forty. (Col. Parl. Papers, 1864, E. 3.)

The correspondent of the *Times* says:

> Allowing that the best way of taking a Maori *pah* is to storm it in front, everything was done that skill and diligence could do to this end.

The premise can hardly be admitted, seeing that Cameron had means of knowing that the *pah* was waterless, and therefore could not be held by the enemy for many hours; nor, even admitting the premise, can the conclusion be granted. One of the rules of war is that, when a force of given strength has to be employed, a homogeneous force is better than a mixed one, unless it be necessary to utilise more than one arm, as, for example, cavalry and infantry. Another rule is to employ for any given service the force best suited by tradition and training for the work in hand.

Cameron had with him nearly 300 officers and men of the 43rd, and more than double that number of the 68th; yet, instead of taking what he appears to have deemed the necessary detachment of men for the assault from one of those corps, he took 150 from the 43rd, and added to them, not 150 from the 68th, but 150 from the Naval Brigade, a force which, looking to all the circumstances, ought, I venture to think, to have formed the reserve, and to have been given no other post. No doubt, the navy craved to be allowed to share the dangers of the storm; but to say that is far from saying that the general was wise in permitting it to do so. It should be added here that at Te Ranga, on

June 21st following, the 43rd amply redeemed its laurels.

The lamentable affair of the Gate Pah cost the British no fewer than 27 killed and 66 wounded. Of this tale, the casualties of the navy were 3 officers and 8 men killed or mortally injured, and 3 officers and 19 men wounded. The officers who lost their lives were Captain John Fane Charles Hamilton, (aged 42; a Capt. of 1858), (*Esk*), Commander Edward Hay, (aged 28; a Com. of 1858) (*Harrier*), and Lieutenant Charles Hill, (survivor of the wreck of the *Orpheus*), (*Curaçoa*); and the officers wounded were George Graham Duff (*Esk*), Lieutenant Robert Frederick Hammick (*Miranda*), and Sub-Lieutenant Philip Reginald Hastings Parker (*Falcon*), (*Gazette*, July 15th, 1864; Corr. of *Times*; Fox.) (A memorial to those of the *Harrier's* people who fell in New Zealand was erected in 1865 in Kingston Church, Portsmouth.)

The Naval Brigade behaved admirably, and retired only when nearly all its leading officers had been shot down. The Commodore and Captain Jenkins had most marvellous escapes. After Commander Hay had been mortally hit, a seaman named Samuel Mitchell went to his assistance, and, although ordered by his officer to leave him and consult his own safety, carried Hay out of the *pah*. The act of devotion gained the brave fellow the Victoria Cross. (*Gazette*, July 20th, 1864.)

In recognition of the gallantry displayed by the navy in New Zealand, and especially in the affair of the Gate Pah, the Admiralty made the following promotions:—

To be Captain: Com. Henry Bourchier Phillimore (July 14th, 1864).

To be Commanders: Lieut. George Graham Duff (Ap. 29th, 1864); Lieut. Charles Frederick Hotham (upon completing sea-time, Ap. 19th, 1865); Lieut. John Thomlinson Swann (July 14th, 1864).

To be Lieutenants: Sub-Lieut. Philip Reginald Hastings Parker (Ap. 29th, 1864) Actg.-Lieut. Archer John William Musgrave (on passing required examination, to date Ap. 29th, 1864); Sub-Lieut. Paul Storr (July 14th, 1864); Sub-Lieut. John Hope (July 14th, 1864).

In addition, the names of Lieuts. Robert Sidney Hunt, and Robert Frederick Hammick, and Lieut. (R.M.A.) Robert Ballard Gardner, were ordered to be favourably noted.

In the latter part of this unfortunate war, which dragged on for a considerable period, and which owed its prolongation not only to the bravery of the enemy, but also to the supineness and divided counsels of the British, the navy had comparatively little share; nor was it called upon to do anything of importance in connection with the repression of the brief New Zealand rebellion of 1869. Among the vessels which were more particularly concerned, especially in the earlier part of the period, were the *Eclipse*, 4, Commander Edmund Robert Fremantle; *Brisk*, 16, Captain Charles Webley Hope; and *Esk*, 21, Captain John Proctor Luce.

Niger & Gambia, 1861

Several effective blows were struck at the West African slave trade in 1861, especially in the Niger, and in the Gambia.

The chief, or petty king, of Porto Novo, in the Niger River, a creature of the King of Dahomey, having been troublesome for some time, Commander Henry Rushworth Wratislaw, of the *Ranger*, 5, screw gun-vessel, put seventeen seamen and marines, and a gunner on board the paddle tender *Brune*, Lieutenant John Edward Stokes, and escorted that craft up to Badagry on February 24th, whence she proceeded alone to Porto Novo. Consul Foote, who accompanied the little expedition, sent ashore a message to the effect that, if his demands were not previously complied with, the *Brune* would open fire on the town at 11 a.m. on the 25th; and then the vessel, dropping three miles down the creek, anchored for the night.

On the following day, though no reply had been vouchsafed, the British waited until 1.20 p.m., when they opened fire, which was returned. During the action a number of friendly Lagos men, who desired to take refuge on board the tender, were mistaken for enemies, and unfortunately fired upon. After some hours' bombardment, the *Brune* returned to Badagry to await results. The king presently sent down to the Badagry chiefs, asking them to intercede for them; whereupon the consul consented to await the arrival of an envoy at Lagos, and to give the king three weeks wherein to comply with his requirements.

The king was so ill-advised as to allow himself to be influenced by the King of Dahomey to refuse satisfaction, and to boom the river. A further expedition was therefore necessary. The consul called on Commodore William Edmonstone, of the *Arrogant*, 47, screw, for assistance; and, in consequence, an expedition, consisting of the *Brune*, *Fidelity*, (hired Liverpool vessel), Lieutenant Robert Barclay Cay, and boats of the squadron on the station, the Commodore accompanying it, moved up from Lagos to Badagry Creek on April 23rd, 1861. On the 26th it proceeded to Porto Novo, and, on approaching the town, opened fire with rockets, grape, canister, and shell, the enemy making a brisk return.

In an hour the place was ablaze; but the natives, driven from the buildings, concealed themselves in the thick grass at the edge of the stream, whence they were not dislodged until a party under Commander Henry James Raby, V.C., of the *Alecto*, 5, paddle, had landed and expelled them. It was computed that about 500 of the enemy fell. The British loss was but 1 killed, and 4 or 5 wounded. As soon as possible, the slave *barracoons* at Porto Novo were destroyed; and the expedition, which had in no way suffered from fever, returned to Lagos on April 28th. The results were excellent, the king conceding all demands. (Foote's Rep.)

At the time of the first attack on Porto Novo, the commodore and part of his command had been occupied to the northward. The King of Baddiboo, on the Gambia, had robbed some British merchants, and, upon being called upon to pay a fine of bullocks, had offered to fight the British. He had been so unwise as to annoy his French neighbours at the same time; and an international expedition had accordingly been organised against him.

The British portion of the force consisted of the *Arrogant*, 47, screw, Commodore William Edmonstone, the *Falcon*, 17, screw, Commander Algernon Charles Fieschi Heneage, and the *Torch*, 5, screw. Commander Frederick Harrison Smith, or detachments from them, together with the 1st and 2nd West India Regiments, the Gold Coast Artillery, and the Bathurst Rifles. The *Forte*, 51, flagship of Rear-Admiral the Hon. Sir Henry Keppel, Captain Edward Winterton Turnour, also proceeded as far as the mouth of the river; but, finding that the services of his ship did not appear to be indispensable, Keppel sailed again at once in order generously to leave the commodore to acquire the whole of whatever credit might result from the coming operations.

A Naval Brigade under the commodore in person, with Lieutenant Walter James Hunt-Grubbe as second in command, was formed; and a landing was effected, under cover of the guns of the *Torch*, in Swarricunda Creek, the banks of which were lined with rifle-pits and held by the enemy. When the natives had been dispersed, the Brigade began a march of several hours' duration in the direction of the strongly stockaded and well-garrisoned town of Saba. On February 21st, the place was vigorously bombarded, rockets as well as shells being employed; and, as soon as the defence showed signs of having been shaken, the position was attacked in flank by the Naval Brigade, which, gallantly led by the commodore, successfully rushed it, and inflicted very heavy loss upon the enemy, but itself lost 6 killed and about 15 wounded.

In December of the same year, part of the West Coast command was employed in retributive operations against the petty King of Quiah, Massongha being captured and destroyed on the 10th, and some stockades at Madonika being taken on the 19th of that month.

Minor Operations, 1861–1863

In 1861 there were frequent and troublesome disputes between the Scots and French fishermen in the home seas, the latter at one time assuming a very offensive attitude. The *Lizard*, 1, paddle. Lieutenant Edward Eyre Maunsell, tender to the flagship at Sheerness, did good work by capturing twenty-four French luggers which, with numerous others, had contravened the fishing regulations, or wilfully annoyed the north countrymen; and the lesson had a most beneficial effect, and was not forgotten for years.

The minor operations of the navy in 1862 were neither numerous nor, except in China, very interesting. During her commission, which had begun in 1860, the *Ariel*, 9, screw, Commanders John Richard Alexander and William Cox Chapman, was particularly successful against slavers on the east coast of Africa, capturing no fewer than eighteen in 1862-4. On the west coast, one of the most energetic cruisers was the *Zebra*, 17, Commander Anthony Hiley Hoskins, which commissioned in the spring of 1862. Among her numerous prizes was the large slaver *Maraquita*, commanded by the famous American skipper, Bowen. On the same station the *Flying Fish*, 6, screw. Commander Warren Hastings Anderson, was also active and successful, especially just prior to her recall in the summer of 1862.

A disturbance at Cape Coast Castle in October, arising out of the mutinous attitude of the Gold Coast Artillery, was put down with the assistance of the *Brisk*, 16, screw, Captain John Proctor Luce, and the *Zebra*. In other seas, it fell to the lot of the squadron under Rear-Admiral Richard Laird Warren, on the southeast coast of America, to carry out a few mild reprisals against Brazil in consequence of a brief and unimportant misunderstanding with that empire, and to that of the *Harrier*, 17, screw, Commander Sir Malcolm MacGregor, Bart., to chastise some troublesome natives of the Fiji Islands.

The minor naval events of 1863 were still more few and unimportant. In consequence of the difficulties with Ashantee, some officers and men from the West Coast of Africa squadron were employed for a time at Cape Coast Castle; and, as in many other years, a small naval expedition ascended the Congo. In the Mediterranean, during the revolutionary troubles in Greece, Captain Charles Farrel Hillyar, of the *Queen*, 74, screw, had occasion more than once to land marines, especially in July, when a force under Lieutenant James Woodward Scott, R.M., undertook the protection of the British Legation at Athens.

Japan, 1861-1865

It is very difficult to understand the nature of the events which led to American and European interference in the affairs of Japan, without first glancing briefly at the ancient political condition of the island empire.

The old constitution of the land was a despotism, feudal, military, and hierarchical, under a *Mikado*. About the twelfth century of the Christian era there arose a "Mayor of the Palace" in the person of an officer known eventually as the tycoon, or, more properly, as the *shogun*—an officer who assumed the political and military management of the country, the *Mikado* retaining, as years passed, little more than the religious headship. The office of *shogun* descended through three families and many vicissitudes; and its powers were gradually modified by the upgrowth of a very large class of *samurai*, or retainers of great nobles—men of birth and education, but hereditary fighters—or, in peace time, hereditary idlers.

The highest class of these, as head retainers of the *daimios*, came to occupy with regard to their nominal masters much the same kind of relationship as was held by the *shogun* to the *Mikado*; for both *Mikado* and *daimios*, brought up apart from the people and surrounded with every indulgence, had temporarily lost the fire and energy of their ancestors. This condition of affairs was a fruitful source of discontent and intrigue.

The position of the *shoguns* was a curious one. They steadily increased their power and importance in the state, yet, though actual rulers of the empire, professed a most abject deference to the person of the *Mikado*, and, moreover, were social inferiors of many of the *daimios*. Indeed, a *shogun*, unless by birth so entitled, was not allowed even to look upon the face of the *Mikado*; while, at the same time, such was his authority that he was able to compel the *daimios* to spend every alternate year at his capital, Jeddo, and to override their views. The *daimios* had a right of appeal to the *Mikado*, but seldom exercised it.

In the nineteenth century the *daimios* had begun to chafe under this state of things; and those of them who came in contact with the *Mikado*, as periodical protectors of his person and palace, resenting the nonentity of their master, set on foot an agitation in favour of a return to a more natural system, with the *Mikado* as ruler, and the *shogun* as commander-in-chief, and no more. When, in 1853, Commodore M. C. Perry first appeared in Japan with an American squadron, and demanded a treaty, threatening hostilities in the event of a refusal, matters were ripening for a change. The *Shogun* and his advisers, called *bakufu* by the Japanese, were thrown into consternation, and having no precedent to guide them—a lack which is as puzzling to the Oriental mind as it is to the British Admiralty—were unable to act with decision. The opinions of the *daimios* were asked, and ideas were welcomed from anyone who was capable of giving them. The Americans, made aware of the perplexities of the situation and of the tumults which took place near Jeddo in consequence, withdrew, to return in the following year; and in the meantime, the *shogun* died, and was succeeded by his son, Jyesada, thirteenth of the Tokugawa dynasty.

In 1854 Perry returned; and hot debates ensued at Jeddo. Prince Mito, a powerful noble, objected to the opening up of the country; but the officials of the *shogun*, better educated, pointed out the impossibility of excluding foreigners at that time, when Japan was unprepared for war, and urged that, while complying for the moment, the country might learn the drill and tactics of the strangers, purchase foreign ships and guns, and, when ready for action, unite and drive the interlopers into the sea, and perhaps even embark on a career of foreign conquest. The result was the signing of the convention with the United States in 1858, and the subsequent conclusion of similar engagements with other powers, Yokohama at the same time being opened for trade.

The *Mikado* and his counsellors at Kioto disapproved of the action of the *shogun*, and unanimously declined to sanction the treaties. This course injured the prestige of the *shogun* in the eyes of the people; and the *shogun*, realising his weakness, selected a regent to support him. The action of the *Mikado* encouraged the prevalent anti-foreign feeling. Of the idle and warlike *samurai*, there were 30,000 in the country, and attacks on foreigners became inevitable.

In the autumn of 1858 the *shogun* died, it is supposed by poison. Prince Mito nominated for the succession his own kinsman, Hitosubashi; but one Jyemochi, of the Kishiu family, obtained the office, whereupon a powerful clique of *daimios*, headed by Mito, privately banded themselves together against the new *shogun*, and memorialised the Mikado to expel the barbarians at once. The regent, on his part, suspecting that Jyesada had met his death by foul play, ordered several of the *daimios* to retire to their estates, and directed Prince Satsuma and others to confine themselves to their palaces in Jeddo. This policy led to fighting, the regent having the best of it, but carrying things with so high a hand as to increase the exasperation of the growing anti-foreign party, and to bring about numerous murders of foreigners and their servants.

In 1860 the regent was assassinated by the followers of Mito, greatly to the loss of the party of the *shogun*, which in consequence was obliged to temporise, and to isolate the foreigners as much as possible. The *shogun*, indeed, who in 1858 had been strong enough to punish even nobles for opposing intercourse with the outer world, dared not in 1860 set the laws in motion against the murderers of Americans and Europeans. The *shogun* tried to improve his position by inducing his friends to bring about a marriage between himself and the sister of the *Mikado*; and the marriage took place in 1861; but it did not mend matters. Prince Mito instigated an attack on the British Legation at Jeddo in the same year; and, as he had in his possession a secret document from the *Mikado*, commanding him to endeavour to reconcile the differences at Jeddo, and to induce the *shogun* to exterminate the barbarians, he had authority for his action.

The *shogun* was then obliged to admit his inability to protect strangers. He made all kinds of efforts, which were not then understood, to persuade the Legations to remove from Jeddo to Yokohama, where they could be more easily defended. The people who had attacked the British Legation were, it is true, executed; but the government was so afraid of popular feeling that it had to announce that the culprits were punished, not for assaulting foreigners, but for highway robbery.

The strength of popular feeling showed itself again in January, 1862, when, although Mito, the great anti-foreigner, had died in the previous September, Ando Tsushima, one of the *shogun's* council, and a protector of foreigners, was nearly murdered in the street, and upon his recovery was made to retire into private life, thanks to the influence of the *Mikado's* party. Up to that time, however, no *daimio* had openly declared himself against the *shogun*, although many retainers of *daimios* had voluntarily outlawed themselves in order to gain freedom of action against the foreigners.

In the spring of 1862 a new force appeared upon the scene, in the person of Shimadzu Sabura, uncle of the then Prince of Satsuma. While on his way to obtain an amnesty for the political prisoners who had been sentenced by the regent in 1860, he was met by a large body of the outlaws, or *ronins*, who begged him to memorialise the *Mikado* to go forth in person against the barbarians, to abolish the *shogunate*, and to punish the *shogun's* council. Shimadzu Sabura presented the petitions, and soon afterwards an amnesty was granted to the political prisoners. Choshiu, Prince of Nagato, was in Kioto at about the same time; and to him and Shimadzu Sabura was entrusted the somewhat difficult task of keeping the *ronins* quiet. Thus, the great clans of Satsuma and Choshiu became for a time associated in a combination against the Jeddo Government, and in an opposition which had the *Mikado* at its back.

Another attack on the British Legation occurred in June, 1862. The *shogun's* council was too feeble to take active measures against the culprits, and, in face of the attitude of the surrounders of the *Mikado*, was unable either to satisfy the foreign representatives or to appease the enmity of its political opponents. In June, 1862, the *Mikado* ordered the *shogun* to expel the foreigners, and to appear at Kioto to consult with the court, leaving proper persons at Jeddo to carry out his functions there. The chief of the persons so left was the same Hitosubashi who had been Mito's nominee for the *shogunate*.

There could have been no more conclusive evidence of the decadence of the once great authority of the *shogun*. In September, 1862, Shimadzu Sabura was greatly incensed at the scant courtesy shown to him by the ministers of the *shogun*, and, it is probable, was only too ready to countenance the outrage, (committed on Sept. 14th 1862), which led, in 1863, to hostilities between Great Britain and Japan.

The *Euryalus*, flagship of Vice-Admiral Kuper, arrived at Yokohama on the day of the outrage, the nature of which will be explained later. Upon representations being made, the *shogun's* council expressed its regret, but frankly admitted its inability to force so powerful a *daimio* as Satsuma to surrender the guilty parties. In the meantime, Shimadzu Sabura had received the thanks of the *Mikado* for his services, and Prince Tosa had arrived at Kioto and joined Satsuma and Choshiu in the policy of opposition to foreigners. This seems to have stimulated the *Mikado's* advisers to order the *shogun*, who had not yet left Jeddo, to take command of the clans in the spring of 1863, when he was due at Kioto, and drive the foreigners into the sea.

The unfortunate *shogun*, continuing to temporise, agreed to obey the commands of the Mikado, and, at the same time, while keeping peace with the foreigners, tried, by making their position intolerable, to induce them to leave the country. The foreign representatives, on the other hand, were daily becoming more and more convinced that the *shogun* had little real power, and no authority to sign treaties.

Strengthened by the arrival of numerous *daimios*, the *mikado* called a meeting at Kioto on April 8th, 1863, a fortnight before the appearance of the *shogun*, and, ordering the expulsion of foreigners from Japan, directed that his will should be conveyed to the *samurai*. Strangers were, in consequence, liable from that moment to be murdered, and were deprived of all protection and all redress, save what might be obtained by the exercise of force.

The Legations were, one by one, driven from Jeddo; and the cordon round Yokohama, where they took refuge, was gradually narrowed in preparation for their final expulsion. A large force of European ships was kept close at hand; seamen and marines were landed to protect the settlement; and, off each of the other ports in which there were Europeans, a man-of-war lay with banked fires, ready, at an instant's notice, to embark the fugitives. The old custom, in virtue of which the *daimios* had spent every alternate year in Jeddo, and had always left their wives and families there, had been abrogated at the end of 1862; so that a wholesome restraint upon the conduct of the malcontent princes, and a formidable instrument of power in the hands of the *shogun*, had disappeared.

On June 5th, 1863, at the instigation of Shimadzu Sabura, the 25th of the same month was fixed as the day on which the complete expulsion of the foreigners was to be effected; and it then became necessary for the *shogun* to make up his mind whether he would carry out the behests of the *Mikado*, or would join hands with the foreigners, bolster up his own power, and try to overthrow his opponents. In his perplexity, he asked for permission to return to Jeddo. It was refused, and his rival. Prince Mito, was sent thither instead of him.

Since April the *shogun's* council had tried to procrastinate in its replies to the demands for satisfaction on account of the outrage of the previous September. It had at last promised to pay the indemnity on June 18th; but as soon as Prince Mito reached Jeddo, a refusal to pay was announced. On June 24th, moreover, a decree was promulgated by the *shogun*, who was stated to have received "orders" to that effect from the *Mikado*, "to close the open ports and remove the subjects of the treaty powers." The indemnity was, however, handed over when the council learnt that the settlement of the business had been placed in the hands of Vice-Admiral Kuper.

A little later the council secretly approached the treaty powers with a request for assistance in overthrowing the *Mikado* and his party. This was refused; but while the answer of the foreigners was still unknown, the council, through Hitosubashi, reported that the orders of the *Mikado* could not be carried out.

The apparent lack of patriotism displayed by the *shogun's* party proportionably increased the fanaticism of the Kioto faction, the result being that on June 25th Choshiu opened fire on some French, American, and Dutch vessels at Simonoseki.

At this crisis the *shogun* behaved very well. He might have made capital by joining the popular movement, and encouraging a general massacre of foreigners; and, as he was at Kioto, he might have pleaded duress.

His council, too, at Jeddo, though playing a double game, succeeded in causing the defence of Yokohama to be handed over to the foreign executive authorities. Choshiu, for his part, received the approval of the *Mikado*; and although, on July 20th, the French Rear-Admiral Jaurès, with a couple of ships, bombarded the Simonoseki batteries, and, landing, spiked some of their guns, the United States corvette *Wyoming*, which tried single-handed to punish Choshiu in the same manner, ran aground under the forts, and did not get off until she had been rather roughly handled. (Griffis, in *N. Amer. Review*, 1875; Adams, *History of Japan*.)

I may now revert to the outrage of September, 1862, and describe the hostilities which resulted from it.

The cause of the quarrel is sufficiently explained in a letter addressed on August 1st, 1863, by Lieut.-Colonel Edward St. John Neale, Her Majesty's *Chargé d'Affaires* in Japan, to the Prince of Satsuma. The important part of this communication is as follows:

> Your Highness,—It is well known to you that a barbarous murder of an unarmed and unoffending British subject and merchant was perpetrated on the 14th of the month of September last . . . upon the Tokaido, near Kanagawa, by persons

attending the procession, and surrounding the *norimon* of, Shi-
nadzu Sabbura, who, I am informed, is the father, (apparently
he was uncle), of Your Highness. It is equally known to you that
a murderous assault was made at the same time by the same
retinue upon a lady and two other gentlemen, British subjects,
by whom he was accompanied, the two gentlemen having been
severely and seriously wounded, and the lady escaping by a
miracle. The names of the British subjects here referred to are
as follows:—

Mr. Charles Lenox Richardson, murdered; Mrs. Borradaile; Mr.
William Clarke, severely wounded; Mr. William Marshal, severely wounded. . . . Ten months have now elapsed since the
perpetration of this unprovoked outrage . . . but I have had occasion to report to my government that, removed in your distant domain from the direct influence of the supreme government, and shielded also by certain privileges and immunities . . .
you had utterly disregarded all orders or decrees of the Japanese
Government calling upon you to afford justice by sending the
real criminals to Yeddo. . . In the meantime, I have received the
explicit instructions of my own government how to act in this
matter. . . . When British subjects are the victims of those acts,
Japan, as a nation, must, through its government, pay a penalty,
and disavow the deeds of its subjects, to whatever rank they
may belong. . . I demanded from the Tycoon's Government an
apology and the payment of a considerable penalty. . . . Both
these demands have been acceded to.
But the British Government has also decided that those circumstances constitute no reason why the real delinquents and
actual murderers should be shielded by Your Highness, or by
any means escape the condign punishment which they merit.
. . . I am instructed to demand of Your Highness as follows:—
First. The immediate trial and execution, in the presence of one
or more of Her Majesty's naval officers, of the chief perpetrators of the murder of Mr. Richardson, and of the murderous
assault upon the lady and gentlemen who accompanied him.
Secondly. The payment of £25,000 sterling, to be distributed to
the relations of the murdered man, and to those who escaped
with their lives the swords of the assassins on that occasion.
These demands are required by Her Majesty's Government to

be acceded to by Your Highness immediately upon their being made known to you. And upon your refusing, neglecting, or evading to do so, the admiral commanding the British forces in these seas will adopt such coercive measures, increasing in their severity, as he may deem expedient to obtain the required satisfaction. . . .

On August 13th the Minister of the Prince of Satsuma replied with a temporising and otherwise unsatisfactory letter; and on the 14th Lieut.-Colonel Neale, by dispatch, requested Vice-Admiral, (temporary rank only), Augustus Leopold Kuper, C.B., Commander-in-Chief on the East Indies and China station, to enter upon such measures of coercion as he might deem expedient.

The vice-admiral's available force consisted of H.M.S.—

Ships.	Guns.	Tons.	Nom. H.P.	Compt.	Commanders.
Euryalus (flag)	35	2371	400	515	{Capt. John James Stephen Josling. {Com. Edward Wilmot.
Pearl . .	21	1469	400	275	Capt. John Borlase, C.B.
Coquette .	4	677	200	90	Com. John Hobhouse Inglis Alexander.
Argus . .	6	981	300	175	Com. Lewis James Moore.
Perseus .	17	955	200	175	Com. Augustus John Kingston.
Racehorse .	4	695	200	90	Com. Charles Richard Fox Boxer.
Havock .	2	235	60	40	Lieut. George Poole.

★★★★★★

The *Euryalus*, a wooden screw frigate, originally of 51 guns, was built at Chatham in 1853. The *Pearl*, a wooden screw corvette, was launched at Woolwich in 1851. The *Coquette*, a wooden screw gun-vessel, was built in 1855. The *Argus*, a wooden paddle-wheel sloop, was built at Portsmouth in 1849. The *Perseus* was a wooden screw sloop, built at Pembroke in 1861. The *Racehorse* was a wooden screw gun-vessel built in 1860. The *Havock*, of the "*Albacore* class," was one of 116 similar wooden screw gun-vessels built at the time of the Russian War.
★★★★★★

From the vice-admiral's dispatch of August 17th to Lieut. Colonel Neale, and from that of August 22nd to the Secretary of the Admiralty, is compiled the succeeding account of what occurred:—

On the forenoon of the 14th inst., Kuper (quitted the *Euryalus* and proceeded in the *Havock* in order to satisfy himself as to the position of three steamers, the property of the Prince of Satsuma, which were lying in a bay to the northward of Kagosima. These steamers were the

England, screw, 1150 tons, purchased for 125,000 dollars; the *Sir George Grey*, screw, 492 tons, purchased for 85,000 dollars; and the *Contest*, screw, 350 tons, purchased for 95,000 dollars. He found deep water in the bay, there being generally fifty fathoms within a hundred yards of the shore. A strong breeze from the eastward had sprung up, and, the rapid falling of the barometer indicating the probable approach of a typhoon or heavy gale, the top-gallant masts were sent on deck.

Kuper received the dispatch of the 14th inst. on the evening of that day; and the *Pearl, Coquette, Argus, Racehorse*, and *Havock* were sent at daylight on the 15th to seize the three steamers already referred to. Captain Borlase, the senior officer, was directed to avoid as much as possible all unnecessary bloodshed or active hostility.

> The steamers were accordingly taken possession of without opposition, and brought down to our anchorage during the forenoon of the 15th, lashed alongside the *Coquette, Argus*, and *Racehorse*, which vessels anchored in the same bay as before. ...
> The weather still looked threatening.
> At noon, during a squall, accompanied by much rain, the whole of the batteries, (about 88 guns and mortars were in position, including at least three 10-in. and two 8-in. guns, and forty 32- and 24-prs), on the Kagosima side suddenly opened fire upon the *Euryalus*, (taken entirely by surprise, the late Sir Alfred Jephson told me that she hastily weighed, while her band played, "Oh dear, what can the matter be?"), the only ship within range; but although many shot and shell passed over and close around her, no damage was done beyond cutting away a few ropes, finding that the springs on the cable would not keep the ship's broadside on, and as it was impossible, with the comparatively small force at my command, to engage the batteries under way.
> And, at the same time, to retain possession of the steamers, I signalled to the *Coquette, Argus* and *Racehorse* to burn their prizes, and then to the whole squadron to weigh and form the line of battle according to seniority, (this order is observed in the tabulated list given earlier), the *Havock* being directed to secure the destruction of the three steamers.
> Previous to this, the *Perseus*, having slipped her cable, was directed to fire on the north battery until the signal was made to form line of battle, which service was executed by Commander

A. J. Kingston with great promptness.

Although the weather was now very dirty, with every indication of a typhoon, I considered it advisable not to postpone, until another day, the return of the fire of the Japanese, to punish the Prince of Satsuma for the outrage, and to vindicate the honour of the flag; and, everything being now ready, I proceeded towards the batteries, opening fire upon the northernmost one with considerable effect; and passed, at slow speed, along the whole line within point-blank range. Owing, probably, to the unfavourable state of the weather, the ships astern did not maintain their positions in as close order as I could have wished, and the *Euryalus* was consequently exposed to a very heavy and well-directed fire from several of the batteries at the same time, and suffered somewhat severely.

About this time, also, and whilst in the thickest of the action, I deeply regret to state that I was deprived, at the same moment, of the assistance of Captain Josling and Commander Wilmot both of whom were killed by the same shot, whilst standing by me on the bridge of the *Euryalus*, directing the fire of the quarters and setting an example of coolness and gallantry which was emulated throughout the entire ship.

★★★★★★

(Captain John James Stephen Josling's commissions bore date: Lieutenant, July 25th, 1847; Commander, Nov. 2nd, 1854; and Captain, Jan. 31st, 1861.)

(Commander Edward Wilmot's commissions bore date: Lieutenant, Sept. 26th, 1853; Commander, Dec. 24th, 1861. He had served in the Black Sea, in the *Royal Albert*, during the Russian War.)

★★★★★★

In consequence of the dense smoke, and occasional heavy showers, it was difficult to ascertain the extent of the damage done to the earthwork batteries, but by the time the *Euryalus* got abreast of the last, or southernmost battery, I could observe the town to be on fire in several places; and, the weather having now assumed a most threatening appearance, I considered it advisable to discontinue the engagement, and to seek a secure anchorage for Her Majesty's ships. The *Racehorse*, owing to a momentary stoppage of her engines, unfortunately took the ground opposite the northern battery: but by the prompt energy of the commanders of the *Coquette, Argus*, and *Havock*, which vessels were despatched to her assistance, she was got off without damage.

The steady fire kept up by Commander C. R. F. Boxer prevented the *Racehorse* receiving any serious injury from the battery, which had already been much disabled by the fire of the other ships. The *Havock* was then ordered to set fire to five large junks belonging to the Prince of Satsuma, which Lieutenant George Poole accomplished in a most satisfactory manner; and these, as well as a very extensive arsenal and foundry for the manufacture of guns, shot, and shell, together with large storehouses adjoining, were also completely destroyed.

During the whole of the succeeding night it blew almost a hurricane, but all the vessels of the squadron rode it out without accident, with the exception of the *Perseus*, which vessel dragged her anchors off the bank into 60 fathoms water, and was compelled to slip her cable during the following afternoon, when the gale had somewhat moderated. The gale subsided gradually during the 16th, and, as I had observed the Japanese at work, apparently erecting batteries on the hill above the anchorage, enveloped in trees and bushes, which might have inflicted much damage upon the small vessels lying within pistol-shot of the shore, I became anxious for their safety, and determined to move the squadron out of the anchorage we had occupied upon the night of our arrival in the gulf, for the purpose of repairing damages, fishing spars, and refitting previous to proceeding to sea.

The squadron accordingly weighed at three p.m. of the 16th, and, passing in line between the batteries of Kagosima and Sakurasima, steamed through the channel and anchored to the southward of the island, taking advantage of the occasion to shell the batteries on the Sakura side, which had not been previously engaged, and also the palace of the prince in Kagosima. A feeble fire only was returned from the batteries which had not been closely engaged in the first attack, and this, happily, without effect upon Her Majesty's ships. . . . With much regret I have to add that the returns received from the various ships present a list of casualties unusually great, being no less than 13, killed and 50 wounded, the half of which occurred in my flagship alone. . . I left the gulf of Kagosima, in company with the squadron, on the afternoon of the 17th inst., on my return to Yokohama. (In addition to the two officers already named, Gunner Thomas Finn, of the *Coquette*, was killed.)

This engagement did much to discredit a type of gun which was then new to the navy. An officer who was present in the *Euryalus* wrote to me:—

We had on our main-deck 32-pr. 56 cwt. muzzle-loaders; and they, of course, gave no trouble. On our quarter-deck we had four 40-pr. Armstrongs, and we got two or three from the port side over to the spare ports on the starboard side to make a larger battery. These all worked well. But in the forecastle wo had a 7-in. B. L. 110-pr. Armstrong. Whether the men in the heat of the action became hurried I cannot say; but certain it is that the breech piece of this gun blew out with tremendous effect, the concussion knocking down the whole gun's crew, and apparently paralysing the men, until Webster, captain of the forecastle and of the gun, roused them by shouting: "Well; is there ere a b—— of you will go and get the spare vent piece?"

It is of first-rate importance that men should have confidence in the safety of their weapons. Naturally the type of gun in question never again commanded much confidence.

During the engagement, a 10-in. shell from the batteries exploded near the muzzle of one of the guns on the main deck of the *Euryalus*, killing seven men, and wounding Lieutenant Alfred Jephson, and five others. The remaining officers wounded were Assistant-Paymaster George Washington Jones, and Gunner W. Sale (*Euryalus*); Carpenter M. Armstrong (*Pearl*); Lieutenant D'Arcy Anthony Denny, and Gunner W. Harris (*Coquette*); and Lieutenant Francis Joseph Pitt, Master Robert Gilpin, and Midshipman John Robert Aylen (*Perseus*). (*Gazette*, Oct. 30, 1863; *Japan Comm. News*, Aug. 26; corr. of *Times*; For. Off. corr.)

The promotions consequent upon this engagement were:—

To be Captains: Coms. John Hobhouse Inglis Alexander (Aug. 16), and Lewis James Moore (Nov. 9).

To be Commanders: Lieuts. James Edward Hunter, and Arthur George Robertson Roe (Aug. 16), and James Augustus Poland, and George Poole (Nov. 9).

To be Surgeon: Asst. Surg. Charles Richard Godfrey (Nov. 9).

Because of the typhoon, and the rolling of the ships, many of the shot intended for the batteries fell in the wood and paper town, and set it on fire. For this, Vice-Admiral Kuper was strongly blamed in the House of Commons; and was as warmly defended by a brother flag-officer, who, in the heat of argument, used the word "damn," and, upon being called to order, created much amusement by apologising for having uttered language which, he said, "so seldom fell from the lips of sailors."

Master William Hennessey Parker, of the flagship, steered his vessel with great judgment, taking her at times within 400 yards of the batteries; yet Kuper continually spurred him with: "Go in closer, Parker; go in closer!" Owing to the heavy sea in which the action was fought, the decks were afloat.

It should be mentioned that, previous to the action at Kagosima, the *shogun* had quitted Kioto, with the expressed intention of returning to Jeddo overland. He had, however, embarked in a steamer at Osaka, and so had reached Jeddo on July 31st. No doubt be feared for his safety.

The effect of Kuper's action was immense, especially on the powerful Satsuma following, that great clan learnt, and never again forgot, that Japan was not the strongest power in the world, and that there were other nations which, though far away, were, even in Japan, to be feared as being both stronger and more civilised. Satsuma's people subsequently took the lead in general progress, and in introducing European machinery and inventions to their compatriots.

Yet, although the conversion of the anti-foreign party had begun, the *shogun* did not regain his prestige. In the autumn of 1863, a European-built steamer, carrying Japanese colours, and bearing envoys from him, was fired upon by Choshiu. Choshiu, however, soon went too far. Early in October, 1863, he formed a plan to carry off the *Mikado* from his palace, one of the gates of which was in charge of the Nagato clan.

The plot was discovered in time; Satsuma's people were summoned in haste; and Aidzu, the *shogun's* Resident at Kioto, with some small *daimios*, rallied to the *Mikado's* person, the upshot being that Choshiu, and many of his confederates, had to withdraw in disgrace. This conspiracy had its influence upon the *Mikado's* advisers; and although the Emperor declared that he was still determined to expel the foreigners, he added that he should delay taking the field. News of this announcement reaching Jeddo, and, it being there interpreted with prudence, the *shogun's* council, on November 12th, withdrew the decree of June 24th, relative to the closing of the ports, and the removal of foreigners; and Satsuma's envoys gave the satisfaction and indemnity which had been demanded by Great Britain.

From that time the scheme for expelling "the barbarians" fell to pieces. The *shogun*, with others, received marks of the *Mikado's* favour, and, at the same time, promised to confine his functions to those of a military vassal, and to endeavour, by improving the military resources of the country, to enable Japan to hold her own against other powers. the authorities thenceforth frankly recognised the superiority of foreign ships and arms; and a decree on the subject was issued by the *Mikado*, and sent to all the *daimios*.

A copy of this decree fell into the hands of the British Minister in April, 1864; and the *shogun's* council was then taxed with cherishing a deliberate intention of expelling foreigners when the time for doing so should have arrived. The council answered blandly that the necessary preparations would take a long time to make, if the foreigners should continue to keep at hand a large coercive force. This led to a permanent occupation of Yokohama by the British and French.

Choshiu, the restless, though in disgrace, was not idle. In February, 1864, he sank a steamer which had been lent to Prince Satsuma by the *shogun*; and in July, 1864, accompanied by an armed body of *ron-*

ins and adventurers, he ascended the river from Osaka, and appeared before Kioto.

The *Mikado* refused to listen to those who advised him to deal leniently with the truculent prince; and heavy fighting resulted, the *shogun's* people, under Hitosubashi, and Satsuma's men, assisting in the defence of the palace, and in the defeat of the assailants, but not until there had been great slaughter, and until thousands of houses, sixty Shinto shrines, and one hundred and fifteen Buddhist temples, had been destroyed.

After the repulse, the *Mikado* ordered the *shogun* to march an army into the rebel vassal's territory at the south-western extremity of Nipon, and in the island of Choshiu, and to bring to his senses "*Matz daira Daizen uo Daibii, Jiusi no Choshiu,*" Prince of Nagato.

Here was a good opportunity for punishing Choshiu for having fired upon European vessels, to aid a government which showed some signs of entertaining wiser and more liberal sentiments than before, and to open the Inland Sea to trade. The *shogun* gave a secret assent to the suggestion that the ships of the powers should assist; and Sir Rutherford Alcock, then British Envoy Extraordinary in Japan, gladly seized so favourable an occasion for dealing a blow at the chief of the anti-foreign party, who, moreover, for the previous twelve months, had interrupted the trade at Nagasaki.

The associated powers were Great Britain, France, Holland, and America. The Americans had no suitable vessel available on the spot; but anxious to take part, they put an officer, some men, and a gun from the U.S. corvette *Jamestown*, on board a chartered steamer, the *Ta-kiang*, and added her to the combined forces, which, when assembled, comprised the following ships:—

Sir Augustus Kuper quitted Yokohama on August 29th, and sailed again from the rendezvous, off Himesima Island, in the Inland Sea, on September 4th, anchoring in the afternoon out of range of the batteries in the Strait of Simonoseki. The defences then existing there are shown in the accompanying plan. The nature of the guns in the various forts is specified in the table following further on.

Kuper, with the French Rear-Admiral Janrès, reconnoitred the position of the various works which were held by the Prince of Nagato; and it was arranged that the attack should be made on September 5th, as soon as the tide should serve.

At 2 p.m. on the 5th, therefore, the ships took up their assigned

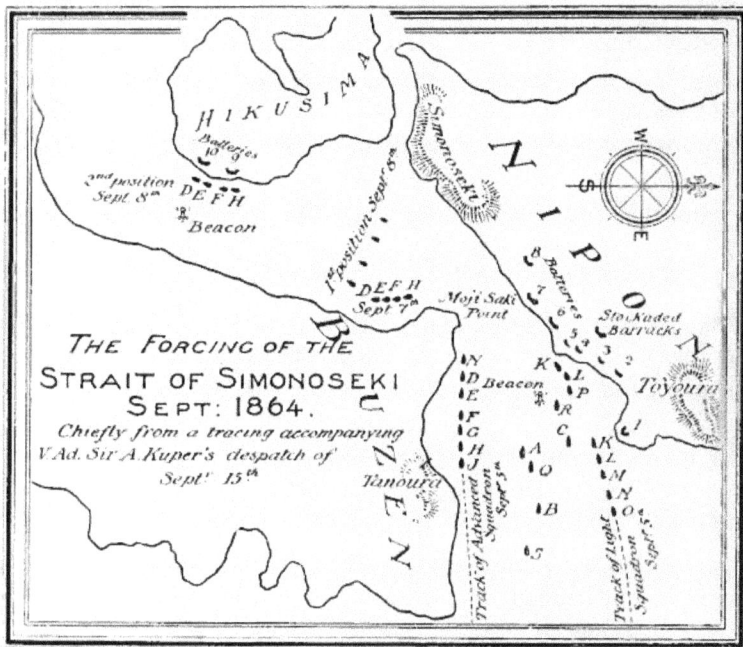

THE FORCING OF THE
STRAIT OF SIMONOSEKI
SEPT: 1864.
Chiefly from a tracing accompanying
V.Ad. Sir A. Kuper's despatch of
Sept. 15th

FOR REFERENCE LETTERS, SEE TABLE FOLLOWING

positions, and, immediately they had reached them, the action was opened by the flagship *Euryalus*, the Japanese replying smartly and with spirit. The positions of the ships, as described in Kuper's dispatch of September 15th, were as follows:—

ALLIED SQUADRONS AT THE FORCING OF THE STRAIT OF SIMONOSEKI,
SEPTEMBER, 1864.

NATION.	Ref. to Plan.	SHIPS.	Tons B. M.	Guns.	COMMANDERS.
Br.	A	*Euryalus*, scr. frig.	2,371	35	{V.-Ad. Sir Augustus Leopold Kuper, K.C.B. / Capt. Jno. Hobhouse Inglis Alexander.
Fr.	B	*Sémiramis*, scr. frig..	..	35	{R.-Ad. C. Jaurès. / Capt. Du Quilio.
Br.	C	*Conqueror*,¹ scr. batt.-ship . . .	2,845	78	Capt. Wm. Garnham Luard.
Br.	D	*Tartar*, scr. corv.	1,296	20	Capt. Jno. Montagu Hayes.
Fr.	E	*Dupleix*, scr. corv.	..	10	Capt. Franlieu.
Dut.	F	*Metalen Kruis*, scr. . . .	..	16	Capt. J. F. De Man.
Br.	G	*Barrosa*, scr .corv.	1,700	21	Capt. Wm. Montagu Dowell.
Dut.	H	*Djambi*, scr.	..	16	Capt. van Rees.
Br.	J	*Leopard*, padl. frig.	1,404	18	Capt. Chas. Tayler Leckie.
Br.	K	*Perseus*, scr. sloop	955	17	Com. Aug. Jno. Kingston.
Dut.	L	*Medusa*, scr.	..	18	Capt. de Casembroot.
Fr.	M	*Tancrède*, scr. disp. v. . . .	..	4	Lieut. Palm.
Br.	N	*Coquette*, scr. g. v. . . .	677	4	Com. Arth. Geo. R Robertson Roe.
Br.	O	*Bouncer*, scr. g. b.	..	4	Lieut. Hy. Lowe Holder.
Br.	P	*Argus*, padl. sloop	281	6	Com. Jno. Moresby.
Dut.	Q	*Amsterdam*, padl. . . .	..	8	Com. Müller.
Am.	R	*Takiang*, chartd. str.	..	1	Lieut. Pearson, U.S.N.
Br.	S	*Pembrokeshire*, collier . . .	..	..	

Advanced Squadron. (rows C–H) Light Squadron. (rows J–R)

¹ Having on board a battalion of Royal Marines.

129

The advanced squadron, under the command of Captain J. M. Hayes, consisting of the *Tartar, Dupleix, Metalen, Kruis, Barrosa, Djambi*, and *Leopard*, moved into the bay off the village of Toyoura, as shown on the plan, within easy range of batteries 3 to 8 (dispatch says "3 to 9" an obvious error), inclusive, while the *Euryalus* and *Sémiramis* opened fire upon the same works. The light squadron, under Commander Kingston, consisting of the *Perseus, Medusa, Tanerède, Coquette*, and *Bouncer*, were directed to take the batteries in flank. The *Argus* and *Amsterdam* being at first kept in reserve to render assistance to any ship that might be disabled or grounded, were afterwards ordered to close and engage; and the *Conqueror*, having the battalion of marines on board, was, in consequence of the difficult navigation, directed to approach only sufficiently near to admit of her Armstrong guns bearing on the nearest batteries.

During this operation, the *Conqueror* grounded twice on a knoll of sand, but came off again without assistance, and without sustaining any damage. The *Takiang* also fired several shots from her one Parrot gun, doing good service. The *Coquette*, towards the close of the engagement, was withdrawn from her position with the flanking squadron, and sent to assist the foremost of the advanced corvette squadron, a service which Commander A. G. R. Roe performed with great promptness.

By about 4.30 p.m. the fire from batteries 4 and 5 evidently slackened; and soon afterwards it ceased. By 5.30 batteries 6, 7, and 8 were also silenced. It was, however, then too late in the day to admit of landing-parties being disembarked. Nevertheless, the *Perseus* and the *Medusa* being very close to battery 5, and it being too dark to signal for instructions. Commander Kingston, with Lieutenant Francis Joseph Pitt, and a party from the *Perseus*, followed by Captain de Casembroot, and Lieutenant De Hart, of the *Medusa*, gallantly pulled ashore, spiked most of the guns in that battery, and returned to their ships without casualties.

A curious and significant feature of this first day's action was the receipt of a request from Buzen, on the side of the strait opposite to Simonoseki, that the people there should be permitted to fire blank cartridges at the squadron during the attack, and yet not be molested. They desired to keep in the good graces of both parties, with a diplomatic view to the future.

At daylight on September 6th, battery 8 re-opened fire upon the advanced squadron, doing some damage to the *Tartar* and *Dupleix*; but, on a return being made by the squadron, it was silenced, only a few straggling shots being afterwards fired from it. Kuper continues:—

The arrangement for the disembarkation having been completed, the allied forces, composed of the small-arm companies of the *Euryalus* and *Conqueror*, under the command of Captain J. H. I. Alexander, of the *Euryalus*, the battalion of marines, and marines of the squadron, under that of Lieut.-Colonel William Grigor Suther, R.M., and detachments of 350 French, and 200 Dutch seamen and marines, the former under the command of Captain Du Quilis and Lieutenant Layrle, *chef d'état major*, and the latter under that of Lieutenant Binkis, were distributed in the boats of the squadron and towed to the opposite shore by the *Argus, Perseus, Coquette, Tancrède, Amsterdam, Medusa*, and Takiang, the *Bouncer* assisting to cover the landing, which was effected without accident, under the able superintendence of Captain W. G. Luard, of the *Conqueror*, assisted by Commander Edward Thomas Nott of that ship; and the force proceeded, under my personal direction, to assault and take possession of the principal batteries; which was accomplished with only trifling opposition.

All the guns having been dismounted and spiked, carriages and platforms burnt, and magazines blown up, and deeming it inexpedient, from the very rugged and almost impenetrable nature of the country, to retain possession of any post on shore during the night, I directed the whole force to re-embark at 4 p.m.

The French and Dutch detachments were already in their boats, when the Naval Brigade stationed at battery No. 5 was suddenly attacked by a strong body of Japanese assembled in the valley in the rear of the battery. Colonel Suther's battalion of marines coming up at this moment, a joint attack was instantly organised, and the enemy driven back upon a strongly-placed stockaded barrack, from which they were dislodged after making a brief but sharp resistance, leaving seven small guns in our possession.

On this occasion, Captain Alexander, while leading his men, was badly wounded in the foot, and numerous other casualties took place. The force re-embarked without further incident. The *Perseus*, while assisting in the landing operations in the morning, was driven on shore by a strong eddy of the current, and remained fast until midnight on the 7th, when, having been lightened, she was towed off undamaged by the good management of Commander Moresby. An extraordinary incident of the second day's work was the arrival of envoys from Choshiu, with a request for a cessation of hostilities for forty-eight hours, it being alleged that the Japanese troops were tired and hungry, but would be prepared to renew the engagement at the expiration of the period. The episode recalls the easy-going behaviour of the Belgian and Dutch troops, who, during the four days' fighting in Brussels in 1830, desisted each day for dinner, as by common consent, and even allowed each other time for a brief *siesta* afterwards.

The batteries from 1 to 8 inclusive being in possession of the Allies, working parties were landed early on September 7th, and began to embark the captured guns. In the afternoon, the *Tartar, Metalen Kruis, Djambi,* and *Dupleix* moved round to the westward of Moji Saki Point, preparatory to an attack on batteries 9 and 10.

On September 8th, accompanied by Jaurès, Kuper shifted his flag to the *Coquette,* and, with the four ships above mentioned, proceeded to open fire on batteries 9 and 10. The fire was not returned; and soon afterwards parties were landed from the squadron to destroy the works and embark the guns, the whole operation being completed by the evening of September 10th. Sixty-two pieces in all were brought away.

On the 8th, while the work on shore was still in progress, an envoy from Choshiu went on board the British flagship under a flag of truce, and produced letters and documents which induced Kuper and Jaurès to allow a two days' truce, at the expiration of which a Japanese officers of high rank brought humble and satisfactory submissions from Choshiu, his promise to erect no more batteries, and his consent to open the strait. (Disps. and letters of Kuper, Alexander, Hayes, and Suther; Journals of Capt. Payne and Chf. Paym. R. R. A. Richards: Corr. of *Times,* and of *A and N. Gazette.*)

In the course of the operations, the allies had 12 people killed, and 60 wounded. The British loss was, *Euryalus,* 5 killed, 18 wounded; *Tartar,* 8 wounded; *Conqueror,* 2 killed, 4 wounded; *Barrosa,* 1 wounded; *Leopard,* 2 wounded; *Perseus,* 2 wounded; *Bouncer,* 1 wounded; and the battalion of Royal Marines, 1 killed, and 12 wounded: total, 8 killed, 48 wounded. No officers were killed, but the following were wounded: Captain John Hobhouse Inglis Alexander, Lieutenant Frederick Edwards, and Midshipman C. W. Atkinson (*Euryalus*); Lieutenant Wil-

BATTERY.	GUNS.	HOWITZERS.	MORTARS.	FIELD PIECES.
No. 1 . . .	1—9-pr.	1—32-pr.	.	2—12-prs.
No. 2 . . .	1—9-pr.			
No. 3 . . .		Removed by the Japanese.		
Stockaded } Barracks } .	..	1—12-pr.	1 coehorn	{ 2—6-prs. 3 swivels.
No. 4 . . .	4—30-prs.			
No. 5 . . .	{ 1—8-ton 6—24-prs.			
No. 6 . . .	{ 2—11-in. 3—78-prs. }	..	..	3—12-prs.
No. 7 . . .	..	..	{ 1—8-in. 1—13-in.	
No. 8 . . .	{ 1—ᵛ-in. 3—24-prs. 7—30-prs. }	2—5-in.		.
Nos. 9 and 10 .	{ 6—30-prs. 1—24-pr. 2—9-prs. }	1—5-in.	..	{ 4—6-prs. 2—3-prs.
Total . .	38	5	3	16

liam Arthur de Vesci Brownlow, and Midshipman Edward John Wing-field (*Tartar*); and Lieutenant-Colonel Charles William Adair, R. M., Captain Nevinson William de Courcy, R.M., and Lieutenant James Weir Inglis, R.M., of the marine battalion.

The promotions consequent upon the action were:—

To be Captains: Commanders John Moresby and Augustus John Kingston (Nov. 21st).

To be Commanders: Lieutenants Henry Lowe Holder, William Henry Cuming, William Arthur de Vesci Brownlow, Richard Hastings Harington, and Richard Edward Tracey (Nov. 21st).

To be Master: Second-Master James Greenwood Liddell (Nov. 18th).

To be Surgeon: Assistant-Surgeon Richard Lovell Bluett Head (Nov. 18th).

Most of the British casualties occurred on September 6th, when the Naval Brigade and marines were engaged on shore. It was then that Captain Alexander was wounded, the command of the Brigade devolving on Lieutenant Harington. In the course of that afternoon's fighting some gallant deeds were done, and no fewer than three Victoria Crosses were gained; one by Midshipman Duncan Gordon Boyes of the *Euryalus*:

133

Who carried a colour with the leading company, kept it with headlong gallantry in advance of all, in face of the thickest fire, his colour-sergeants having fallen, one mortally and the other dangerously wounded, and was only detained from proceeding further yet by the orders of his superior officer. The colour he carried was six times pierced by musket balls. (Alexander to Kuper, Sept. 10th.)

The others were gained by Thomas Pride, captain of the after-guard, who, until he fell disabled, had supported Boyes; and by William Seeley, seaman, who daringly ascertained the position of the enemy, and afterwards, though wounded, continued in the front of the advance. (*Gazette*, April 21st, 1865.)

In addition to most of the officers who have been already named, the following were mentioned in the dispatches:—

Lieutenants Robert Peel Dennistoun (flag), Cottrell Burnaby Powell, and Alfred Jephson; Masters George Williams, John Charles Solfleet, and John Emanuel Chappie; Paymaster Hemsley Hardy Shanks (Secretary); Surgeons David Lloyd Morgan, and Christopher Knox Ord, M.D.; Assistant-Surgeons Samuel M'Bean, Edward Alfred Birch, and John Thomson Comerford; Midshipmen Henry Hart Dyke, and Edward Plantagenet Hume; Clerk Robert N. Haly; Lieut.-Colonel Penrose Charles Penrose, R.M.; Captain Ambrose Wolrige, R.M.; Lieutenant John Christopher Hore, R.M.; Lieutenant William Henry Townsend Morris Dodgin, R.M.A.; and a Prussian officer, Herr von Blanc, who was attached to the *Tartar*.

After much further negotiation, some internal outbreaks, and a demonstration by the fleets of the powers at Osaka, the *mikado* ratified the treaties at the end of 1865. In 1866 the *shogun*, or *tycoon*, Jyemochi, died, and was succeeded by Hitosubashi, under the name of Keiki. At about the same time Choshiu, who had previously repulsed the *shogun's* forces, became reconciled both with the *Mikado* and with Satsuma. In 1867 the *Mikado* also died, and the crown devolved upon Mutsu Hito, then a boy of fifteen, who later distinguished himself as a most successful and enlightened ruler. There was thenceforward no serious difficulty with foreigners. An attack in May, 1867, on two British subjects who were travelling between Osaka and Jeddo was promptly punished; and the murder of two men of H.M.S. *Icarus*, at Nagasaki, was as quickly inquired into, the perpetrators being executed. In November of the same year, the dual government was terminated by Keiki's surrender of the remains of his power to the *Mikado*.

It is not necessary to follow further the evolution of the modern regime in Japan. It was not accomplished without much violence; and in 1868 seamen and marines had again to be landed on Japanese soil, this time at Kobe. They had, however, little or no fighting to do; and, soon afterwards, the conservative chiefs formally admitted that the long efforts to close the country were a mistake, and prayed that relations of amity with foreigners might be encouraged. In March, 1868, the European and American ministers were invited for the first time to visit the *Mikado* at Kioto. Isolated outrages continued for some time; and even on the occasion of this visit to the *Mikado*, the British minister narrowly escaped assassination; but proper punishment was instantly meted out to the offenders; and it was generally admitted that these crimes were the work of individual fanatics, and were in no sense instigated by the government.

Japan, under the Emperor Mutsu Hito, began, very soon afterwards, to astonish her friends by the rapidity with which it assimilated European methods and civilisation; and, ere the end of the nineteenth century, she won her way to recognition as one of the great powers of the world.

Niger, 1864-1866

In 1864, and again in 1865 and in 1866, various expeditions proceeded up the Niger to maintain British prestige, and to keep the turbulent chiefs in order. For this work the *Investigator*, (built at Deptford in 1861), 2, paddle, drawing as she did only about 4 feet 4 inches of water, proved most useful. She was employed almost constantly during those three years, either up the river, or in the Lagos lagoons, where, in March, 1865, she participated in the action at Ikorudu. Among the officers who successively commanded her on these services were Lieutenant Charles George Frederick Knowles, Lieutenant John George Graham M'Hardy, Lieutenant George Truman Morrell, and Lieutenant John William Jones. In the Congo, in 1865, the boats of the *Archer*, 13, screw, Captain Francis Marten, were engaged against the river pirates.

Early in 1865, while the *Dart*, 5, screw. Commander Frederick William Richards, lay at Akatoo, on the West Coast of Africa, a rumour arose to the effect that the natives were about to plunder the British factories. One factory, indeed, had been actually looted, and a schooner had been stripped and set adrift. Richards therefore landed some men from his gun-vessel, and, also a small detachment from the *Lee*, 5, screw. Lieutenant Oliver Thomas Lang. Several boats were capsized in the surf, and two people drowned; and, in a subsequent collision with the natives, one seaman was wounded.

Of the captures of slavers made in the same year, no case was more gallant and creditable than one in which the pinnace and cutter of the *Wasp*, 13, screw, Captain William Bowden, were concerned. On May 12th, the boats in question, containing 24 seamen and two Midshipmen, under Lieutenants Charles Compton Rising, and Charles Barstow Theobald, found an Arab *dhow*, with 283 slaves and a crew of 76 Arabs on board, about nine miles off Zanzibar, and captured her, after the enemy had made a desperate resistance, and had killed the pinnace's coxswain, John New, and wounded 11 people, including Rising, (com., Nov. 26, 1865, pension of £100 for wounds, Aug. 9, 1866), Theobald, (com., Nov. 16, 1865), and Midshipman William Wilson, (*Gazette*, July 21, 1865.)

The *Wasp* made several more captures, resistance, however, not being offered in most cases. Another vessel which, at about the same time and on the same station, greatly harassed the slave-trade, was the *Lyra*, 7, Commander Robert Augustus Parr. At her paying off, in April, 186S, after a fifty-two months' commission, she had eleven *dhows* to her credit.

Minor Operations, 1865

In June, 1865, while surveying off the south cape of Formosa, a boat party from the screw gunboat *Dove*, Master George Stanley, was set upon by cannibal natives, and had one man wounded. The vessel, upon the return of the party, opened fire with effect upon the assailants, who crowded the beach. The scene of the outrage is now known as Attack Bay.

In consequence of the long-continued outrages committed by certain of the inhabitants of the New Hebrides, Commodore Sir William Saltonstall Wiseman, Bart., in the *Curaçoa*, 28, screw, bombarded Tanna and Erromanga in 1865. At Tanna one British seaman was killed by a native. On the native side the damage done was confined chiefly to property.

On December 12th, boats' crews from the *Salamis*, paddle despatch-vessel, Commander Francis Grant Suttie, and *Janus*, gunboat, Lieutenant Cecil Frederick William Johnson, had a brush with some

Chinese pirates at Tia Nia, on the west coast of the island of Tonqua. Acting on information received from the *mandarins*, Commander Suttie landed with 45 officers and men, and, approaching three *junks* and five snake-boats which lay in a creek, was fired upon from several directions by a force of about 200 people, who presently fled to the hills. Lieutenant Johnson, with only six men, followed the main body of these, and fought them gallantly until he was recalled. About a dozen of the enemy were killed and wounded, and all their craft were destroyed. On the British side there were no casualties.

Among the numerous engagements which took place during these years between H.M. ships and Chinese pirates, few were more noteworthy than one fought by the gunboat *Grasshopper*, Lieutenant George Digby Morant, in November, 1865. The vessel, on several other occasions, rendered useful service of the same sort, and, at her paying off, she was able to claim prize-money in respect of 20 pirate vessels, and 483 men. Morant, while lying in Chimmo Bay, near Amoy, learnt that three pirate *lorchas*, which were then at Port Matheson, had lately captured five cargo *junks*. Arriving off Pyramid Point at about 8 a.m. on November 23rd. Morant found the three pirates under sail, and their prizes at anchor inside of them.

He gave chase, and, at 8.45, fired a gun to bring them to. They replied at once, and formed line of battle at the shoal end of the bay, tacking backwards and forwards. Having little more water under him than he drew, Morant was obliged to engage them at 1200 yards. At 11 a. m, one of his 68-pr. shells blew up the magazine of the largest pirate, a Macao *lorcha*, and set fire to the hull. The other two tried to make off through a rocky channel. The *Grasshopper* steamed round outside, and drove them back, and, upon the tide rising, was able to close within 800 yards. At 12.45 the people of one of the *lorchas* began to jump overboard; whereupon Morant ordered his gunner, Mr. H. Gardner, to take the cutter and capture her. This was done.

The third *lorcha* kept up the engagement until 1.15, when she struck, her crew leaving her. Morant, in the gig, went and took possession of her. The gunboat had no casualties, and was hulled only twice. Upon seeing the *Grasshopper* approach, the pirates had deliberately beheaded 34 of the prisoners whom they had on board, and disembowelled two boys, sons of the masters of two of the prizes. Lieutenant Morant, who was promoted, (com., Feb. 6th, 1866), for this affair, was fortunately able to capture 23 of the scoundrels who had jumped overboard. The largest of the *lorchas* mounted two long 16-prs. and six

6-prs. Each of the others had five guns, and among them the three had about 150 men on board. (Morant to King.)

In the previous month, the *Opossum*, 2, Lieutenant Henry Craven St. John, tender to the *Princess Charlotte*, had been sent in search of some pirates who were reported to be lying in Mirs Bay. She had there found two pirate *junks*, which she burnt, and their prize, which she restored to her owners, from whom St. John received news which induced him to proceed at once to Tooniang Island, where he discovered three more piratical craft in a creek. Having landed a force to take them in rear, he attacked in the gunboat from seaward, the result of his excellent dispositions being that he captured all three without suffering any loss. This exploit was, for the moment, the last of a series of operations, during which, in about a year, St. John had captured 35 pirate vessels, mounting, in the aggregate, 140 guns.

Haiti, 1865

One of the most brilliant bits of hard fighting done by the navy in the second half of the nineteenth century stands to the credit of the paddle-sloop *Bulldog*, 6, of 1124 tons, and 500 nominal horsepower. She was on the North America and West Indies station in 1865, when Sylvestre Salnave was endeavouring to wrest the presidency of the Haytian Republic from Fabre Geffrard. On October 22nd, off Acul, and in sight of the sloop, a Salnavist steamer, the *Valorogue*, fired into a British Jamaica packet. Captain Charles Wake, of the *Bulldog*, having approached, and inquired into the matter, informed the commander of the *Valorogue* that, unless he ceased firing, his ship should be sunk under him. The rebel officer thereupon desisted, and took his vessel into Cape Haytien. As soon as he heard what had happened, Salnave ordered the arrest by force of a number of fugitives who had sought refuge in the British Consulate there.

On the morning of the 23rd, Wake who was accompanied by three Geffrardist war-steamers, appeared off the mouth of the harbour. (The two lieutenants of the *Bulldog* were John Lewis Way, and Frank Rougemont.) The consul had informed him in the interval that the refugees had been not only seized but also shot, that the Consulate had been wrecked, and that the flag had been insulted in other ways. Wake demanded satisfaction, and, getting only a refusal, began to shell Fort Cirolet at 8.45 a.m. The work replied five minutes later. Pushing further in, and engaging all the batteries. Wake presently caught sight of the *Valorogue*, which, perhaps rather unwisely, he endeavoured to ram at full speed.

Unfortunately, he was in waters which were strange to him; and his navigating officer, Acting-Master Edwin Behenna, was a young man fresh to the station. The result was that the sloop ran on a reef within short musket-shot of the enemy's vessel, and within point-blank range of a masked shore battery, which instantly opened on her. Nevertheless, the *Bulldog* sank the *Valorogue* at 9.45; and at 10.10 a.m. the largest schooner of the Salnavist fleet was also sunk. In addition, the sloop blew up the Salnavist powder-magazine, set fire to the town, and dispersed with grape and canister the riflemen who had assembled on the shore.

At 11.30, Wake sent a message to the United States' war-steamer *De Soto*, requesting her captain, Lieutenant-Commander Howell, to tow him off. Some steps in this direction seem to have been taken, but in vain, by the Americans, who, at noon, through Lieutenant Sumner, kindly offered to receive and tend the sloop's wounded. This Wake thought proper to decline at the moment. During the whole time, and, indeed, until dark, the engagement continued. When the firing had ceased, the gallant British captain, who had no intention of allowing his ship to fall into the hands of the blacks, and who had little ammunition left, set fire to and abandoned her, transferring himself, his people, his wounded, and his killed (with the exception of a few who were sent to the friendly *De Soto*), to the Geffrardist steamer *Vingt-deux Décembre*. The sloop, still fast aground, finally blew up.

Of her complement of 175 officers and men, the *Bulldog* had 3 killed, and 10 wounded. A court-martial, which was held at Devonport, considered that Wake and Behenna were to blame for having run the sloop on to the reef, and that she had been abandoned and destroyed prematurely; and it severely reprimanded Wake, and reprimanded Behenna. Captain Wake called the attention of the Admiralty to his sentence, which, according to public opinion, was a somewhat harsh one, and was informed that their lordships "did not consider that any imputation was cast on his honour or his courage." (Disps.: Wake's account in *Army and Navy Gazette*, Dec. 2nd, 1865; letter of officer of the *De Soto*. Mins. of C.M., Jan. 15th, 1866.) This gallant officer, as will be seen on reference to the Flag-Officers' List, died in 1890. It is pleasant to be able to add that he was soon again employed afloat.

★★★★★★

Punch ended some verses on the affair and its sequel with:

"*Then here's three cheers for Captain Wake; and, while we sail the sea.*

May British Bulldogs always find Captains as stout as he.
That's all for biting when they bite, and none for bark and brag,
And thinks less about court-martials than the honour of the flag."
★★★★★★

On November 9th, following, the offending forts at Cape Haytien were bombarded, and silenced one after the other, by the *Galatea*, 26, scr., Captain Rochfort Maguire, and *Lily*, 4, scr. Commander Algernon Charles Fieschi Heneage. The firing lasted from 9 a.m. until 6 p.m. The *Galatea* had no casualties; but the *Lily* had several people hurt. As the forts were reduced they were occupied by the Geffrardists.

In opening the Legislative Session of 1865, Governor E. J. Eyre, of Jamaica, made the following reference to the part played by the navy in repressing the very serious disturbances which had then recently taken place in the island:—

> To the senior naval officer, Captain de Horsey, of H.M.S. *Wolverene*, we owe it that we were enabled to carry out with promptitude and efficiency the arrangements necessary to control and suppress the rebellion. The *Wolverene* and her gallant captain were kept almost unceasingly at work, day and night, in all weathers, and off a lee coast; but all was done with hearty good will, zeal, and cheerfulness. . . . Lieutenant Brand, of H.M.S. *Onyx*, is entitled to the highest praise for the unceasing and valuable services rendered by the little gunboat under his command.

Captain de Horsey was the Admiral Algernon Frederick Rous de Horsey, the dates of whose commissions, etc., will be found in the Flag Officers' List. Lieutenant Herbert Charles Alexander Brand, commanding the *Onyx*, one of the smallest of the gunboats which had been built for the purposes of the war with Russia, became a victim of a hot and foolish agitation in England, the result of which was that, with Brigadier-General Nelson, he was arraigned at the Old Bailey on a charge of wilful murder. The prisoners were happily acquitted; and, after further honourable service, Brand retired in 1883 with the rank of Commander. He died in 1901.

Arab Pirates, 1865–1866

In 1865 the piratical depredations of the Arabs on the west coast of the Persian Gulf, and especially of those of El Kateef, became so troublesome that, towards the close of the year, the screw corvette

Highflyer, 21, Captain Thomas Malcolm Sabine Pasley, was sent thither to exact satisfaction. Failing to obtain it, Pasley, in January, 1866, destroyed two forts, and burnt some *dhows* belonging to the marauders. Misapprehending the nature and strength of a fort near El Kateef, he subsequently sent his boats ashore there, and landed a party which, in an attempt to rush the work, succeeded in getting inside the outer wall only, and was at length obliged to retreat thence with a loss of 3 killed and 8 wounded, (among the wounded was Lieut. John Fellowes: see Disps.), one of the latter also dying on the following day. After the repulse, the *Highflyer* sent in her boats, and shelled the fort at long range, but apparently did it little damage. (*Bombay Gazette.*)

The Fenian Revolt in Canada, 1865–1867

During the Fenian disturbances in Canada, in 1865–67, a number of Her Majesty's ships and vessels were employed, under the direction of Captain de Horsey, on the River St. Lawrence, and lakes Ontario, Erie, and Huron. Their services were not, for the most part, of a very exciting character, being mainly of a preventive nature; but, in respect of them, a medal and clasp were granted in 1899 to officers and men who were in the following vessels on the occasion:—

Aurora, 35, screw, Captain Algernon Frederick Rous de Horsey; *Pylades*, 21, Captain Arthur William Acland Hood; *Niger*, 13, screw, Captain James Minchin Bruce; *Rosario*, 11, screw. Commander Louis Button Versturme; the gunboats *Heron*, Lieutenant Henry Frederick Stephenson; *Britomart*, Lieutenant Arthur Hildebrand Alington; and *Cherub*, Lieutenant Spencer Robert Huntley; and the armoured hired gunboats *Canada*, Lieutenant Thomas Hooper; *Royal*, Lieutenant .John Henry Vidal; *Hercules*, Lieutenant Archibald Lucius Douglas; *St. Andrew*, Lieutenant Seymour Spencer Smith; *Michigan*, Lieutenant Frederick William Burgoyne Heron Maxwell Heron; and *Rescue*, (twin-screw, of 248 tons, and 100 H.P.), Lieutenant Henry James Fairlie.

The Cretan Revolt, 1866–1867

The Cretan revolt, which began in 1866, caused so little anxiety to the British authorities in the Mediterranean that it is not mentioned in the autobiography and journals of Vice-Admiral Lord Clarence Edward Paget, who was commander-in-chief there at the time. Nevertheless, precautions were taken for the protection of British interests; and for some months in 1866-67, the gunboat *Wizard*, Lieutenant Patrick James Murray, was stationed off the coast for that purpose.

Chinese Pirates, 1866

Lieutenant Henry Craven St. John, who was reappointed to command the gunboat *Opossum*, 2, at the beginning of 1866, signalised his fresh term of command, and earned his promotion, by the zeal which he again displayed in the repression of Chinese piracy. In February, he left Hong-Kong on a cruise, and, hearing of the presence of a number of pirates near Pakshui, on the west coast beyond Macao, he at once went in search of them. He discovered fifteen vessels at the head of a small creek, mounting among them 43 guns, and protected by a battery mounting three others. He had but about thirty men on board; yet he silenced the battery, and drove the pirates from their vessels, which he seized, and many of which he destroyed, handing over the rest to the Imperial Chinese authorities. His loss was 5 people wounded.

Two days later, he recaptured a *junk* which had been stolen from her owners and used for piratical purposes by her skipper. Not long afterwards, he made another prize. After his promotion, which was dated April 12th following, he made a further attack on Pakshui, where he captured nine snake-boats, and again destroyed a battery. He was then superseded by Lieutenant Karl Heinrick Augustus Mainwaring. In June, 1866, the *Osprey*, 4, Commander William Menzies, with the *Opossum*, left Hong-Kong in search of some more pirate *junks*, which, to the number of twenty-two, were found in Sama Creek. Among them they mounted upwards of 200 guns. The *Osprey* approached within 1200, and the *Opossum* within 700 yards, and, after a two hours' cannonade, landed parties, which took the *junks* in rear, and compelled their abandonment. The vessels were all burnt, and the village of Sama, which had sheltered them, was destroyed. The only person killed on the side of the attack was a Chinese *mandarin*, who had accompanied it in order to identify the freebooters. (*A. and N. Gazette*, Sept. 22, 1866.)

Minor Operations, 1867-1868

In the course of the year 1867 several of Her Majesty's ships were actively employed on the coast of Ireland in connection with the repression of the Fenian disturbances there. The navy took part, however, in no fighting deserving of the name.

Early in the same year, the British consul at Cartagena, Colombia, having complained that his letters were opened and detained by the local authorities. Commodore Sir Francis Leopold M'Clintock, in charge at Jamaica, despatched to the spot the *Doris*, 24, screw, Captain Charles Vesey. Vesey made certain demands which the governor of the town declared that he had not power to grant; whereupon, on February 26th, the Colombian Government steamer *Colombiano* was seized by an armed party in three boats from the frigate. This measure induced the governor to adopt new views as to his powers, and, matters having been settled satisfactorily, the steamer was released on March 1st.

On June 26th, the gunboats *Bouncer*, Lieutenant Karl Heinrick Augustus Mainwaring, and *Havock*, Lieutenant Yelverton O'Keefe, with a *mandarin* accompanying them from Kowloon Bay, found two piratical Chinese vessels at anchor in Starling Inlet, and, getting out their boats, took and destroyed both, and released their prize, a trading *junk*. Such pirates as escaped were followed to the shore, but in vain. On the 28th, fifty miles further up the coast, the same gunboats attacked, captured, and destroyed a considerable flotilla of piratical craft, preserving, however, one prize which, on the 29th, was towed by the *Havock* into Hong Kong. In the course of 1867, when the treaty port of Cheefoo, in north China, was threatened by a large horde of rebels, a British force was landed there for its defence. The senior officer on the spot at the time was Commander Frederick William Hallowes, of the paddle-sloop *Argus*, 6.

On July 17th, 1867, Her Majesty Queen Victoria reviewed a large fleet at Spithead. Admiral Sir Thomas Sabine Pasley was in command, with his flag in the *Victoria*, screw wooden three-decker. The port column on this interesting occasion consisted exclusively of vessels of the old and doomed types. The starboard column, under Rear-Admiral Frederick Warden, who had his flag in the *Minotaur*, consisted exclusively of ironclads, and included not only iron-hulled armoured battleships, like the *Bellerophon*, but also wooden-hulled ones, like the *Lord Clyde*, together with coast-defence turret-ships, such as the *Royal Sovereign* and the *Prince Albert*, and armoured gun-vessels, such as the *Vixen* and the hydraulic-driven *Waterwitch*. No non-steamers were present in the lines.

Accompanying the queen were the Sultan of Turkey and the Viceroy of Egypt. Lieutenant William Robert Kennedy acted as Flag-Lieutenant to the Board of Admiralty at the review, and was promoted, on the following day, to be Commander. In August, 1869, when their Lordships went for a cruise in the *Agincourt* with the Channel

143

H.M. PADDLE, WOODEN ROYAL YACHT *VICTORIA AND ALBERT*.
(*Built at Pembroke*, 1855.)

Length, 300 ft. ; beam, 40 ft. 3½ in. ; mean draught, 16 ft. 11 in. ; displ., 2470 tons ; I.H.P., 2980 ; speed, 15·7 kts.
Complement, 151.

Squadron, which was then commanded by Vice-Admiral Sir Thomas Matthew Charles Symonds, in the *Minotaur*, Captain James Graham Goodenough, Lieutenant the Hon. Edward Stanley Dawson was appointed Flag-Lieutenant to the Board. The Admiralty flag was hauled down on September 30th, and Mr. Dawson received his promotion on the following November 11th.

Numerous acts of piracy and murder by the natives of the Nicobar Islands led to the despatch thither from the Straits Settlements on July 19th, 1867, of the *Wasp*, 13, screw, Captain Norman Bernard Bedingfeld, and the *Satellite*, 17, screw, Captain Joseph Edye, the latter having native troops on board. Some villages and war-canoes were burnt, and one or two prisoners were released; but, disturbances having in the meantime broken out at Penang, the ships had to return thither in the middle of August. The *Wasp* had been originally commissioned in November, 1868, for the suppression of the slave-trade on the east coast of Africa. One of her exploits there in the year 1865 has been already recorded.

The Abyssinian Expedition, 1868

The navy had but a modest, though an altogether creditable share in the Abyssinian Expedition of 1868. The naval arrangements in the Indian seas were in the hands of Captain Leopold George Heath, C.B., who flew a broad pennant, as Commodore of the First Class, in the *Octavia*, 35, screw, Captain Colin Andrew Campbell. To the *Octavia* was attached, as Director of the Transport Service, Captain George Tryon, who had on his staff Paymasters Thomas Henry Lovelace Bowring, and Thomas Nelson Firth, and Assistant-Paymaster Thomas Edmund Goodwin. These officers did most of their work at the base at Zoulla, in Annesley Bay, one of the hottest places on earth, and were fully employed, seeing that no fewer than 291 transports, besides tugs, lighters, and native craft, were engaged in the operations. (Fitzgerald, *Life of Tryon*.)

More interesting experiences fell to the Naval Brigade which, with rockets and Sniders, was landed at Zoulla on January 25th, under Commander Thomas Hounsom Butler Fellowes, of the *Dryad*, 4, screw, (in his absence the *Dryad* was temporarily commanded by Lieut. George Woronzow Allen), and which accompanied the army to Magdala. The ships which chiefly contributed were the *Octavia*, the *Dryad*, Commander Fellowes, and the *Satellite*, 17, screw, Captain Joseph Edye; though medals for the campaign were also granted to the

Star, 4, screw. Commander Richard Bradshaw; *Argus*, 6, paddle. Commander Frederick William Hallowes; *Daphne*, 4, screw, Commander George Lydiard Sulivan; *Nymphe*, 4, screw, Commander Thomas Barnardiston; *Spiteful*, 6, paddle. Commander Benjamin Langlois Lefroy; and *Vigilant*, 4, screw. Commander Ralph Abercrombie Otho Brown; these ships being engaged on various services in connection with the campaign.

The Brigade marched on February 29th, reached Senafé on March 5th, and, advancing again on the 7th, arrived at Antalo on March 16th. It consisted of but 100 European officers and men, with 2 farriers, 13 grasscutters, 3 water-carriers, 6 sick-bearers, 1 hospital-sweeper (Indian natives), and 88 battery mules, 54 baggage and provision mules, or their equivalent in camels, 11 officers' horses, and 3 bullocks for carrying water. At Antalo it was attached to the 2nd Brigade, 1st division. At Lat, on March 23rd, it joined the first division under Major-General Sir Charles Staveley, and thence continued on the 25th towards Magdala.

On joining Lieutenant-General Sir Robert Napier, the commander-in-chief, at Santara, on March 30th, the force was drilled, and fired rockets, under His Excellency's inspection. It was then attached to the 1st Brigade under Brigadier-General Schneider, which moved forward on the 31st. On April 10th it rendered valuable service during the action in the Arrogie Pass, where it led the attack up the King's Road. On April 13th it threw rockets into Magdala, and took part in the assault on the place. Two or three days later it again used its rockets to disperse Galla plunderers. In the distribution of the loot, the Brigade received as its trophy "a valuable and handsome shield, with gold filigree and lion's skin, and a solid silver cross." At the review on Dalanta Plain, on April 20th, the Brigade was placed on the right of all the troops, excepting the cavalry. The return march was begun on the 22nd. In the meantime, another Brigade, under Captain Colin Andrew Campbell had been landed for the defence of Senafé, but was not required there, and was re-embarked. (In his absence Com. William Henry Maxwell commanded the *Octavia*.)

Throughout the operations the men behaved admirably, and marched very well indeed, although, in many cases, their boots gave out. Commander Fellowes, who was himself mentioned in the despatch of Sir Robert Napier, specially brought to the notice of the Admiralty (in his despatch dated Marrawah, May 2nd) the names of the following officers and men of his little command: *viz.* Lieutenant Charles Searle Cardale (*Satellite*), Assistant-Surgeon Henry Nanton Murray Sedgwick (*Octavia*), Chief-Gunner's Mate Charles Henry Jones, Gunner's Mate Robert Smith, Boatswain's Mates Thomas Vaughan, and John Graham, coxswain of the barge Benjamin Starkes, and second captain of the foretop Charles Austin. There were no casualties. (*Gazette*, June 16th, 1868. Fellowes to Admlty., May 2nd, in *A. and N. Gazette*, June 27th, 1868. Hozier, *Brit. Exped. to Abyssinia.* Heath to Admlty., June 10th, 1868. The last makes favourable mention of a number of officers.)

For their services Commodore Heath received a K.C.B., and Captains Edye, Tryon, and Fellowes each a C.B. (All dated Aug. 15th, 1868. Capt. Edye died on Sept. 13th, 1868, at Hong Kong.) In addition, Commanders Fellowes and Barnardiston were posted; Lieutenants John Fiot Lee Pearse Maclear, Edmund Lyons Green, and Charles Searle Cardale were made Commanders; acting Sub-Lieutenant George Lambart Atkinson was made acting Lieutenant; Navigating-Lieutenants Daniel John May, and Thomas Pounds were made Staff-Commanders; Surgeon James Nicholas Dick was made Staff-Surgeon; Assistant-Paymaster William Edwin Boxer was made Paymaster; and Engineer William Henry Grose was made Chief-Engineer. (All dated Aug. 14th, 1868.)

Pirates, 1868-1869

This year is remarkable for the unusual number of cases of piracy and outrage which, in various quarters of the world, necessitated the active employment of ships of the navy.

Lieutenant Compton Edward Domvile, of the *Algerine*, 1, screw, who had already done useful service against Chinese pirates, continued to be very active in the summer. On May 26th, 1868, the gun-vessel left Hong Kong in search of a piratical *junk* or snake-boat, which had committed piracy just outside the harbour. She found a *junk* of about 100 tons in an inlet of Mirs Bay, and, acting upon information received, took her, burnt her, and drove her people away, then proceeding to Stanley for further directions. Early on the 31st she again started, calling at Macao, and thence going to Namoa. On her way back, when between that place and St. John's, on June 3rd, she fell in with a squadron of thirteen heavily-armed pirates. Domvile hailed them, and demanded their papers, whereupon they fired into him. The *mandarin* with him assured him that they were pirates, and the fire was promptly returned.

In a few minutes the action became general. The gun-vessel rolled badly, but made fairly good practice. She cut off and boarded one junk, which was endeavouring to run inshore, and then she chased the others, which were going off in a body to the westward. She got up with them at about dusk, having first engaged them at a little after 3 p.m. A fresh and close action followed, and lasted for an hour and a half. Owing to the darkness and the shoaling water the pursuit had then to be abandoned; but the already captured *junk*, which made off to seaward, was retaken two hours after dark, and towed into Hong Kong on June 9th.

Whether the Chinese were really pirates is more than doubtful; for, on trial, the prize was judged to be a trader, and was released. Domvile, indeed, though with the best intentions, acted too hastily. Otherwise the affair was most creditable; for while on the Chinese side about 800 men and 130 guns seem to have been engaged, the *Algerine* had on board but one large and two small pieces, and about 20 people; among whom there were, strange to say, no casualties. (*China Mail*; Admiralty Corr. in *A. and N. Gazette*, May 22nd, 1869.) On July 15th the *Algerine* captured three other alleged piratical *junks* in a bay in Tychan Island. Domvile was promoted on September 2nd following. British officials, both consular and naval, were at that time rather too ready to employ force in China. In 1869 the Foreign Office strongly censured Consul Sinclair, of Foochow, for having unnecessarily induced Lieutenant Leicester Chantrey Keppel, of the *Janus*, 1, to intervene on behalf of a certain missionary.

At Yangchow, on August 22nd, 1868, the unpopularity of the British missionaries led to a serious outrage, which only by great good fortune did not terminate in the whole household of the Rev. Mr. Taylor being burnt. Happily, the entire British party escaped to Chinkiang. Consul Walter Medhurst, and the *Rinaldo*, 7, screw, Commander William Kemptown Bush, proceeded as soon as possible from Shanghai to Chinkiang, whence, with an escort of 80 officers and men from the sloop, the consul went to Yangchow on September 8th, and made certain demands. Some of these the local authorities professed themselves powerless to grant, whereupon the consul and his party moved up to Nankin; but, Commander Bush falling ill, the *Rinaldo* was withdrawn; and the governor-general, seeing the consul deprived of his supports, assumed an intractable attitude.

Medhurst had to return to Shanghai, and refer the matter to Pekin. The affair was most injurious to British prestige, and Commander

Bush was much blamed for withdrawing his sloop instead of leaving her at Nankin and himself going to Shanghai in one of the regular steamers. (*Shanghai News Letter: Friend of China.* Shanghai Corr. of *Times* in letter of Oct. 13th, 1868.) After some negotiations. Sir Rutherford Alcock was obliged to place the matter of the attack on the missionaries in the hands of Vice-Admiral the Hon. Sir Henry Keppel, who, accordingly, sent up the *Rodney*, 78, screw (flag; but Keppel was temporarily elsewhere, in the *Salamis*). Captain Algernon Charles Fieschi Heneage, *Rinaldo*, 7, and *Slaney*, 1, screw, Lieutenant William Francis Leoline Elwyn, to Nankin, where the *Icarus*, 3, screw. Commander Lord Charles Thomas Montagu Douglas Scott, and the *Zebra*, 7, screw, Commander Henry Anthony Trollope, subsequently joined them. The squadron seized the Chinese gunboat *Tien Chi*, on November 8th, as a material guarantee; and a strong landing party, under Captain Heneage, was then despatched, in November, to Yangchow, where it remained until the whole of the British demands had been conceded. (Keppel, *A Sailor's Life*, iii.)

There were other outrages, arising chiefly out of the local opposition to missionaries, and the attempt of the Chinese to monopolise the camphor trade, in the island of Formosa. Claims for redress were evaded, and at length Consul Gibson requested Lieutenant Thornhaugh Philip Gurdon, commanding the *Algerine*, 1, screw, to occupy the Amping and Zelandia forts, which constituted the key to the capital, Taiwan. At Amping, forty-one guns were already in position. To prevent the mounting of more, Gurdon, on November 25th, 1868, opened fire with his pivot-gun at 2000 yards; but, finding that he could not stop the construction of earthworks, he very pluckily landed at night in his gig and cutter, accompanied by two officers and twenty-three men.

The gig was swamped, but he disembarked in safety through the surf, two miles below the town. Advancing carefully, as it was moonlight, he took shelter under some rising ground, 800 yards from the works, until 2 a.m., when he made a rush, and carried the place almost instantly, killing several Chinamen, and driving off the rest. At daylight he also took possession of Zelandia, and, when attacked there by a force from Taiwan, repulsed it with heavy slaughter. This brilliant action led to the submission of the local authorities, the punishment of those who had committed the outrages, and the breaking down of the camphor monopoly. On the other hand. Consul Gibson, Lieutenant Gurdon, and Sir Henry Keppel were severely attacked, besides being blamed by the Admiralty, for having had recourse to such active measures, although, in fact, fruitless negotiations had been going on for five months ere any blow was struck. (Keppel, *A Sailor's Life* iii.; *A. and N. Gazette*, Feb. 13th and Mar. 13th, 1869.) Gurdon was, however, promoted on June 1st, 1869.

On February 2nd and 3rd of the following year, the *Algerine*, then commanded by Lieutenant Henry Rowland Ellison Grey, destroyed twelve piratical snake-boats off Tonqua, subsequently releasing four valuable prize *junks*. (*Hong-Kong Daily Press*, Feb. 10th, 1869.)

The town of Choochi, on the River Han, above Swatow, was long the headquarters of a band of pirates, who interfered with the transport of merchandise from the interior to the coast, and even plundered vessels in sight of Swatow itself. In 1868 some of these people foolishly fired upon and robbed a boat which, in charge of a British subject, was bringing down stores for the *Bustard*, 2, screw. Lieutenant Cecil Frederick William Johnson. Johnson demanded the punishment of the offenders, but the local *mandarin* declared that Choochi was fortified, and far too strong for him to meddle with; whereupon, on June 29th, the *Bustard* steamed up the river, and anchored a mile and a quarter from the pirate stronghold. The co-operation of some *mandarins*, with 300 Chinese troops, had been obtained.

The town having been summoned, and having refused to surrender, Johnson landed, and led the troops to the attack of the place, which was stoutly held and mounted two guns. The Chinese soldiers did well until they became entangled among spikes and other obstructions under a heavy fire inside the outer stockade. Johnson was then obliged to retire, as he had with him too few Europeans to attempt a storm, and the enemy could concentrate 600 men at any given point. Returning to the gunboat, he began a bombardment which he kept up until dark. In the night he landed sixteen of his men with a 24-pdr. howitzer, which, posted within 600 yards of the works, opened fire at dawn on the 30th.

When, after some hours, the inner fortifications were breached, the Chinese troops were again induced to advance. Johnson led them gallantly, but they were once more repulsed. On the two following days the bombardment was continued. At length, the town being on fire in several places, Johnson, with twenty-four of his own small ship's company, succeeded in taking it. After levelling the works and burning the stockades, he handed it over to the Chinese authorities. (*Hong-Kong Daily Press*, Aug. 10th, 1868. Johnson to Keppel.) Johnson was recommended for his services, but was not promoted until 1873.

Owing to Mr. Baker, a missionary, and some of his dependents having been murdered, the *Challenger*, 18, screw. Commodore Rowley Lambert, C.B., proceeded in August, 1868, to Rewa, in the Fiji Islands, and despatched her launch, and first and second cutters, under Commander Charles James Brownrigg, who shelled one or two villages as a punitive measure, and, it was believed, killed several natives. On the British side two persons only were wounded. On September 11th and 12th the *Blanche*, 6, Captain John Eglinton Montgomerie, executed similar punitive measures at Rodora Bay, in the Solomon Islands.

As in so many previous years, some of the piratical tribes on the Congo gave trouble in 1868. They were effectively punished, particularly at Maletta Creek in November. The vessels whose officers and men participated in the affair were the *Myrmidon*, 4, screw, Commander Henry Boys Johnstone, *Pandora*, 5, screw. Commander John Burgess, and *Plover*, 3, twin screw. Commander James Augustus Poland.

Towards the end of the year a schooner under the British flag was captured by pirates near Malluda Bay, and three of her people were killed. Upon hearing of the outrage, the governor of Labuan went in pursuit in the *Dwarf*, 2, screw. Lieutenant Charles Francis Walker. The pirates made a stand on the island of Ubean, and, refusing to deliver up their leader, were punished by a landing party, which burnt their village, and brought about their submission. Governor John Pope Hennessy left the question of compensation to be settled by an official of the Sultan of Sulu.

The Arabian Gulf, 1868–1869

Piracy in the Arabian Gulf received a check at the hands of Commander Benjamin Langlois Lefroy, of the *Spiteful*, 6, paddle, who, during a month's cruise in the early part of 1868, captured and destroyed six vessels, and rescued 200 slaves. Two of the slavers taken were armed with 6-pr. carronades. On one occasion determined resistance was offered; and on another the fugitive crew of a captured *dhow* returned, and made a bold but vain effort to regain the prize, which had to be blown up.

In the late summer of 1868, as soon as she could be spared from service with the Abyssinian Expedition, the *Vigilant*, 4, screw, Commander Ralph Abercrombie Otho Brown, was sent, with three vessels, (*Sir Hugh Rose, Sinde,* and *Clyde*), of the Bombay Marine, to deal with the troublesome chief, Mahomet ben Kuleef, of Bahrein, in the

Persian Gulf, and with his neighbours and allies, who had greatly oppressed Indian traders. Mahomet ben Kuleef's fort, war-vessels, and guns were destroyed after a two days' bombardment; reparation was made; fines were imposed; and certain chiefs were deposed and outlawed. The Bombay vessels subsequently proceeded to Muscat, which was found to have been captured by rebels on the day previous to their arrival; and assistance was rendered to the *Sultan*. (*Times* of India, Oct. 2, 1868; *A. and N. Gazette*, Nov. 7, 1868.)

At Bahrein matters did not remain quiet for long; and towards the end of 1869 it became necessary again to take action there. The matter was entrusted to Commander George Amelius Douglas, of the *Daphne*, 4, screw, who, accompanied by the *Nymphe*, 4, screw, Commander Edward Spencer Meara, and two vessels of the Bombay Marine, proceeded to the spot, and, in October and November, blockaded the island of Bahrein, took the fort of Menameh, and seized or obtained the surrender of several truculent chiefs, who were presently carried to Bombay as prisoners. It may be added that, previous to this expedition, both the *Nymphe* and the *Daphne* had been unusually successful while slave-cruising. During the commissions which they were then serving they captured between them about sixty slave vessels of one kind or another. The *Star*, 4, screw, Commander Walter Sidney de Kantzow, was also conspicuously successful.

Another craft which, on the same station, did good service against slavers in the years 1868 and 1869 was the *Dryad*, 4, screw-sloop. Commander Philip Howard Colomb, who subsequently wrote an interesting account of his work, and published it under the title of *Slave-Catching in the Indian Ocean*.

Minor Operations, 1869

Early in January, 1869, when Vice-Admiral the Hon. Sir Henry Keppel happened to be with the British Consul at Canton, information reached him from Captain Oliver John Jones, commodore at Hong Kong, concerning an outrage which had just been committed by the Chinese in the vicinity of Swatow. The crew of the *Cockchafer*, 2, screw, while exercising in the boats up the River Han, under the commander of the gunboat, Lieutenant Howard Kerr, had been attacked by the inhabitants of some neighbouring semi-piratical villages, and, having been landed, had found itself opposed by about 600 people, and ultimately obliged to retire, with a loss of 11 wounded.

Keppel communicated with the Chinese authorities, who undertook to co-operate in punishing the assailants; and he ordered the commodore to proceed to the spot with the *Rinaldo*, 7, screw, Commander Frederick Charles Bryan Robinson, *Perseus*, 15, screw. Commander Charles Edward Stevens, *Icarus*, 3, screw, Commander Lord Charles Thomas Montagu Douglas Scott, *Leven*, 2, screw, Lieutenant Orford Somerville Cameron, *Bouncer*, 2, screw. Lieutenant Rodney Maclaine Lloyd, and a detachment of seamen and marines from Keppel's flagship, the *Rodney*, which was making good defects at Hong Kong. Keppel did not intend Jones to act before his senior's arrival, and, having proceeded to Hong Kong, sailed thence on January 30th, 1869, in the *Salamis*, 2, paddle. Commander Henry Matthew Miller.

The impetuous commodore, however, probably fearing to be superseded in the command of the expedition, did not wait for the arrival either of his chief, or of the whole of the Chinese forces, but, having landed a sufficient detachment, advanced on January 28th along the banks of Outingpoi Creek, burnt two or three villages, killed or wounded 88 natives, re-embarked, and returned to his ships. The British loss was only five wounded, including Lieutenants Herbert Frederick Gye (*Rodney*), Philip Bennet Aitkens (*Rinaldo*), and Rodney Maclaine Lloyd (*Bouncer*). (Keppel, *A Sailor's Life*, iii.; untrustworthy especially as regards names. *A. and N. Gazette*, Feb. 20th, March 6th, March 13th, and March 27th, 1869. *Saturday Review*, May 29th, 1869.)

The slave trade persisted on the east coast of Africa many years after it had become practically extinct elsewhere; and, indeed, slavers continued to he captured there, though with diminishing frequency, until the end of the nineteenth century. In 1869 the traffic was extremely active, as may be judged from the fact that between January 4th and April 9th of that year, the *Nymphe*, 4, screw. Commander Edward Spencer Meara, took no fewer than sixteen slave-*dhows* on the station. On April 11th, when the sloop was at Zanzibar, her two cutters were ordered away, at the request of the *Sultan*, to stop another *dhow*, which was putting to sea. She was made prize of, but in the struggle, and by subsequent fire from the shore, a seaman was killed, and two officers were wounded. (Sub-Lieut. Norman Leith Hay Clark, who commanded, and Sub-Lieut. Thomas Tarleton Hodgson, severely. Both were presently promoted.)

On May 21st, while on her way to Aden, the *Nymphe* took two more large slavers, making nineteen in less than five months. Other vessels were almost equally successful at about the same period.

An expedition, consisting of the *Lynx*, 4, twin screw. Commander James Wylie East, and the *Pioneer*, 2, paddle. Lieutenant William Wiseman, (afterwards Capt. Sir Wm. Wiseman, 9th Bart., died Nov. 1, 1893), left Lagos, on July 21st, 1869, in order to proceed as far as possible up the Niger in support of British trade and influence. The bar of the river was crossed on July 23rd, but only very slow progress could be made, owing to the sandbanks and natural obstacles. After a point upwards of 400 miles from the sea had been reached, the vessels, which had become very sickly, returned; but the difficulties of navigation prevented them from recrossing the bar until September 13th. On the arrival of the *Lynx* at Ascension, every one of her people except four had to be sent to hospital. The expedition was purely a peaceful one, yet it narrowly escaped being of the most costly nature.

In June, 1869, the *Bouncer*, 2, Lieutenant Rodney Maclaine Lloyd, tender to the *Princess Charlotte*, receiving-ship at Hong-Kong, proceeded, in company with two Chinese gunboats, on a cruise in search of pirates. On the night of June 12th, off Gowtow Island, in the Gulf of Tonquin, the *Bouncer* took five large *junks*, after her landing-party had had a sharp engagement with some of the freebooters on shore, who, swimming off at length, turned the guns of one of the *junks* upon the others as they were attacked. A marine, James Murphy, had previously distinguished himself by swimming in the darkness to reconnoitre the enemy's position. By the 26th the *Bouncer* had captured twelve piratical craft, and her consorts nine more. Some of the prizes were excellently armed. Lloyd was specially thanked by the Hong Kong Government, and promoted on his return to England.

Upon the death in England of the American philanthropist, George Peabody, who had contributed half a million sterling to the relief of the poor of London, it was decided by the British Government, at the suggestion of H.M. the Queen, to send the body of England's dead benefactor across the Atlantic in a man-of-war, in order to let it be seen how greatly his generosity was appreciated by the nation. It was at first intended to employ the large iron cruiser *Inconstant*, but the new turret battleship *Monarch*, Captain John Edmond Commerell, C.B., V.C., was ultimately selected as being more worthy of the occasion. Mr. Peabody's coffin was, accordingly, placed in the specially fitted stern cabin of the ironclad at Portsmouth on December 11th, 1869, under a salute of twenty minute guns; and the ship then went to Spithead, where, however, she was delayed for several days by heavy weather; and she did not sail for Boston until December 2lst. She was escorted by the U.S. corvette *Plymouth*. (*A. and N. Gazette*, Dec. 11th,

18th, and 25th, 1869.)

In the same year, when an iron government floating-dock, then the largest in the world, was towed across the Atlantic to Hamilton, Bermuda, one of the vessels which convoyed her was the twin-screw gun-vessel *Lapwing*, 3, Commander Philip Ruffle Sharpe. (Her length overall, 381 ft.; width at entrance, 84 ft.; lifting power, 11,000 tons.) Towards the end of the year, having seen the dock to its destination, the *Lapwing* was usefully employed off Nassau in watching and intercepting blockade runners bound for Cuba. She captured four of these craft; and she also disarmed and embarked 296 filibusters whom one of them had landed on Nurse Key.

Minor Operations, 1870-1871

On January 28th, 1870, when the twin-screw gun-vessel *Growler*, 4, Commander Edward Hobart Seymour, was lying in the mouth of the Congo, she was boarded by some men belonging to the British schooner *Loango*, who reported that their vessel had been attacked by pirates on the previous afternoon. The *Growler* weighed at once, and steamed up to the scene of the outrage. At 1 p.m., having sighted the schooner, she manned and armed three boats, which pursued the freebooters, who abandoned their prize. Thirteen canoes and a prisoner were captured ere the boats returned. It was discovered that the *Loango* had been pillaged, and that her master and a boy were missing.

Seymour suspected a chief named M'pinge Nebacca to be implicated, and decided to surprise him in his town. On the 29th, three boats were again manned and armed. First a visit was paid to a village belonging to the chief's brother, and some plunder was there recovered. The expedition then pushed on, and landed two miles from the town, towards which the force advanced under a dropping fire from the retreating natives. In the place the missing master, badly wounded, was discovered by Sub-Lieutenant Henry Bingham Chesshyre Wynyard; and much gunpowder, which had been looted from the schooner, was found and blown up. The town was burnt before the force retired.

Still anxious to find the missing boy, Seymour sent his cutter, with the wounded master, back to the *Growler*, and, with his gig and whaler, moved up two miles further to Nebuila. He landed in a narrow creek, exposed to a desultory fire, which wounded Navigating Sub-Lieutenant William Stephen Robert Gow, and, after the village had been burnt, struck down Seymour himself. When the party had withdrawn, word was sent that, in exchange for a certain quantity of cloth, the missing boy would be released. Seymour, however, replied that, unless the boy were released unconditionality, all the villages in that direction would be burnt, whereupon the youngster was at length sent down to the ship. Seymour's wound, a serious one in the right leg, obliged him to invalid some weeks later. (*A. and N. Gazette*, July 23, 1870.) Only a few months earlier the recall of the cruisers from the West African coast had been foolishly urged upon the Admiralty.

In consequence of the piratical depredations of certain Malays, and of the resistance offered by them and their friends to the colonial officers sent to secure the culprits, Colonel Anson, Administrator of the Straits Settlements, desired Commander George Robinson (2), of the *Rinaldo*, 7, screw, to take under his orders the colonial steamer *Pluto*, and to proceed with her to Selangor. The two vessels anchored off the mouth of the Selangor River early on July 3rd, 1871; and the sloop's boats, being manned and armed, were sent with a field-piece party to the *Pluto*. The party from the *Rinaldo* consisted of ninety-five officers and men under Commander Robinson, Lieutenant Grosvenor Stopford, and Acting-Lieutenant Eustace Downman Maude, (wounded.)

At 7.30 a.m., the *Pluto* got under way to proceed with the boats, but at 9 a.m. grounded, and did not arrive off Selangor until 2 p.m. Parties were detached to search the houses, shipping, and river banks. Lieutenant Maude's party, in a cutter which was armed with a rocket-tube, landed, and, upon returning to the beach, was fired at, one man at once falling mortally wounded. The party, pursued by a hot fusillade, made the best of its way to the *Pluto*, which then returned the fire. In the scuffle and the retreat, seven members of the party were injured. The Malays, however, seem to have suffered much more heavily.

Commander Robinson ordered the *Pluto* to weigh, her position and that of the boats being unduly exposed. Later in the day he sent her to Penang with the wounded, and with a request for troops and a surgeon. (The *Rinaldo* was without any medical officer, her surgeon being ill, and her assistant-surgeon having been appointed by the C.-in-Chief to the Naval Hospital at Hong Kong. *A. and N. Gazette*, Sept. 16, 1871.) On the 4th, the *Rinaldo* steamed into the river alone. At 6.15 a.m. the forts near the southern side of the entrance opened on her at about 400 yards, the northern forts soon afterwards joining in with such good effect that in less than five minutes the sloop had three men wounded, and her hull and rigging much cut. She replied, and, steaming on, took the batteries from the rear, quickly knocking them to pieces and dismounting their guns.

At 6.40 a.m. Robinson anchored off the town, and laid out an anchor astern so as to keep his battery bearing on the forts. By 8 a.m. he had driven the enemy from all his works. Occasional guns were fired during the day to prevent the Malays from remanning their pieces. At 4.30 p.m., after having been aground for several hours, the *Rinaldo* weighed, and steamed leisurely down again, ceasing fire at 5.30, and re-anchoring in the road at 6. The *Pluto* returned on the 5th with a detachment of Royal Artillery, and another of the 19th Madras Native Infantry. On the 6th, these troops were landed, but there was no further resistance, and the place was quietly occupied. (Robinson to Anson, July 6; Robinson to Admiralty. Col. Papers, c. 460: 1871.)

On September 20th, 1871, Bishop J. C. Patteson, of Melanesia, was murdered by a native of Nukapu Island, one of the Swallow group of the Santa Cruz archipelago in the Pacific. At about that time, largely, it must be admitted, in consequence of the iniquities of the labour traffic, the natives were exceedingly hostile to white men, and had recently committed numerous outrages. Not too soon, therefore, did the *Rosario*, 3, screw, Lieutenant Albert Hastings Markham (acting Commander), undertake a cruise among the islands where the worst troubles had arisen.

★★★★★★

Com. Henry Joseph Challis, of the *Rosario*, had been appointed acting Captain of the *Blanche* on Oct. 12, 1871, and his place had been taken by Lieut. Markham, who retained it until Feb. 10, when Challis, superseded in the *Blanche*, relieved him.

★★★★★★

In the middle of November, 1871, she reached Havannah Harbour, in Vate, one of the New Hebrides, and thence sent her boats to Montague Island, (otherwise Nguna), hard by to enquire into the murder of some people belonging to the schooner *Fanny*.

The natives declined to give up the murderers, and, attacking the party, were punished by the destruction of their village. On the 15th the *Rosario* steamed round, and made a harmless but effective demonstration with her guns. On November 23rd, the sloop anchored off Cherry Island, in connection with an outrage on the people of the ship *Marion Rennie*, (*Fiji Times*, Feb. 1, 1871); but, although the natives seemed friendly, no satisfaction could be got out of them. Probably they were innocent.

On the 29th, the sloop reached Nukapu. Markham's object was to acquire information concerning the murder of the Bishop. He sent in a boat, which was fired at with arrows. It was recalled, but, being sent in again, was again fired at, whereupon the *Rosario* opened with her two 40-pr. Armstrongs and her 7-inch muzzle-loader. At high-water a party landed and destroyed the village and canoes. Two of the sloop's crew were wounded in this affair, one mortally; and about five-and-twenty natives are said to have been killed. (Markham himself seems to doubt whether any were killed. *Cruise of the Rosario.*)

Nitendi, or Santa Cruz, where Goodenough fell in 1875, and Espiritu Santo, the largest of the New Hebrides, were also visited. At Cape Lisburn, the south-west point of the latter, the natives were interrogated, on December 16th, as to the murder of the crew of the New Zealand craft, *Wild Duck.* They admitted having killed the men, and were believed to have also eaten them. Markham would have let them off very mercifully with a fine of twenty-five pigs, but, as only four of these were paid, he burnt the village and destroyed the canoes. Pentecost and Aurora Islands were next touched at. At Aurora, where the natives at first seemed friendly. Paymaster Shuldham Samuel Crawford Hill, who had confidingly sat down to rest on the beach, was treacherously clubbed and badly hurt on December 27th; and there also the villages and canoes were wrecked in retaliation. The sloop returned to Sydney on February 8th, 1872. (*Sydney Empire.* Feb. 9, 1872: *A. and N. Gazette,* Ap. 6 and 20, 1872. Markham, *Cruise of the Rosario.*)

The fact that the offending natives were treated with a consideration which they did not merit is proved by Markham's offer to allow the Nitendi people to compound by the payment of a few pigs for the murders which they admitted having been guilty of. Nevertheless, the proceedings of the *Rosario* gave great offence to certain pseudophilanthropists in England. Questions on the subject were even put in the House of Commons, where eventually Mr. Goschen quieted clamour by laying the despatches on the table. On the other hand, the Pacific natives were sometimes frightfully ill-treated. A letter written from the *Basilisk*, 5, paddle, Captain John Moresby, and dated from Cardwell, Queensland, February 5th, 1872, contains the following:—

This morning at about 11 o'clock, just after we had passed the entrance to the bay, there was the report of a sail, and the captain, wishing to send letters, stood for her. She was soon made out to be a schooner of about 80 tons. When we got close to her we saw a lot of Polynesians in her. We immediately sent the first lieutenant and the gig to board her; but, as they seemed inclined to show fight, we sent the cutter, armed, to assist. When they got on board they found twelve blacks all right, one dying, and three dead of starvation, the ship stinking like a pest house, so that all our men were as sick as possible.

It appears she was a kidnapping schooner from Samoa, and, running short of provisions, besides being waterlogged, the white men, supposed to be Portuguese, deserted her four days ago, and left nothing for the poor blacks (seventeen) but a bucket of water, and not a scrap of provisions, so that they had eaten one of their own number. They were the most frightful looking wretches I ever saw, being so fearfully attenuated, and quite naked. The very bones were sticking through their skin; and, as for the dead men, they were quite putrid and blue, so that, when they hoisted them out of the hold, a hand or a foot would be left behind. . . .

This schooner was the *Peri*. Subsequent inquiry showed that she was from Rewa, Fiji, not from Samoa, and that she had sailed, with 50 Polynesians and three white men on board, on December 27th, 1871. It was suspected that the natives had really risen and murdered their kidnappers: but the truth seems never to have been fully ascertained. (Many examples of the barbarity of the kidnappers are given by Markham.)

During the same cruise, the *Basilisk* sent an expedition, under Lieutenant Francis Hayter, which severely punished some Australian aborigines who had murdered part of the crew of the brig *Maria*, wrecked on the Great Barrier Reef. (*A. and N. Gazette*, June 15, 1872.) Navigating-Midshipman Hubert Heath Sabben, who had charge of a schooner, tender to the *Basilisk*, went in a boat with a small party early in 1872 in search of survivors of the brig's people. He was attacked by a large body of natives, and being shamefully deserted by his crew, and left ashore with only a single supporter, a gallant bluejacket named Springay, he was in serious peril. The two Englishmen, however, drove off the enemy, no fewer than sixteen of whom were killed or wounded by the steady fire from their Snider rifles. (*A. and NK. Gazette*, July 20, 1872.)

In May, 1872, while the *Nassau*, 4, screw surveying vessel, Commander William Chimmo, was engaged in the performance of her

The Jubilee Review at Spithead.
July 23rd 1887

duties in the Sulu Sea, she had occasion to land a boat's crew on the north-east end of Sulu Island, where it was desired to take bearings. The party was attacked on May 11th by forty or fifty Illanoon pirates, and had to retreat fighting, several people, including Navigating-Lieutenant Francis John Gray being wounded, (transferred on Apr. 1, 1873, to the lieutenants' list with seniority of Mar. 2, 1866, in recognition of this service.) Attempts were made to secure satisfaction, it being at first supposed that the natives had mistaken the British for Spaniards; but, as the enemy, during prolonged negotiations, displayed a truculent attitude, the *Nassau* eventually shelled and destroyed their village, Carang-Carang. (Strait *Times.*) During the operations about 190 of the pirates were believed to have been killed.

A very creditable capture of a slave-*dhow* was made in the same year by the boats of the *Vulture*, 8, twin-screw, Commander Robert Barclay Cay, off Ras-el-Had, in the Persian Gulf. The affair, which gained promotion for Sub-Lieutenant Frank Hannam Henderson, revealed in their most repulsive forms some of the horrors of the middle passage. Of 169 slaves on board, no fewer than 36 were found to be down with smallpox. Forty-four wretches, who, before the capture, had been recognised by the crew and slave-merchants to be infected, had been flung overboard alive; and when it had been seen that this procedure did not check the spread of the plague, the owners had run to the other extreme, and had forced sick and sound to huddle together until the vessel became so foul that the captors could hardly endure to board her. (*Times of India*; *A. and N. Gazette*, Oct. 26, 1872.)

Minor Operations, 1872

The *Bittern*, 3, twin-screw. Commander the Hon. Archibald St. Clair, rendered some useful services on the West Coast of Africa. In January, 1872, she undertook active operations against the piratical natives of Corisco and Elobey Islands, after the loss of the mail steamer, *McGregor Laird*, and succeeded in capturing Coomba, the chief of Corisco. She was subsequently engaged in the mouth of the Congo in protecting the Banana Creek factories from native attack.

For many years the ownership of the San Juan, or Haro Islands, an archipelago lying between Vancouver Island and the mainland, had been disputed by Great Britain and the United States. In July, 1859, when the group was in the joint occupation of the two powers, (under a provisional arrangement come to in 1855), General Harney, commanding in Washington Territory, largely reinforced the American

161

garrison in San Juan, and made an unqualified declaration of United States sovereignty. The governor of British Columbia remonstrated, but General Harney persisted, and, indeed, persisted in a most provocative manner.

Happily, the government of the United States assumed a more friendly attitude, and despatched to the scene of the dispute General Winfield Scott, with whom it was amicably arranged that the American reinforcement should be withdrawn, and that both powers should maintain only a very small number of troops in the islands, pending the ultimate settlement of their ownership. In consequence of the temporary friction, a small British squadron had been ordered to the scene. This thereupon dispersed, leaving behind it, however, a few Royal Marines to serve as garrison under the agreement. Thenceforward, for many years, marines were stationed in the islands. After General Harney's recall, in 1860, the joint occupation was managed with good feeling on both sides. At length, by arbitration of the German Emperor, on October 21st, 1872, the dispute was settled in favour of the United States; and the British marines, then commanded by Captain William Addis Delacombe, evacuated the islands on November 22nd following.

Among the vessels most active in their operations against the slave-trade on the east coast of Africa and in the Red Sea at about the time when Sir Bartle Frere, as envoy to Zanzibar and Muscat, was specially exerting himself against it, were the *Columbine*, 3, screw, commanded in 1871-3 by Commanders John Collier Tucker, and Edward William Hereford; the *Daphne*, 5, screw, Commander Richard Sacheverell Bateman; and the *Thetis*, 13, screw, Captain Thomas Le Hunte Ward. The *Columbine* took numerous *dhows*, especially in 1871; the *Daphne*, which also made many prizes, had the misfortune to lose one of her officers, Sub-Lieutenant Marcus M'Causland, in a treacherous affair with natives at Kiunga, near Barawa, on the Somali coast, in the autumn of 1873; and the *Thetis*, though then only passing through the station on her way to China, captured ten *dhows* in May, 1873. Most of them, however, seem not to have been slavers, for they were not condemned.

After the murder at Kiunga, Sub-Lieutenant Percy Hockin, (promoted to be Lieutenant, Sept. 23, 1873), who was boat-cruising in company with the *dhow* from which M'Causland had landed, took his men ashore with great determination, and forcibly obliged the murderers to give up the body. He afterwards proceeded to the southward, until he fell in with some boats of the *Briton*, 10, screw, under Lieutenant Arthur Stephens Phillpotts, with whom he returned, and partially destroyed Kiunga. (*A. and N. Gazette*, Nov. 22, 1873.)

Honduras and Guatemala, 1872-1873

In 1872-73, disputes relative to the then partly-built interoceanic railway led to the overthrow of President Medina, of Honduras, and to the installation in his place of Señor Arias. A movement was thereupon begun in Honduras and Guatemala for the reinstatement of Medina, who lay imprisoned at Comayagua; and the troops assembled for the purpose from both states were placed under the orders of General Palacios, who had been Guatemalan minister in London. As the railway was being built largely with British capital and under British supervision, British interests suffered considerably from the disturbances, and from the consequent insecurity. Puerto Cortez, the Atlantic terminus of the line, lies near the Honduran town of Omoa; and at Omoa is the ancient Spanish casemated fort of San Fernando, which was occupied by a certain General Streber, on behalf of Arias; the old governor, General Alvarez, being superseded, but remaining as commandant of the port.

In view of this situation, the *Niobe*, Commander Sir Lambton Loraine, Bart., was despatched from Jamaica to Omoa in June, 1873, with instructions to protect British interests and to enforce treaty obligations.

★★★★★★

A few months earlier. Sir Lambton had exhibited a salutary display of determination at Puerto Plata, San Domingo, where three refugees had been kidnapped from the British Consulate. The governor himself was forced to remove the shackles from the feet of his prisoners, and then to deliver them up onboard the *Niobe*. The San Domingan troops were also obliged to replace the ensign above the consulate, and to salute it with twenty-one guns. *A. and N. Gaz.* May 17, 1873.

★★★★★★

On her way, she called at Truxillo, where Loraine was informed of certain acts of oppression which had been committed in the Bay Islands against neutral persons who were under treaty protection. At Puerto Cortez Streber was found to have made military exactions from the railway company, and to have tried to force the company's labourers to join him. He was duly cautioned; and the *Niobe* then proceeded to Belize, (arriving on July 12th), to gain further intelligence from the lieutenant-governor, and from Mr. Debrot, British vice-consul at Omoa, who had taken refuge in British Honduras, to escape from the outrages and tyranny of Streber. That general had also obliged the Spanish and Portuguese consuls to flee with their families; and the people had taken up their residence on the Zapotillo Cays, dependencies of British Honduras; whither Streber had had the audacity, on July 4th, to send an expedition which captured and handcuffed the fugitives, and carried them off, after threatening the inhabitants. They were fortunately retaken on their way to Omoa by a steamer belonging to Palacios.

When Sir Lambton Loraine returned to Omoa, he learnt that, in his absence, Palacios had secured military possession of the railway works at Puerto Cortez, and, by occupying San Pedro, had wholly cut off Streber from connection with Arias and the interior. Streber was communicated with, and was induced to promise that, upon proof being given that British territory had been violated, he would give satisfaction, and that, in the meantime, he would abstain from further raids in that direction. The discussion about the Zapotillo affair occupied nearly a fortnight; and, during much of that period, the *Niobe*, as she had yellow fever onboard, usually kept under sail in the offing, or visited Puerto Cortez.

Thus, her commander could not continuously observe what was going on in Omoa; nor did he learn immediately after the occurrence that on July 29th some of Streber's soldiers had rifled a building belonging to Mr. Debrot. Indeed, though he was at Omoa on the 30th and 31st, he heard no news of the outrage until his return on August 15th from a cruise to the Bay Islands. He was then met with sworn evidence, not only of the events of July 29th, but also of further outrages, including the tearing down of the British flag, the robbing of Mr. Debrot's premises, the firing on the troops of Palacios under a flag of truce, and the sacking of Omoa in celebration of this treachery, foreign property suffering to the extent of £20,000, and four British subjects being imprisoned, after one of them had been flogged.

Having satisfied himself as to the facts. Sir Lambton Loraine took on board the acting British vice-consul, Mr. Bain, and, on August 18th, anchored in a suitable position opposite the fort of San Fernando. Early on the following morning Streber was supplied with a precis of the evidence, and desired to give his explanations, to deliver up the prisoners, and to state what reparation he purposed to offer.

Four hours were allowed him for a reply. In the interim General Alvarez visited the *Niobe*, informed himself as to what terms would be accepted, expressed his sense of their fairness, and obtained an additional three horn's' delay. At the end of that time, it being 2 p.m.,

Alvarez returned with a verbal refusal of satisfaction from Streber, whose folly he denounced, and who, at the moment, paraded his troops on the ramparts, and fired shots of defiance, though not towards the *Niobe*. Loraine sent ashore a letter stating what course he intended to pursue, and, at 2.30, Alvarez remaining onboard, opened a bombardment of the fort with his 7-in. and 40-pr. guns. The troops promptly disappeared from the ramparts, and returned the fire only with badly aimed musketry. The *Niobe* pounded the 20-foot walls for three hours and three quarters, and then withdrew until 1 a.m. on August 20th, when she closed again, and fired at long intervals until 4 a.m. At 9 a.m. a white flag was shown, and Streber's secretary went off to the ship with a verbal request for a 72 hours' truce.

This was refused, and a renewed bombardment promised for 2.30 p.m. unless a satisfactory written communication should be received in the interval. Nevertheless, some further delay was accorded; and it was not until 1 p.m. on the 21st that Streber at last yielded, promising surrender of the prisoners, restitution of stolen goods, and compensation for damage done. He subsequently signed a formal declaration to the same effect; but he so badly carried out parts of his undertaking that, on September 10th, a detachment had to be landed from the *Niobe* to secure and seal up the plundered houses, and to nail a British flag over the vice-consulate. The vessel sailed on September 13th for Jamaica. She had suffered neither loss nor damage. (Disps. Priv. accounts of eyewitnesses. *A. & N. Gazette*, Oct. 18, Oct. 25, 1873.)

Sir Lambton Loraine's proceedings in this matter were so warmly approved by the British at Belize, and so well supported by Commodore Algernon Frederick Rous de Horsey and Vice-Admiral George Greville Wellesley, Commander-in-Chief, that Mr. Gladstone's government, perhaps unwillingly, realised their necessity, and stood by the action of the commander, who, very soon afterwards, had a further opportunity of showing his readiness to assume serious responsibilities.

Chinese Freebooters 1873

Some piratical Chinese freebooters in the Larut River, on the Perak coast, gave much trouble in 1873, especially in connection with an attack which they made upon the British steamer, *Fair Malacca*. At length it was decided to take the severest measures against them; and, on September 19th, by arrangement, the *Thalia*, 6, screw, Captain Henry Bedford Woollcombe, met the *Midge*, 4, twin-screw. Commander John Frederick George Grant, which already had had peculiar experience both of the local waterways and of the habits of the pirates throughout the Straits of Malacca. Indeed, on September 16th, while two of her boats were searching a creek, they had been set upon by row-boats, supported by fire from a 7-gun stockade. After a hot action, in which the British had employed both small-arms and rockets, the Chinese had been driven off with heavy loss, but not until Sub-Lieutenants William Rooke Creswell, and Abraham Hamilton Lindesay had been badly wounded.

At the mouth of the river the two commanders consulted; and, on the morning of September 20th, towed by the *Midge*, and by the yacht of the friendly Rajah Muntri, the ships' boats went up the stream. At about 11 a.m., being near the fort, the stockade, and the three heavy war *junks* which belonged to the pirates, the boats cast off, led by the *Thalia's* galley under Woollcombe in person, and covered by the fire of the *Midge*, while, soon afterwards, the *rajah's* yacht, brought up by Grant, steamed close to the fort, and there anchored. The enemy fired briskly; but, apparently the attack was delayed owing to the yacht drifting ashore under the Chinese guns. She was, however, got off, thanks largely to the energy of Gunner Alexander Ellis, of the *Thalia*, who gallantly laid out an anchor for the purpose; and, soon after 2 p.m., the attack was most daringly delivered.

The Chinese fought stubbornly, and, being about 4000 in number, while only 150 seamen formed the assaulting party, were a formidable enemy.

But at length they were driven from all their positions, and the fort, the stockade, and the three *junks* were taken possession of, and destroyed, all the guns being spiked. The boats then proceeded further up the river in company with the yacht, burnt a fourth *junk*, captured a fifth, and destroyed a second stockade; whereupon the pirate chiefs surrendered unconditionally with the whole of their forces. They had lost about 200 men in the fighting. (*Penang Gazette*, Oct. 4, 1873. Disps., especially Woollcombe's of Oct. 4. Col. Papers, c. 1111, 1874. *A. & N. Gaz.*, Aug. 19, 1876.)

The British had two people (one mortally) wounded.

Cuba, 1873

In the same year there occurred an affair which has provided the international lawyers with some famous precedents, and which is also interesting as an illustration of the kind of good work which is often done for humanity at large by the British Navy.

The *Virginius*, an American steamer secretly engaged in the cause of the rebellion in Cuba, after causing some anxiety and trouble to the British authorities at Jamaica, who suspected her true character, but could obtain no proof of it, sailed from Kingston on October 23rd, 1873, ostensibly bound for Port Limon, in Costa Rica, for which place she had been advertised to sail with passengers, having been cleared in due form by the United States Consul. She carried 155 people, of whom 103 were passengers, while the remaining 52 included the crew and certain poor persons who had been engaged to work their passage to Port Limon. Among the 155 were 32 British subjects, and 14 citizens of the United States. The rest were principally Cubans; and four of them were chiefs of the Cuban rebellion, and were named Varona, Cespedes, Del Sol, and Ryan. The steamer was commanded by Captain Fry, formerly of the United States Navy.

Soon after leaving Jamaica the *Virginius* began to leak, and directed her course to Haiti, ostensibly for repairs, but really to embark arms and ammunition. This done she left her anchorage on October 30th, and steered for the coast of Cuba, to the dismay of the British passengers and all who, like them, had paid their passage money to Costa Rica.

On the afternoon of October 31st the *Virginius* was sighted eighteen or twenty miles off the coast of Cuba by the Spanish man-of-war *Tornado*, whose commander, suspecting her intentions, gave chase, and, though without any international right to do so, captured her that same night on the high seas while running towards Jamaica. It is said that the arms embarked at Haiti had been thrown overboard during the chase.

On the following day, November 1st, the *Tornado* arrived with her prize at Santiago de Cuba. All onboard the *Virginius* were at once declared by the Spanish authority, and in defiance of public law, to be pirates. Their property was taken from them. The crew, brought into harbour ironed and corded, was then conveyed on board Spanish gunboats to await trial by a naval court-martial. The passengers were thrown into prison to await trial by a military one.

Brigadier-General Don Juan Nepomuceno Burriel y Lynch was at that time departmental governor of the district of which Santiago is the capital. This officer found himself in the fortunate position—so far as concerned the immediate purposes which he cherished— of being cut off for a time from his superior authority at Havana, as well as from Spain and all Europe, by the fortuitous interruptions of telegraphic communication between Santiago and the western end of the island.

It may be added that General Jovellar, then Captain-General of Cuba, and Señor Castelar, head of the republican government in Spain, both stated afterwards that they had received no information of the proceedings at Santiago until it was too late to interfere. General Burriel, on his own part, had mendaciously affirmed to his interlocutors, all through, that he was acting under the orders of superior authority.

General Burriel's first step was to stop the sending of telegrams to Jamaica (that line being open) on the part of the United States Consul at Santiago, to whose protests against the *Virginius's* capture and the impending trials by courts-martial he had responded insultingly. On November 4th the four captured insurgent chiefs were shot. This news reached Jamaica on November 5th. The fate of the Cuban chiefs inspired there no particular regret, and, had the justly exasperated Spanish authorities gone no further, their illegalities of procedure might have been condoned by the British. When, however, the following day brought to Jamaica further telegrams from Santiago to the effect that thirty-seven of the *Virginius's* crew—half of them British subjects and mostly innocent cooks, stewards, servants, and firemen—were about to be condemned to death, the community received a shock.

Sir John Peter Grant, Governor of Jamaica, and Commodore Algernon Rous de Horsey, commanding the West Indies division, at once telegraphed strong protests against these summary and bloodthirsty proceedings, and H.M.S. *Niobe*, Commander Sir Lambton Loraine, Bart., was ordered by the commodore to sail the same night (November 6th) for Santiago de Cuba to stop them.

The protests just mentioned, together with the prospect of a man-of-war's interference, had no other effect than to cause General Burriel to hurry on his summary courts and to execute their sentences with all rapidity. The naval court-martial sat through the night of the 6th, and on the morning of the 7th the aforesaid thirty-seven captives— among them Captain Fry, with eight other Americans and nineteen innocent British subjects—were sent from the Spanish men-of-war to the gaol under sentence of death. Their consuls had been denied access to these friendless persons, and, on protesting, had received contemptuous replies. The Spanish priests, however, had free access to them, and seized the opportunity to assail the faith of all who did not belong to their own communion.

At about 4 p.m. the thirty-seven were marched from the gaol, bound with cords and followed by the exultant shouts of the crowd, to the common slaughter-house of the town; and there, ranged in line against the wall surrounding this place, all on their knees and facing the wall, they were shot. So clumsily was the execution performed that, although four soldiers were detailed to each victim and ordered to pour their fire into his back at close quarters, seven minutes of struggling and butchery were counted by a spectator before the last man was completely despatched. The bodies were carted off in loads and shot into a trench hard by.

On the following morning, November 8th, at 7 a.m., and while the *Niobe* was nearing her goal, twelve of the more prominent Cuban prisoners were shot in like manner. At 9.30 a.m. the *Niobe* arrived and cast anchor. Not many minutes afterwards, her commander, accompanied by Mr. Theodore Brooks, British acting vice-consul, presented himself at Government House and called for a cessation of the executions. He was passionately answered by Burriel that the prisoners were in the power of Spain, and that any more of them sentenced to death would infallibly be shot. Written arguments impeaching the legality of his proceedings were next addressed to the governor by the commander.

Burriel only found fault with his interference, and would give no guarantee. All, indeed, that could be obtained from him was permission for Sir Lambton Loraine and the acting vice-consul to visit the prison, with liberty there to see and question in open court such of the accused as were of their own nationality. The British commander, therefore, authorised his Consulate to give out that the shedding of more innocent blood would be the signal for him to sink the Spanish man-of-war lying nearest to the *Niobe*.

Nothing was heard of executions thereafter; and Burriel, for the first time, consented to refer to his captain-general. But for this check on his vindictive intentions, it is probable that of the remaining prisoners fifty-seven would have been shot, and forty-five (being mere youths and boys) sent to penal servitude for life. All instead were freed. The citizens of Santiago, ultra-patriots all, had been looking forward eagerly to their governor prolonging the executions through several days. "*No hay carne fresca esta mañana?*" (Is there no fresh meat this morning?) they would say. In the written language of the commander of the *Tornado*, their "enthusiasm was turned into frenzy." Meanwhile, the British commander, attended by the acting vice-consul and two Spanish magistrates, examined, in the hall of justice in the gaol, the prisoners claiming to be British.

In course of time, the circumstances became known in Europe and America, and on November 15th (a week after the last executions) a telegram reached Santiago de Cuba to announce that the British Government had notified Spain that her government and all concerned would be held responsible for any further executions of British subjects. This was the *coup de grace*, and it was followed next day by the necessary telegraphic orders from Spain, extended so as to apply to the prisoners of all nationalities.

Up to that time no foreign power but Britain had been represented in Santiago harbour; and the foreign consulates were without instructions. Of Spanish men-of-war there had been six present; but two were detached on November 13th to escort the *Virginius* to Havana. The town itself and the fortifications of the harbour were amply garrisoned. Even when, at length, ships of war from the United States and from France appeared on the scene (November 26th–December 2nd), it was left to the *Niobe*, on an occasion when the Spanish governor, Morales, acting in Burriel's place, clandestinely removed the prisoners in the night (December 3rd) and shipped them off in a gun-vessel outside the harbour, to pursue that vessel as far as Havana, and there procure orders from the Captain-General of Cuba for her immediate return, with the prisoners, to Santiago.

The first result of diplomatic negotiations was that, on demand of the United States, the *Virginius* was, surrendered to the American flag. This took place at Bahia Honda on December 15th. Next, the surviving prisoners, 102 in all, were delivered up to the U.S. corvette *Juniata* at Santiago on the 18th, the *Niobe* being present. There, for the last time, a refined cruelty was practised by the Spanish officials on the captives, in informing them they were being taken out of prison to be shot. The *Virginius* herself speedily came to an end. She sank off the American coast while being towed from Bahia Honda towards New York. The released captives were in due time dispersed by the United States' authorities to their own homes. In the sequel the British Government demanded from Spain a national recognition of the wrong

170

done to Great Britain, and compensation to the families of the British subjects executed. The United States demanded further the trial of General Burriel, but that was not conceded; and after a time, the man was appointed to an important governorship in the Peninsula. He died in January, 1878.

For his services in this affair, Sir Lambton Loraine received the thanks of the British and French Governments, the freedom of the city of New York, and other well-deserved recognition, but, probably because he was only a commander, not the honour of a C.B.

The Carlist War, 1873–1876

Early in 1873, King Amadeus, after a brief and anxious experience of its discomforts, resigned the crown of Spain, and, quitting the country, left it a prey to various factions. Of these the strongest for the moment was the republican party, which, under Señores Salmeron and Castelar, assumed power at Madrid; but in the north the Carlists were active, and in more than one town on the Mediterranean littoral a separate cantonal government of communist type was proclaimed.

One of the places to take this course was the important naval port of Cartagena, in Murcia, where the *Intransigentes* seized a considerable part of the Spanish fleet, including the four ironclads, *Numancia*, *Vitoria, Tetuan*, and *Mendez Nuñez*, together with several unarmoured craft. On July 20th, President Salmeron proclaimed these vessels to be pirates, and his foreign minister duly brought the fact to the notice of the diplomatic corps in Madrid.

In the meantime, in consequence of the action of the British consul at Valencia, the British and German senior naval officers on that part of the coast had entered into an agreement each to afford protection to the subjects and interests of the other as well as of his own nationality. The senior German officer was Captain Werner, of the ironclad *Friedrich Carl*. He at once quitted Valencia for Alicante, where the Intransigentes were believed to be about to cause trouble. The British force on the coast was small, but information as to the state of affairs at Cartagena and elsewhere was promptly despatched to Malta, whence, in pursuance of orders from the Admiralty, the ironclad *Swiftsure*, Captain Thomas Le Hunte Ward, departed westward on July 25th, followed, on the 26th, by the ironclads *Lord Warden*, Captain Thomas Brandreth, bearing the flag of Vice-Admiral Sir Hastings Reginald Yelverton, K.C.B., *Invincible*, Captain John Clark Soady, and *Pallas*, Captain Charles John Rowley. The *Helicon*, dispatch vessel, Lieutenant

171

Frank Egremont, was left behind to await the arrival of the English mail, *via* Italy, and then to press after the other ships with all speed.

Werner's prompt appearance before Alicante checkmated the designs of the Cartagena *Intransigentes* there. He discovered the *Vitoria*, which, with the revolutionary leader Galvez Arce onboard, had sent in a demand for the instant payment of a war contribution of $80,000, and which, upon the refusal of the local authorities to comply, had already bombarded the place, but had wisely desisted upon learning of the *Friedrich Carl's* approach. The pirate had committed this outrage under the red flag, but she hoisted, and saluted with, the Spanish flag when Werner was sighted. She then steamed to sea, and as soon as she was out of gunshot rehoisted the red flag.

On July 22nd, as Werner was about to return to Cartagena, Salmeron's proclamation of the 20th was brought onboard to him by the German consul. He reached Cartagena on the 23rd at 1 a.m., and found the *Vitoria* already anchored there. As day broke there came in the dispatch-vessel *Vigilante*, which hoisted the new unauthorised flag, and, moreover, had been seen on the previous day in company with the *Vitoria*. She paid no heed to Werner's orders, enforced with an unshotted gun, to bring to; and, as soon as the German captain had been assured by his consul that the newcomer was one of the *Intransigente* ships, he decided to take possession of her. He instantly seized her, capturing with her the insurgent leader Galvez Arce; and she was placed securely in a berth between the *Friedrich Carl* and the British gun-boat *Pigeon*, 2, Lieutenant John Archibald Harvey Trotter, which had arrived that morning, and which happened to be the craft with whose commander Werner had made the compact at Valencia a few days earlier. The Cartagenans were furious, and threatened reprisals.

With the co-operation of a British captain, who soon afterwards reached the spot, Werner arranged with the *Intransigentes* that no ship should quit Cartagena until July 28th, by which date he hoped to receive instructions from his government. Galvez Arce and his friends promised to take care of the lives of all German and British subjects on shore, and when, in addition, they formally admitted that the *Vigilante*, having been taken under unrecognised colours, was good prize, Werner released his prisoners.

In the interim the whole Spanish coast, from Barcelona to Cadiz, was carefully watched by British and German vessels; and a large international squadron began to assemble in Spanish waters.

Early on August 1st, the *Friedrich Carl* appeared off Malaga, which was threatened with bombardment by the *Intransigentes*. A few hours later, the *Swiftsure*, which, as has been shown, had left Malta on July 25th, also arrived there. Malaga, like Cartagena, had declared itself independent of the central government at Madrid; but this fact did not prevent the Cartagenans from desiring to levy a contribution from the town, money being very scarce in Murcia. At Malaga lay the French frigate *Jeanne d'Arc*.

Werner and Ward put to sea together, and found in the offing the *Intransigente* ironclad *Vitoria*, and frigate *Almansa*, flying no flags, and declining to hoist any, until a shot from the *Friedrich Carl* across the *Almansa's* bows brought the Spanish flag to the peak, and a flag of truce to the truck. Werner then ordered the insurgent General Contreras to quit the *Almansa* and go on board the *Friedrich Carl*. The rebel chief did so, and was made prisoner; the *Almansa* was taken possession of by the Germans, and simultaneously the *Swiftsure's* people seized the *Vitoria*. The two captains were about to conduct their prizes back to Cartagena, and there to liberate them, when they were fallen in with by Vice-Admiral Yelverton, who directed that the vessels should be retained, and that Contreras should be kept as a hostage, but that the crews might be released upon certain conditions. Werner and Ward, accordingly, took the ships to Cartagena, and on August 3rd anchored them in Escombrera Bay. Yelverton, who was overtaken by the *Helicon* shortly before he reached Gibraltar, anchored there on August 2nd.

At Cartagena the people belonging to the prizes were put ashore. Malaga was delighted at Werner's conduct, and the British captains were loud in their praises of his behaviour. Unfortunately, he was disavowed by his political superiors in Berlin, and, on August 14th, was superseded, though he was immediately employed elsewhere. Berlin made a mistake, and a few months later Werner's successor found himself obliged to deliver an ultimatum to the Cartagenan insurgents, and to claim payment of an indemnity of $15,000 under threat of bombardment. Had Werner's action been supported throughout, German interests would have been respected by the *Intransigentes* from August 1st onwards.

The *Vitoria* and *Almansa* remained in Escombrera Bay in charge of Yelverton, who proceeded in person to the scene. He was anxious to hand them over to the Madrid Government, which, however, seemed at the time to be almost impotent, and which was then able to send to sea only a wooden frigate and three old paddle-vessels. Occasional shots from the insurgent batteries fell near the British ships and boats, but Yelverton diplomatically assumed that these were fired unintentionally in his direction.

While he waited at Cartagena with the ironclads *Lord Warden, Triumph*, Captain John Dobree M'Crea, and *Swiftsure*, the *Helicon*, and the gun-vessel *Torch*, 5, Commander Hugh M'Neile Dyer, he kept the *Pallas*, and the *Rapid*, 11, Commander the Hon. Victor Alexander Montagu, at Barcelona; the *Hart*, (later summoned to Cartagena), 4, Commander Thomas Harvey Royse, at Valencia; the *Pheasant*, (later summoned to Cartagena), 2, Lieutenant George Woronzow Allen, at Malaga; the *Invincible* at Cadiz; and the rest of his immediately available force (including the detached squadron under Rear-Adm. Fredk. Archibald Campbell), at Gibraltar.

Towards the end of August, as the Spanish Admiral Lobo seemed to be less able than ever to meet the *Intransigentes* with any reasonable prospect of beating them, Yelverton made up his mind to remove the prizes to an anchorage where their custody would be less troublesome to him. On August 31st he caused all the merchantmen in harbour to be towed out of the way, ordered all his ships to get up steam and to be prepared to slip, and warned the Consul and British subjects ashore to be ready to go off to the squadron in case of need; and, on September 1st, in spite of the threats of the insurgents, he brought out the *Vitoria* and *Almansa*, under their own steam, and with British crews on board. The prizes and their escort passed the three ironclads, *Numancia, Mendez Nunez* and *Tetuan*, and the forts, all of which had their guns loaded and run out; but nothing happened. Had a shot been fired, the three ironclads were to have been taken or sunk by the *Lord Warden, Triumph* and *Swiftsure*, and the forts were to have been afterwards silenced.

The *Vitoria* and *Almansa*, which were in a disgustingly filthy condition when captured, were convoyed by the *Swiftsure* and *Triumph* to Gibraltar, where they arrived on August 3rd. They were eventually handed over to Admiral Lobo, who was waiting there for them, and who, on October 11th following, employed them in a long-range indecisive engagement, which he fought off Cartagena. As for the rest of Yelverton's squadron, after the bringing out of the prizes it returned to its anchorage in Escombrera Bay, where it was not molested. (Disps., Brit, and German: Tesdorpf, *Gesch. der k. d. Marine*; *A. and N. Gazette*, Aug. 16, Aug. 30, Sept. 6, Sept. 13, 1873.)

After the action of October 11th, Yelverton sent Lieutenant Tynte Ford Hammill to Cartagena, and Commander Royse to Admiral Lobo with offers of surgical assistance. Lobo professed to have no killed or

THE GOLD COAST

AND PART OF

ASHANTEE.

Scale of English Miles.

wounded. The *Intransigentes* appeared to need no help. In the middle of the mouth, Sir Hastings was happily instrumental in preventing the insurgent ships from Cartagena from bombarding Valencia. A blockade of the port was afterwards established.

The Gold Coast, 1867-1873

On March 5th, 1867, a convention had been concluded between Great Britain and the Netherlands, in virtue of which a transfer of territory had taken place in that part of West Africa known as the Gold Coast. Great Britain handed over to Holland Apollonia, Dixcove, Secondee, Commenda, and the protectorate of Denkira, East and West Wassaw, and native Apollonia, while she received part of Accra, Cormantine, Moree, and Apam.

The tribal people were not pleased with the transaction. The King of Apollonia, and other chiefs, protested; and the people of Commenda, refusing to accept the arrangement, attacked a boat's crew from a Dutch man-of-war, killed some seamen, captured others, and were punished by having their town bombarded. At Dixcove there was another conflict; nor were affairs much more satisfactory in the new British protectorate.

It seemed, however, that the country might soon settle down if the whole coast were subjected to a uniform system of customs duties, and if only one European flag flew there; and as the Dutch were not enthusiastically in love with their possessions, it was found easy to begin negotiations with them for the cession to Great Britain of all their remaining Gold Coast territory.

The attitude of the coast tribes for generations had been greatly influenced by that of the King of Ashantee, a considerable tract of country forming the Gold Coast hinterland. In 1868 a new king, Coffee Calcallee, young, warlike, and ambitious, mounted the Ashantee throne, and embarked at once upon an anti-European policy. He committed several outrages to the westward, in the neighbourhood of the River Volta; and a relative of his, Prince Atjempon, stirred up some of the Fantees and Denkiras to assist him in an attack upon the Dutch forts at Elmina. (General authorities for the history of the causes and events of the Third Ashantee War, 1873-4, include Winwood Reade, *The Ashantee Campaign*, this is also republished by Leonaur).

Mr. Salmon, British Administrator of Cape Coast Castle, interfered to prevent tribes under British protection from going to war with Great Britain's allies, and checked the formation of a Fantee Confederation, which had been projected by speculative traders and ambitious natives.

On the other hand, the attack on Elmina rendered Sir Arthur Kennedy, Governor of the British West African settlements, unwilling to contemplate the proposed transfer of Elmina to Britain so long as there was danger of Ashantee complications arising out of the transaction. The position of Holland was that Ashantee had no claim whatsoever upon Elmina. Coffee Calcallee, however, maintained that from time immemorial the Elmina forts had paid regular tribute to his predecessors, and that Elmina was practically his. It had brought him in, he said, £80 a year; but the Dutch contended that the £80 was neither tribute nor rent, but merely a present.

To induce Coffee Calcallee to adopt their view, the Hollanders arrested his relative, Atjempon, and stopped the payment of the £80; and by these and other methods they secured from Coffee an unwilling retraction of his former statement.

This seemed to remove the objections on the part of Great Britain to accepting the transfer of Elmina; and when, in April, 1872, Mr. John Pope Hennessy succeeded to the governor-generalship, he arrived with instructions to complete the business. The cession was thereupon effected, mainly on the strength of British confidence in Dutch representations.

Coffee Calcallee was displeased; and, upon demands being made to him for the release of some missionaries and others who had been taken prisoners during the raids to the westward in 1869, he declined to surrender them, save upon payment of 1800 oz. of gold. The result was a blockade of the trade-routes leading from the coast into Ashantee.

If the British Government, as represented by Mr. Pope Hennessy, had been firm and consistent in its attitude, it is possible that war might have been avoided, in spite of the disturbances which broke out at Elmina and elsewhere when it became known that the transfer had been decided on. Unfortunately, Coffee Calcallee was by turns threatened and cajoled. He was given to understand that on no account would the British pay him the 1800 oz. of gold, but it was suggested that perhaps the missionary society whose missionaries had been captured might be disposed to spend £1000 on effecting their liberation. Moreover, a present of gold-embroidered silks was forwarded to the king: he was told that his roads should be opened again to traders; and he was promised a yearly gratuity double that which he had received from the Dutch.

In addition, a turbulent Ashantee, who had been imprisoned at Cape Coast Castle, was liberated, and his expenses up country were paid. But the still more turbulent and dangerous native, Atjempon himself, was arrested, and then inconsequently released before the European captives had been freed; and although the imprisoned missionaries had been sent down as far as the River Prah, and their society had supplied the £1000 for their ransom, it was foolishly determined that the money should not be handed over until the poor people were safe at Cape Coast Castle.

The indecision, weakness, delay, and haggling of the administration, coupled with the fact that Atjempon returned to Coomassie, the capital of Ashantee, on the eve of a "grand custom," or court orgie, brought matters to a crisis. Coffee Calcallee, flattered by his subjects, spurred on by his war chiefs, annoyed by the story of Atjempon's imprisonment, and excited by what he had eaten and drunk, swore that he would conquer all lands from Coomassie to the sea, and would wash his royal stool in British blood at Cape Coast Castle.

On January 22nd, 1873, he began his invasion of territories which, though absolutely undefended, were under nominal British protection. The chiefs of Assin, Abrah, Annamaboe, and Mankassim applied in terror for aid. Fifty Houssa police were sent from Lagos, but only as far as Dunquah, where, even had they been ten times as numerous, they would have been useless. Sixty thousand Ashantees, having crossed the Prah, were advancing in three armies towards the coast. At that time Mr. Pope Hennessy was relieved by Mr. Keate.

The idea of a Fantee Confederation, for defence, was revived; volunteers were organised; and arms and ammunition were sent to a native contractor named Bentill, who had offered to raise 20,000 men: but the tide of invasion was almost unchecked; and on March 1st the victorious Ashantees occupied Yancomassie, only about five-and-twenty miles from Cape Coast Castle. The Fantee allies proved useless; and as for the available regulars, all of them, and more, were needed for the defence of the coast settlements.

On April 11th a great but indecisive battle was fought between Dunquah and Yancomassie, and 40,000 Ashantees, under Amanquatia, received a slight check. On the 14th, there was another action, the result of which was that the Fantee allies, after committing some outrages, dispersed. It was vain to attempt any more fighting in the field at that time. Cape Coast Castle, Annamaboe, and Elmina were garrisoned as well as might be by the aid of detachments from the *Druid*, 10, Captain William Hans Blake, *Argus*, 6, paddle, Commander Percy Putt Luxmoore, *Merlin*, 4, Lieutenant Edward Fitzgerald Day, *Decoy*, 4, Lieutenant John Hext, and *Seagull*, 3, Commander Ernest Augustus Travers Stubbs. Even then Colonel Harley had barely a thousand men with whom to defend the coast settlements.

The news of the situation reached England in the middle of May; whereupon the government, instead of sending out at once a body of troops sufficiently large to permit of the offensive being assumed, contented itself with slightly reinforcing the West India and Houssa detachments in the colony, and with despatching thither 110 Royal Marines, (with two mountain guns and 200 rockets), under Lieutenant-Colonel Francis Worgan Festing, while augmenting the small squadron on the coast by adding to it the *Barracouta*, 6, paddle. Captain Edmund Robert Fremantle. This craft reached Elmina on June 7th, when Fremantle became senior naval officer.

In the meantime, the Ashantees, instead of making straight for Cape Coast Castle, had struck somewhat to their right, in the direction of Elmina, in and around which town they had many sympathisers; and Atjempon, with 8000 fighting men, had proceeded further to the westward in order to attempt to raise the Apollonia tribes against the British. Had Coffee Calcallee pushed ahead from the beginning, things must have gone badly with the defence.

It was quickly seen that the state of affairs at Elmina was most dangerous. The suburb known as King's Town was furnishing the enemy with arms, stores, and information, and the local chiefs were disaffected. Harley ordered these last to come in and surrender their weapons. They did not obey; and it was determined to punish the Elmina rebels swiftly and severely.

On the night of June 12th, Festing occupied the land side of Elmina with marines, West India and Houssa troops, and volunteers to the number of 300. As many officers and men from the squadron were told off to co-operate; and the twenty-one boats containing them were all ready, inside the bar of the river, by daybreak on the 13th. There were four paddle-box boats, each with a 20-pr. R.B.L. gun on a swivel mounting; one cutter with a 7-pr. gun; eight cutters with rocket-tubes; two pinnaces also with rocket-tubes; five whale boats; and one jolly-boat, all posted opposite the hostile quarter of the town, above the bridge that led from the loyal quarter to the esplanade of the castle. The officers in command were Captain Fremantle, Lieutenant

Hext, who was to lead, as he knew the river mouth well, and Lieutenants Lewis Fortescue Wells, William Marrack, Edmund George Bourke, and Gordon Charles Young.

A final summons was addressed to the rebels, and delay was granted for the removal of their women and children. Then, at noon on June 13th, a bombardment of their town began both from the boats and from the castle. In ten minutes Elmina was on fire in several places, and the natives, leaving it, took to the bush, whither they were pursued by Festing, Fremantle, with most of the bluejackets, also landing to assist. While the boats continued to ply their guns and rockets, Hext and Young, with a very few men, and at considerable risk, went along the windward side of the native town with torches, and completed its destruction.

Scarcely had the bluejackets and troops returned from the pursuit ere an attack was made upon the loyal part of the town by about 600 Ashantees. A brisk engagement resulted; but the Ashantees fired badly, and, though sometimes at very close range, succeeded in hitting only about half-a-dozen of the defenders, of whom three were killed. The enemy drew off towards 6 p.m., having lost very heavily. They carried away their wounded, but left behind them some hundreds of dead, and six prisoners.

It was by that time evident that the Ashantee war was not to be concluded without a serious effort; for the Ashantees, while not again attacking Elmina, lay around both that place and Cape Coast Castle, confined the British and their allies within a comparatively small tract beyond range of the guns of the ships and forts, and plainly awaited only what they should deem a good opportunity for sweeping the whites into the sea. Yet in England the situation was not grasped for some time; and, in the interim, little more than purely defensive measures could be undertaken by the feeble forces on the spot.

In those services the navy proved very useful, especially on August 28th, at Aquidah, ten miles from Dixcove, where the *Druid* co-operated with the Dixcove natives in taking revenge upon their Aquidah cousins, who had attacked them without provocation. The corvette shelled the offending village, and then covered the successful attack of the native allies by sending in three of her boats. During this waiting period two strong outposts were formed inland, about six miles behind the two threatened towns. Fort Abbaye, to the rear of Elmina, and Fort Napoleon, to the rear of Cape Coast Castle, served as stations from which any movement of the enemy could be observed promptly, and whence information could be sent to the shore in such a manner as to prevent undue panic there.

In August, when at length the home authorities were beginning to take a proper view of their difficulties. Commodore John Edmund Commerell, V.C, C.B., in the *Rattlesnake*, 17, Commander Noel Stephen Fox Digby, arrived on the scene; and it was decided, pending the receipt of further military forces from England, to make a reconnaissance up the River Prah, which comes down from the Ashantee country, passes through or near the district then held by the right of the Ashantee army, and falls into the sea at Chamah, midway between Commenda and Secondee. It was supposed that on an island in that river, which is navigable for about twenty-five miles inland, there was a large force of the enemy. It was an unfortunate and costly decision.

On August 13th the Commodore went to Secondee, and at 9 a.m. on the following day quitted the *Rattlesnake* with the following boats manned and armed, *viz.*, the steam-cutter of the *Simoon* troopship which had arrived, (Capt. Mountford Stephen Lovick Peile), lent for the occasion, under Lieutenant Frederick Edwards, of the *Rattlesnake*, who had with him Navigating Sub-Lieutenant Peregrine William Pepperell Hutton; the gig of the *Rattlesnake*, under Sub-Lieutenant Archibald James Pocklington; the *Rattlesnake's* whaler, under Surgeon Charles Frederick Kennan Murray, M.D.; the colonial steam-launch, under Sub-Lieutenant Charles Henry Cross, of the *Argus*, and, towed by the latter, his own galley, in which were himself. Commander Luxmoore, and Captain William Helden, (2nd W.I. Regt.), civil *commandant* at Secondee.

Commerell landed unarmed at Chamah, and had what was deemed to be a friendly interview with the chiefs there, who, however, expressed a wish to be neutral in the quarrel, and who declined to allow two of their number to accompany the expedition. Soon afterwards the *Rattlesnake* anchored off Chamah, while the boats entered the liver, the colonial launch, however, breaking down almost immediately, and being left behind, with the gig to assist her.

Supposing the Chamah people to be neutral, if not actively friendly, the commodore ascended the stream on the Chamah side. The stream is seventy or eighty yards broad, and the banks are covered with dense brushwood. The boats had advanced about a mile and a half against a two-knot stream when, without the slightest warning, they were saluted with a most murderous fire from the Chamah bank, where an ambuscade had been prepared. The fire was returned, but the rockets could not be used, as they were in the *Simoon's* steam-cutter, which was then towing the two other boats. Commerell, Luxmoore, and Helden were severely hit at the first discharge, and a number of men were wounded. The boats were ordered into mid-stream, and, in view, of the numerous casualties, were then directed to return to the *Rattlesnake*. Luxmoore behaved most pluckily. He continued to carry on, and no one save himself knew that he was wounded until he nearly fainted.

At 6 p.m. the *Rattlesnake* was reached, and the injured people were transferred to her. On the way down Surgeon Murray not only attended to them, but also steered, and directed the fire of, the whaler.

In the meantime, another act of treachery had been perpetrated. It had been arranged that the fort at Chamah was to be occupied by ten policemen. A cutter, under Sub-Lieutenant William Pitt Draffen, took these men ashore from the *Rattlesnake* while the other boats were still up the river. After Draffen and the police had landed, the cutter was swamped in the surf; and while Midshipman Richard Henry Francis Wharton Wilson, (wounded), and the crew were endeavouring to right her, and to land the stores, they were fired into by the natives on the beach. Draffen, (slightly wounded), who had remained at hand, coolly did all that was possible, by forming up the police, and throwing them out as skirmishers, to cover the people in the water; and he certainly saved many lives; but a seaman, a *Krooman*, and two Fantee policemen were killed, and several of the boat's crew were wounded.

As soon as he saw what was happening on the beach. Commander Digby despatched further boats under Lieutenants Henry Holden Wilding and John Dundas Nicholls; but, ere they reached the shore, the natives had made off to the bush. Upon the return of the boats from the river, the *Rattlesnake* was cleared for action, and the town of Chamah was bombarded and burnt. It was not, however, believed that the treacherous natives suffered heavily from the fire either of the boats or of the corvette. During the bombardment, the *Merlin*, 4, arrived on the scene.

The commodore at once sent her to Secondee with Sub-Lieutenant Edward Henry Bayly, of the *Rattlesnake*, who was ordered to take the place of the wounded Captain Helden as civil commandant there. Commerell subsequently himself proceeded to Secondee, whence he sent on the *Merlin* to communicate with Dixcove and Axim. Although severely wounded in the right side, he decided to endeavour to continue to exercise the command of the squadron. Word to that effect was carried to Cape Coast Castle by the *Simoon's* steam-cutter. On the 14th, Commander Digby, and Assistant-Paymaster William Nichols Thomas, the Commodore's Secretary, held a palaver with such of the Secondee chiefs as could be induced to attend; and on the 15th, the *Argus* having arrived that morning, the *Rattlesnake* weighed, and proceeded for Cape Coast Castle. In addition to the officers already named, Commerell mentioned Charles Godden, coxswain, and William Sermon, ordinary seaman, both of Lieutenant Wilding's party, who, he said, had "evinced great pluck."

The total casualties in these two lamentable affairs amounted, on the British side, to 4 killed and 20 wounded. (Wilding to Commerell, Aug. 14; Commerell to Admlty., Aug 15, 1873.)

During August and the first half of September great preparations were made in England for the prosecution of the military part of the campaign; and on September 11th, Major-General Sir Garnet Joseph Wolseley, who had been selected to conduct it, embarked with his staff for Africa. On October 2nd he landed at Cape Coast Castle; but he preceded the greater portion of the force which was to be employed under him. Nevertheless, he began work without delay, and set to work at once to clear the enemy from the neighbourhood of Elmina.

Commerell, greatly to his disgust, had been obliged to relinquish active command, (he left for the Cape on Aug. 22), his wound at length vanquishing his will; and Fremantle was left senior naval officer upon the coast. The first operation undertaken owed much of its success to the navy, for, except officers, the only white people taking part in it were 22 bluejackets and 1 marine, with a 7-pr. gun, from the *Barracouta*, 158 Royal Marine Artillery and Light Infantry, from the *Simoon*; 38 seamen and 19 marines from the *Argus*; and 15 seamen and 10 marines from the *Decoy*. The total force landed from the ships, including 19 Kroomen, and 17 officers, numbered 299, the officers being:—

Captain Fremantle, Lieutenant Thomas Edward Maxwell, Staff-Surgeon Francis Hamilton Moore, and Assistant-Paymaster Edmund Hickson (*Barracouta*); Captain John Frederick Crease, R.M.A., Captain William Winkworth Allnutt, R.M., Lieutenant Thomas Moore, R.M.A., Lieutenant Montague Philip Hall Gray, R.M., and Surgeon Archibald Adams, M.D. (*Simoon*); Commander Luxmoore, Lieutenants Gordon Charles Young, and John Leslie Burr, Sub-Lieutenant Edward John Sanderson, and Staff-Surgeon Leonard Lucas (*Argus*); and Lieutenant John Hext, Boatswain William Jinks, and Surgeon James William Fisher, M.D. (*Decoy*).

Some miles in rear of Elmina was an Ashantee camp at Mampon. To the westward of Elmina, and along the coast between it and Commenda, were the disaffected villages of Amquana, Akimfoo, and Ampanee; and between these villages and Mampon was the town of Essaman, which the Ashantees held. The ships, (*Barracouta* and *Decoy; Argus* was already to the westward), left Cape Coast Castle on the night of October 13th, ostensibly for the eastward, a baseless rumour having been intentionally allowed to circulate to the effect that Commander John Hawley Glover, R.N. (retired), Official Administrator of Lagos, who was raising native forces for an expedition up the Volta, was in difficulties at Ada, at the mouth of that river. (Glover: Born 1825; Com. 1862; retd. 1870: G.C.M.G. 1874; later Govr. of Newfoundland and of Leeward Islands; died 1885.)

Instead of going eastward, the ships steamed westward; and at 3 a.m. on the 14th disembarked the major part of the intended landing force at Elmina, the *Decoy* and *Argus* then proceeding, and anchoring off the coral reef in front of Akimfoo and Ampanee, while the *Barracouta's* steam-launch and the *Argus's* paddle-box boats placed themselves inside the reef. Meantime, the land forces, including the main part of the Naval Brigade, marched from Elmina, and at 7 a.m. on the 14th approached Essaman.

The enemy was on the alert, and opened fire. Though the Ashantees were completely concealed in the bush, the fire was returned; and the party pressed on, the gun and rocket-trough being quickly placed in position within 200 yards of the place. By 8.30, after some sharp fighting, the enemy retired, and Essaman was taken. It was promptly burnt. From Essaman the column marched six miles to Amquana, which was taken and set on fire. Most of the marines were left there temporarily, and the rest of the force proceeded four miles along the shore to Akimfoo, where, at 3 p.m., it was joined by the landing-parties from the *Argus* and *Decoy*, which vessels had been engaged during the day in shelling Akimfoo and Ampanee. Both villages were found to be deserted, and were destroyed; but, upon leaving Ampanee, the party was attacked by an ambushed force of the enemy, and while the Naval Brigade was being re-embarked, a further attack was made upon it, the West India troops, (200 of these were with the column), however, driving the Ashantees back.

This day's work went far towards securing the safety of Elmina and Cape Coast Castle, and, indeed, it caused the whole of the Ashantee

Army to fall back several miles; but it was not earned out without some loss. Fremantle was wounded severely; four other people from the ships were injured, and on the side of the land forces there were 21 casualties. (Wolseley to Sec. for War; Wolseley to Col. Sec, both of Oct. 15; Fremantle in *Gazette* of Nov. 11.)

Although nothing like a general advance could yet be attempted, owing to the non-arrival of troops from England, the navy did not cease to be engaged almost continuously up and down the coast. On one occasion a party from the *Argus* landed at Tacorady to destroy some canoes, but had to retire with a loss of 12 wounded, including Lieutenant Gordon Charles Young, who commanded it. Brief bombardments of the unfriendly coast villages occurred frequently. On October 28th, Bootry, three miles east of Dixcove, was shelled by the *Argus* and *Decoy*, and was then burnt by a landing-party under Lieutenants J. Hext and G. C. Young. There were no casualties. (Luxmoore to Fremantle, Oct. 28.)

At about the same time Sir Garnet Wolseley undertook another short inland expedition with the object of endeavouring to break up a detached Ashantee force which, he had reason to believe, was near Dunquah, some miles on the main route between Cape Coast Castle and the interior, *via* Mansu. He sent a small military force from Cape Coast Castle to Dunquah on October 25-26th, and on the 26th another force marched out of Elmina, which was garrisoned in its absence by a party from the *Druid*, while a third force, with which were Sir Garnet and a detachment of bluejackets and marines, from the squadron, moved out to Assayboo in support.

★★★★★★

Under Captain Fremantle: from the *Barracouta*, 64 men under Lieut. Lewis Fortescue Wells; from the *Simoon*, 66 men under Capt. Mountford Stephen Lovick Peile, and 101 marines under Capt. William Winkworth Allnutt, R.M.; and from the *Bittern*, 3, twin-scr., 34 men under Com. Prescot William Stephens; besides 48 *Kroomen*. Owing to lack of marine officers, Lieut. Horatio Fraser Kemble (*Bittern*), and Sub-Lieut. Francis Avenell Brookes (*Barracouta*) did duty as such. Capt. Allnutt breaking down on the march, Capt. Crease, R.M.A., took his place.

★★★★★★

At Assayboo some Houssas and native levies were picked up, and thence an advance was made to Abrakrampa, where more native troops were found, some of these being under Lieutenant George

185

Northmore Arthur Pollard, R.N.; but in such fighting as occurred on October 27th and 28th near Dunquah the Brigade had little share. After that fighting. Lieutenant Wells, with 50 men, was left to form part of the garrison of Abrakrampa, and the rest of the landed force returned to Cape Coast Castle. (*Gazette*, Nov. 25, 1873.)

On November 5th, Abrakrampa, where Major Baker C. Russell commanded, was attacked by the enemy in force, just as Lieutenant Wells, with his seamen and marines, was about to set out on his return to Assayboo and the coast. The firing was heavy, and the little garrison, though well entrenched, was for a time hard pressed. News of its precarious situation reached Wolseley at 2 a.m. on the 6th, and he appealed at once to Fremantle for a landing force wherewith to attempt a relief. The navy, of course, responded with cordiality, every man who could be spared being put promptly ashore, and the Brigade, (325 officers and men from the *Barracouta, Simoon, Beacon, Bittern*, and *Encounter*), with Wolseley and Fremantle accompanying it, marching inland soon after 7 a.m., together with some Houssa artillery and miscellaneous troops.

The march was most exhausting. At Assayboo, 100 bluejackets and marines were left, but at Accroful a detachment of the 2nd West India Regiment was added to the expedition, which pushed on, and reached Abrakrampa at 6.30 p.m., while fighting was still in progress. It soon, however, ceased. This march, and a demonstration made on the following morning by some cowardly native levies, caused a regular panic among the Ashantees, who retired hastily, abandoning many stores, and, indeed, almost everything except, as Wolseley put it, "the actual weapons in the hands of the fighting men." In these operations no white man was wounded, though many suffered terribly from the heat.

Thenceforward the enemy stood almost exclusively on the defensive, and soon recrossed the Prah, retiring on Coomassie. Its retreat was hastened by Colonel Evelyn Wood, (later Gen. Sir Evelyn Wood, he had begun his career in the navy), who, however, experienced a check on November 27th at Faysowah, on the road between Mansu and Prahsu; whereupon a small naval contingent, (3 officers and 50 men), which afterwards became the nucleus of the Naval Brigade in the general advance, was despatched to reinforce him at Sutah.

On November 14th, Fremantle was superseded as senior naval officer, Commodore William Nathan Wrighte Hewett, V.C, who had succeeded Commerell, arriving in the *Active*, 10, screw. Commander

Robert Lowther Byng. Fremantle had done so well that Wolseley paid him the compliment of saying that, but for him, the operations leading to the retreat of the Ashantees could not have been carried out.

This was, no doubt, perfectly true; but Wolseley's praise of Fremantle was constructive censure of the authorities at home, who, for nearly a year after the commencement of hostilities, had left the colonies without white troops, and who had thus obliged the navy to undertake work for which it was never intended. When, at the end of the year 1873, troops in plenty arrived on the scene, the Naval Brigade might well have been released from further service ashore. It continued, however, to be employed, and although its unnecessary employment was economically unsound, the Brigade, by its gallant and cheerful behaviour, gained further laurels, which, perhaps, even the bitterest critics of the administration would have been sorry to see it shut out from.

In December, 1873, the troopships *Himalaya*, Captain William Burley Grant, and *Tamar*, Captain Walter James Hunt-Grubbe, and the hired transport *Sarmatian*, arrived off the coast with the 42nd Highlanders, the 2nd battalion of the Rifle Brigade, and the 23rd Regiment, but were sent to sea again until all was ready for the advance. Other troops also, and Royal Marines, went out. On December 26th Wolseley left Cape Coast Castle for Prahsu; on the 27th, a new Naval Brigade landed, and marched up to Prahsu, which it reached on January 3rd; and on January 1st the troops were disembarked.

Almost at the last moment before the general advance was begun a somewhat amusing affair occurred to the westward. The Commenda natives, burning to prove their loyalty by attacking Chamah, begged the British to convey a body of them across the mouth of the Prah. The *Encounter*, 14, Captain Richard Bradshaw, and *Merlin*, 4, Lieutenant Edward FitzGerald Day, accordingly transported 635 natives to the west bank of the Prah on December 24th. A day later the valiant natives, who were like to have been annihilated by the Chamah people, were glad enough to be ferried back again. On the 26th, Bradshaw, before returning to Cape Coast Castle, bombarded and burnt a village on Alboaddi Point, where the Chamah natives had congregated. The three boats concerned in this affair were respectively commanded by Lieutenant Day (*Merlin*), and Lieutenants Edward Seymour Evans, and Alfred Churchill Loveridge (*Encounter*). (Hewett, of Dec. 26; Bradshaw, of Dec. 24 and Dec. 26.) Ere the loyal natives were removed, they succeeded in burning Chamah, and in capturing about 50 canoes.

During the final advance, the chief difficulties which the Naval Brigade had to contend with were natural ones; and it was not until the last five or six days of the campaign that it took part in any serious fighting. It was the first European part of the expedition to cross the Prah, which it passed on January 20th. The force, which was about 500 strong, was commanded by Commodore Hewett.

On January 29th, there being a hostile force under the King of Adansi on the left flank of the British advance, Borumassie was captured, and the enemy driven out of it. A much more important battle was fought on January 31st, at and around Amoaful, on the main line of the advance. Says Hewett, (Feb. 2; Hunt-Grubbe, of Feb. 18; Luxmoore, of Feb. 7):—

Without attempting to give the details of the general's plan of operations, I will endeavour to afford such particulars as will enable their Lordships to gain some idea of the position occupied by the Naval Brigade during the engagement. The first encounter took place at 8 a.m., when the village of Egginnassie, about a mile from Amoaful, was carried by a rush of the scouts under Lord Gifford. The Naval Brigade was divided into two wings, one, under Captain Walter James H. Grubbe, of Her Majesty's ship *Tamar*, being attached to the left column, and the other, under Acting-Captain Percy P. Luxmoore, of Her Majesty's ship *Druid* to the right. (Capt. Wm. Hans Blake died of dysentery on Jan. 22, 1874. Com. Luxmoore had taken his place upon his being invalided.)

On the advance being made, the right and left columns were ordered to cut paths at right angles to the main road for a distance of 300 yards into the bush and then to form upon the flanks of the 42nd Regiment, who, in the front column, were making their way through the thick bush on either side of the road. The enemy's centre was at Amoaful, and, throwing out two columns towards us in a diagonal direction, they formed, as it were, a broad arrow with the main path, in which order they received our attack.

After suffering very heavy losses, the 42nd Highlanders eventually captured the town at 1.45 p.m. I have great pleasure in acquainting their Lordships with the steady behaviour of the Naval Brigade. During a very trying time they showed the greatest coolness, and, advancing slowly under a continuous and heavy fire, steadily drove back the enemy until 3 o'clock, when they forced them to make a precipitate retreat, and the day was ours.

On February 1st, the Brigade was sent on to Becquah, three miles beyond Amoaful, where a large force of Ashantees was attacked, and driven back with considerable loss.

The naval casualties during these three days were as follows:—

At Borumassie, Jan. 29th: two seamen of the *Active*, and one seaman and one marine of the *Argus* wounded.

At Amoaful, Jan. 31st: Capt. Hunt-Grubbe (*Tamar*), Lieut. Angus MacLeod (*Barracouta*), Actg.-Lieut. Gerald Rivers Maltby, and Sub-Lieuts. Robert Leyborne Mundy, and Wyatt Rawson (*Active*), and Mids. Charles Goodhart May (*Amethyst*), wounded. Petty officers, seamen, and marines, twenty wounded (*Active, Druid, Amethyst*, and *Argus*).

At Becquah, Feb. 1st: one seaman killed (*Active*), and three petty officers and seamen wounded (*Active*).

On February 4th, there was further fighting at Ordah-su, where the Naval Brigade had an officer, (Lieut. Adolphus Brett Crosbie, R.M.L.I.; *Active*), and four men wounded; and in the afternoon of that day the army entered Coomassie, which Sir Garnet Wolseley, on the 6th, ordered to be burnt. A few days afterwards. Commander Glover, who had advanced by way of Akim, from the Volta, joined hands with the main force. On his way, on January 16th, he had captured the town of Obogo just in time to save the lives of 40 slaves who were to have been sacrificed that day at the funeral of a local chief. On February 18th peace was concluded.

Among the officers favourably mentioned in the despatches of Wolseley and Hewett, or in their enclosures, were:—

Lieutenant Ernest Neville Rolfe, Naval A.d.C. to the Commander-in-Chief, Captains Hunt-Grubbe, Richard Bradshaw (*Encounter*), Alfred John Chatfield (*Amethyst*), and George Henry Parkin (*Victor Emmanuel*); Commanders John Hawley Glover (retd.), Thomas Henry Larcom, Percy Putt Luxmoore, Herbert Franklyn Crohan, John Hext (actg.), and Robert Lowther Byng; Lieutenants Robert Beaumont Pipon, Edward FitzGerald Day, Gerard Henry Uctred Noel, George Henry Moore, Gerald Rivers Maltby, William Frederick Stanley Mann, and Angus MacLeod; Sub-Lieutenants Henry Ponsonby, Henry Horace Adamson (retd.), Wyatt Rawson, and Harry Seawell Frank Niblett; Navigating-Lieutenant Hugh Halliday Hannay; Captain (R.M.) James William Vaughan Arbuckle; Lieutenant (R.M.) Adolphus Brett Crosbie; Midshipman Charles Elsden Gladstone; Gunner Thomas Cowd; Staff-Surgeons Ahmuty Irwin, James William Fisher, John Watt Reid (2), and William James Hamilton; Surgeons Henry Fegan, Henry Thompson Cox, and Walter Reid: and Assistant-Surgeon James Mc-Carthy. (Glover, of Feb. 25; Hewett, of Mar. 3; Hunt-Grubbe, of Feb. 19; Hewett, of Mar. 4, 1874.)

In addition to numerous promotions for services in the campaign, the following honours to naval officers were gazetted:—

To be K.C.B., Capt. John Edmund Commerell, V.C.; Capt. William Nathan Wrighte Hewett, V.C.

To be C.B., Capt. Walter James Hunt-Grubbe; Capt. Hon. Edmund Robert Fremantle; Capt. Percy Putt Luxmoore; Dept. Insp. of Hosps. Ahmuty Irwin; Staff-Surg. Henry Fegan; and Col. Sir Francis Worgan Festing, R.M.A.

To be K.C.M.G., Col. Francis Worgan Festing, C.B., R.M.A.
To be C.M.G., Capt. Hon. Edmund Robert Fremantle, C.B.

Her Majesty's ships which were concerned from first to last in the campaign, and their commanding officers (where these have not been already named), were:—

Active, Amethyst, Argus, Barracouta, Beacon (Com. Hamilton Dunlop), *Bittern, Coquette* (Lieut. Edward Downes Law, and later Lieut. William Eveleigh Darwall), *Decoy, Dromedary* (Nav.-Lieut. William Wallis Vine), *Druid. Encounter, Himalaya, Merlin, Rattlesnake, Seagull, Simoon, Tamar,* and *Victor Emmanuel.*

On April 23rd, 1874, the queen graciously inspected the Ashantee Naval Brigade, and the Royal Marines who had been sent to Africa. The *Barracouta's* and *Simoon's* officers did not, unfortunately, arrive in time to be present; but in the grounds of the Royal Clarence Victualling Yard, Gosport, there were 61 naval officers and seamen, 11 officers and 209 men of the Royal Marine Light Infantry, and 8 officers and 104 men of the Royal Marine Artillery.

The Zanzibar & Madagascar Slavers, 1874-1875

At about this time much success attended British efforts to repress the slave-trade, especially on the east coast of Africa.

On March 13th, 1874, the *Daphne*, 5, screw. Commander Charles

Edward Foot, made prize, off Madagascar, of one of the finest slave-*dhows* ever taken in those seas, a vessel of upwards of 200 tons' burden, with 230 slaves and forty other people onboard. She had then been eight days at sea, and had already lost thirty slaves. Unfortunately, owing to the unwillingness of the acting agent of the Union Steamship Company at Mozambique to incur the responsibility of taking over, and giving a receipt for the captives, Foot, after carrying them thither, was obliged to proceed with them to Zanzibar; and on the way, he encountered a cyclone, the results of which, and the insanitary nature of the surroundings, cost the loss of about forty more of the poor wretches ere the survivors could be landed. (*A. and N. Gazette*, May 10, June C, July 18, 1874.)

The affair naturally made some stir at the time, it being at first believed that Commander Foot was to blame for the terrible mortality, or that it was in consequence of orders from the Commander-in-Chief in the East Indies that the slaves could not be landed earlier.

In April, 1874, Captain George Lydiard Sulivan, who was selected on account of his wide experience in dealing with the slave trade, was appointed to the *London*, storeship at Zanzibar. During his period of command, he displayed great and ceaseless activity; and no fewer than 39 *dhows* were captured by the boats of the ship between October, 1874, and April, 1876. (He was superseded on Sept. 27, 1875, by Capt. Thomas Baker Martin Sulivan, who was also very active.) He was also instrumental in quelling a dangerous native insurrection which, at the end of 1874, broke out at Mombasa, about 140 miles north of Zanzibar.

Mombasa, or Mombas, which was visited by Vasco da Gama, was for many years a station of the Portuguese, who built there a fort called Mozambique in 1594, and a citadel in 1635. The Portuguese were, however, expelled by the Imam of Oman in 1698; and soon afterwards the town passed into the possession of the Mazara family, which placed it under British protection in 1823. The British soon abandoned it; whereupon, after much fighting, it was secured, in 1834, by Sayyid Said, of Zanzibar.

The outbreak of 1874 was the work of a rebel named Abdallah, who, with about 400 fighting men, seized the Portuguese fort, provisioned it for a year, and set himself up as independent. Early in January, 1875, he attacked the *Sultan's* people and burnt the town of Mombasa; and the *Sultan*, while preparing to send a force of his own to the scene of trouble, asked for British assistance.

Captain Sulivan, with 100 of his bluejackets and marines, and accompanied by the British Consul, Captain W. F. Prideaux, of the Indian Army, proceeded northward at once in the screw surveying vessel *Nassau*, 4, Lieutenant Francis John Grey. The *Rifleman*, 4, Commander Stratford Tuke, also went to the spot, and on January 19th, 1875, the vessels and their boats, after a five hours' bombardment, drove out the rebels, who lost 17 killed and 51 wounded, and occupied the fort, subsequently handing it over to the *Sultan's* representatives. The British suffered no casualties.

In the following November, some of the *London's* people, and five of her boats, under Lieutenant William Martin Annesley, were engaged at Tangata, where two hostile villages were taken and burnt.

★★★★★★

A daring act of bravery was related by the Zanzibar correspondent of the *Western Morning News*. Richard Trigger, captain of the *London's* launch, and two bluejackets named Quint and "Hope," were cruising in Captain Sulivan's yacht *Victoria*, off Pemba, when they saw a *dhow* becalmed about seven miles away. With an interpreter, they manned their dingy, and, after a two hours' pull, reached the *dhow*. There was some opposition; but Trigger, with his cutlass between his teeth, boarded over the bows. He and his comrades, seeing that the craft was full of slaves, knocked down and tied up the Arab master, put him into the dingy, made sail on the *dhow*, and, with the dingy in tow, fetched back to the *Victoria*. The *dhow* was eventually condemned at Zanzibar. This was in 1875. I believe that these men were Richard Harris Trigger (Boatswain, Sept. 30, 1876), Stephen Quint (Gunner, July 26, 1883), and Stephen Hopes (Gunner, Sept. 10, 1881).

★★★★★★

Another vessel which, at about the same period, and on the same station, was most useful in the repression of the slave trade was the screw corvette *Thetis*, 14, Captain Thomas Le Hunte Ward. During her commission, 1873-77, her boats were repeatedly employed, especially in river work, on the east coast of Africa; and on one occasion they came into collision with the natives of Madagascar. The *Flying Fish*, 4, Commander Herbert Franklyn Crohan, was also active and successful. The supply of steam-boats, in addition to pulling and sailing boats, for use by men-of-war was then a novelty. It greatly increased the utility of such cruisers as were provided with the new craft, and led to the capture of numerous *dhows* which otherwise must have escaped. (*Western Daily Mercury*. Zanzibar letter of July 2, 1875.)

The Pacific, 1874–1875

On July 2nd, 1874, the sailing schooner *Sandfly*, 1, Lieutenant William Henry George Nowell, cleared Sydney Heads for a cruise among the Pacific islands. Nothing of importance befell her until she reached Tapoua, or Edgecumbe Island, one of the Santa Cruz group, where the natives, at first very friendly, made a sudden and unprovoked attack upon the vessel on September 17th. They were then fired at and dispersed, twenty of their canoes were destroyed, and two of their villages were burnt. On September 20th, the schooner anchored off Nitendi, or Santa Cruz Island. Armed canoes quickly put out, and presently a general attack was made upon the *Sandfly*, many of the natives having previously climbed onboard.

Something like a hand-to-hand fight took place ere the assailants, who lost about thirty men, were driven off. Nowell then lowered his boats, destroyed as many abandoned canoes as he could lay hands on, and burnt two villages. On the 21st and 22nd the parties sent ashore for water had to be covered by rifle-fire, and a couple of shells were thrown into the bush. On the 23rd, the natives were again dispersed. These collisions were the cause of the visit which Commodore Goodenough paid to the island nearly a year later, and which had so fatal a result. In the course of the cruise, the *Sandfly* also called at Api, or Tasiko Island, in the New Hebrides, where she shelled a village by way of punishing certain natives who, some time before, had murdered and eaten a boat's crew belonging to a vessel named the *Zephyr*. She returned to Port Jackson on December 10th, 1874.

On May 22nd, 1873, Captain James Graham Goodenough had been appointed to the *Pearl*, 17, as Commodore on the Australian station; and in the following August he arrived at Sydney. (*Sydney Empire*, Dec. 11, 1874.) After having taken part in the inquiries which preceded the annexation of the Fiji Islands in October, 1874, he conveyed Sir Arthur Hamilton Gordon, (1st Baron Stanmore, 1893), as Governor, to Levuka, and then sailed for a cruise to the New Hebrides and Santa Cruz groups. He visited Ambrym, Mallicolo, Saint Bartholomew, Espiritu Santo, and Vanikoro. On August 12th, 1875, accompanied by some officers and men, the commodore landed in Carlisle Bay, Santa Cruz Island, his intention being to conciliate the natives, and to open friendly intercourse with them.

The people assembled on the beach, showed no signs of hostility, and were ready to barter. They even received Goodenough in their village, and allowed him to mix freely with them. But, as the party was re-embarking, a man discharged a poisoned arrow, which struck the commodore in the left side; and, before the British could get to their arms, several flights of arrows were fired at them, and six people were wounded, (including Sub-Lieut. Henry Colley Hawker), Goodenough also being again hit, though slightly. On returning to the ship the commodore resolved to punish the act of treachery by burning the village which had been the scene of the attack; and he therefore sent in four boats for the purpose; but he expressly ordered that no life should be taken.

He might, with reason, have been much more severe, for, as has been noted, the *Sandfly* had been attacked at the same place in the previous September. Moreover, he had more than a suspicion that the wounds had been inflicted with poisoned arrows, and would prove fatal. Unhappily, they did so, in three cases out of seven. A seaman died on August 19th, Goodenough himself on the 20th, and another seaman on the 21st.

The *Pearl* returned to Sydney on the 23rd with the commodore's body, which was publicly buried on the 24th at St. Leonard's cemetery in the presence of thousands of people, and of officers, seamen and marines, from the *Pearl* and *Sappho*. Goodenough's grave lies near that of the eminent surveyor and Arctic navigator, Captain Owen Stanley, who died in 1850. That officer's brother. Dean Stanley, in a sermon at Westminster Abbey on November 1st, 1875, spoke of the commodore as:

> One of England's best seamen, a man tender as he was brave, a man of science, full of the highest aspirations, fit for any great work—such a one as no nation can afford to lose lightly.

It is a strange coincidence that Goodenough's last public act in New South Wales was to unveil at Randwick a statue of Captain James Cook (1), an officer who, besides having many characteristics in common with him, met death in almost exactly the same way—at the hands of savages who attacked without provocation. (C. R. Markham: *Commodore J. G. Goodenough*. Goodenough to Admiralty, Aug. 19th, 1875.) Goodenough had received the C.M.G. in 1874, and the C.B. in 1875.

PART OF THE
MALAY
PENINSULA

0 10 20 30 40 50 60 70 80
Scale of Miles.

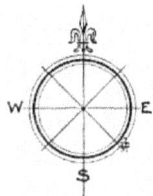

W E
S

Pulo
Penang
R.Krean
R.Kulong
Kurou R.
Silensing R.
Larut R.
Telok Karlang
Bruas R.
R.Dinding
Dinding I.
Perak R.
Bernam R.
PERAK R.
Wellesley
Province

Wellesley Prov.
Bast R.
R.Krean
Plus R.
Perak River
Qualla Kangsa
Kangsa R.
Kinta
Blanja Balli
Kinta River
Passir-Salat
Banda Baru
Kota Stia
R.Durian
Durian S'batang
S'batang
Bernam

Scale of Miles.
0 10 20 30

Pahang
China Sea
Selangor
Jellebu Johpolo
Dato Muti
Sungei Ujong Srimanti
Johole
LANGAT
Rambow
Janina
Malacca
Territy
Moar
S.LUKUT
R.LIMGIT
MALACCA
MALACCA R.
Malacca Strait
Sumatra
Johore
SUNGA River
I. of Singapore

The Malay Peninsula, 1873-1876

In November, 1873, Sir H. St. George Ord, C.B., had been succeeded as Governor of the Straits' Settlements by that distinguished
administrator. General Sir Andrew Clarke, K.C.M.G. Up to that date
the relations between the British authorities and the various native
states of the Malay peninsula had been generally unsatisfactory. It is
true that these relations had been regulated by treaties, as, for example, those of 1818 and 1826 with Perak, and those of 1818 and 1825
with Selangor; but frequent civil wars, chronic piracy, the tyranny,
weakness, and self-indulgence of the local princes, and the numerous
disputes between the dominant chiefs and the Chinese settlers within
their territories prevented the development of the country, especially
on the west coast, crippled trade, and gave perpetual cause for active
British intervention.

The new governor might have found plenty of excuse for con-
quering and annexing the more troublesome provinces. Instead, he
set about thoroughly mastering the origin and history of the disor-
ders which prevailed among his semi-civilised neighbours, and then,
while maintaining a firm and inflexible attitude with regard to piracy,
embarked upon a policy of attempting to arrange all difficulties by
pacific methods, and of endeavouring to induce the chiefs to accept
British counsel and assistance in the management of their affairs. The
work which he thus mapped out for himself was of a very laborious
nature, and for a time the results were disappointing; but the outcome
of Clarke's wise and far-sighted action was ultimately the addition to
the British Empire of a number of protected states which, while retaining much of their independence, submitted contentedly to British
methods of government, and became valuable outworks of civilisation
instead of instating centres of turbulence along its borders.

As early as January 20th, 1874, Sir Andrew concluded with Perak
a treaty in virtue of which the Raja Muda was recognised as *Sultan*
of that long distracted country, and a resident and an assistant-resident
were appointed to aid him in preserving order in his state. Later in
the same year residents were also appointed to Selangor and Sungei
Ujong. Even that measure of success, however, was not secured until
the imagination of the chiefs had been stimulated by naval demon-
strations, which, owing to the fortuitous presence in that part of the
station of Vice-Admiral Charles Frederick Alexander Shadwell and a
considerable part of the China command, could, when desirable, be

carried out upon an impressive scale.

The coast of Perak at that time swarmed with pirates; and on the night of December 11th, 1873, the *Avon*, 4, Commander John Conyngham Patterson, being near the Dindings, was so fortunate as to come upon three trading craft at the moment when they were being attacked by six boats full of these cut-throats. (Patterson had retired with the rank of captain Oct. 1, 1873, but remained in command pending the arrival of his successor.) She fired upon the scoundrels, and drove them off with loss, but did not succeed in capturing any of them at the time. Proceeding in January, however, to Silemseng, near the mouth of the Larut River, and taking with him the armed steamer *Johore*, Sub-Lieutenant Charles Skelton Nicholson, Patterson, who had satisfied himself as to the complicity of some of the local people, enforced the surrender of a number of *junks*, many men, and a quantity of arms, and burnt some houses. (Patterson to Woollcombe, Dec. 13, 1873; Jan. 21, 1874.) This action sufficed to convince the people of Perak that the British were in earnest. To convince the other states, more imposing action was employed.

Previous to the inception of negotiations with Selangor, it was deemed necessary to induce the *Sultan* of that state to promise to make reparation for certain serious piratical acts which, not long before, had been committed by some of his subjects to the prejudice of British residents at Malacca; and, to attain the object in view, Vice-Admiral Shadwell himself appeared in his flagship, the *Iron Duke*, Captain William Arthur, off the mouth of the Klang and Langkat Rivers, where, by appointment, he met the governor on February 6th, 1874.

There were also assembled the *Thalia*, 6, Captain Henry Bedford Woollcombe; *Salamis*, 2, dispatch-vessel, Lieutenant the Hon. Algernon Charles Littleton; *Rinaldo*, 7, Commander George Parsons; *Frolic*, 4, Commander Claude Edward Buckle; *Midge*, 4, Commander John Frederick George Grant; *Avon*, 4, Commander Armand Temple Powlett; and the colonial steamer *Pluto*.

Shadwell and Clarke went up the Klang River to Langkat on the 7th, and, on the three following days, effected a satisfactory arrangement with the Sultan of Selangor, who agreed upon measures for the punishment of the pirates, and assented to the destruction of certain stockades. Captain Woollcombe remained as senior officer, with the *Thalia, Rinaldo, Midge*, and *Avon*, and eventually occupied two stockades near the mouth of the Jugra River. These, after having been held for a fortnight, were burnt. (All corresp. relating to these events is to be found in Command Paper 1111, of 1874.)

Another focus of piratical activity was the Lingie River, between the British state of Malacca and the friendly native state of Sungei Ujong, where stockades had been erected under the alleged authority of the chief of Rumbow. At the beginning of May, 1874, Sir Andrew Clarke went to the Lingie River in the *Charybdis*, 17, Captain Thomas Edward Smith, accompanied by the *Avon*, 4, Commander Armand Temple Powlett, and the colonial steamer *Pluto*. The chief of Rumbow made excuses for not attending a conference to which he had been invited, whereupon the governor, on May 4th, gave his support to the chief, or *klana*, of Sungei Ujong, who, without opposition, occupied the offending stockades at Bukit Tiga. They had been abandoned a few hours earlier. This action was of great commercial importance, as it reopened the Lingie River to the trade to and from the rich tin mines in the interior.

In the following September the *Charybdis* and *Avon*, together with the *Hart*, 4, Commander Thomas Harvey Royse, took part in an expedition to the Indau River, a stream which runs into the sea on the east coast of the peninsula, and which forms the frontier between Johore and Pahang. Sir Andrew Clarke's object in going thither was to compose some differences between the rulers of those two states. He was very successful.

Soon afterwards serious disputes arose in Sungei Ujong between the *klana*, or ruling chief, and the *bandar*, a feudatory of great wealth and influence. As the former had already asked for a British resident to be sent to his court, and as the latter was intractable in spite of Sir Andrew Clarke's repeated efforts to persuade him to adopt reasonable courses, it was decided to support the *klana*, who had been forced to begin hostilities on November 16th, 1874. On November 24th, accordingly, Clarke proceeded to the mouth of the Lukut River in the *Charybdis*, with the *Hart* in company, and a small military force including men of the 10th Regiment and of the Royal Artillery.

On the 26th the troops were disembarked, together with a small Naval Brigade, (officers 6, seamen and marines 67: from the *Charybdis*), under Lieutenant John George Jones, Acting-Lieutenant Gerard Marmaduke Brooke, Lieutenant Robert Evans Montgomery, R.M.L.I., Surgeon George Gibson, Gunner Edwin Bishop, and Midshipman Charles Brownlow Macdonald, and on the 27th began to march inland, (Smith to Shadwell, Nov. 26; Jones to Smith, Dec. 10, 1874), ten marines under Montgomery being, however, left in charge at Lukut.

Clarke in the meantime went on in the *Hart* to Langkat, in order to warn the Selangor authorities against affording assistance to the insurgents.

The force which included the Naval Brigade had a most trying two days' march ere it arrived, on November 28th, within three miles of Campayang, the *bandar's* headquarters, where a halt was called. A reconnaissance, however, brought on some firing, and the advance was resumed in consequence. As soon as the leading body, under Brooke, showed itself, it was fired at from the stockades. A rocket-tube was brought up; and after about half-an-hour's action, in the course of which Robert Chambers, captain of the main-top, was fatally wounded, the enemy was nearly silenced. As darkness was falling the expedition withdrew for the night. On the following morning it was announced that Sir Andrew Clarke had sent up orders that the *bandar* was to be given twenty-four hours in which to come to terms.

On the 30th, no reply having been received from the rebel, the force again advanced, but discovered to its disgust that the place had been evacuated by the Malays, and occupied by a number of Chinese *coolies*, who were already quarrelling over the loot, and who did not desist until about fifty of them had been killed. (Corr. of A. and N. Gazette, Feb. 20, 1875.) The guns found were four of iron, about 12-prs., and two of brass, about 2-prs. Yet another gun, which had been captured from the British on some previous occasion, was recovered. The place was burnt. Parties were afterwards sent out in all directions to look for the *bandar*; but he could not be caught, and the Naval Brigade had to return empty-handed to the *Charybdis*, which was reached on January 10th, 1875. The chief surrendered later.

Towards the middle of 1875 Governor Sir Andrew Clarke was succeeded by Sir W. F. D. Jervois. The affairs of the peninsula had settled down, and the general outlook was exceedingly encouraging when, on November 2nd, 1875, Mr. J. W. W. Birch, the resident in Perak, was murdered near Passir Sala, together with several of his attendants. Jervois at first mistook the outrage for one of a personal and isolated character, and ordered to the spot 100 troops from Singapore, 60 from Penang, and armed police from various quarters. He also went thither himself. Upon arriving in the Perak River on November 8th, he learnt that on the 7th a small party, including a naval officer and four seamen with a rocket-tube, had attacked the village in which Birch had been killed, and had been defeated with loss.

★★★★★★

Sub.-Lieut. Thomas Francis Abbott, of the *Thistle*, had been left at Banda Bahru, with four men, for instructional purposes. Stirling to Jervois, Oct. 16, 1875; Jervois to Carnarvon, Nov. 16, 1875. Abbott behaved admirably. Going up under fire from Banda Bahru to Passir Sala, upon hearing of the murder, he took charge of the residency, and entrenched himself on the island on which it was built. It was after this that he joined in the attack on the village. He was promoted Jan. 28, 1876.

★★★★★★

Jervois then came to the conclusion that the disturbance was much more serious than he had at first supposed; and he applied for rein-forcements, naval and military.

The only men-of-war on the spot were the *Thistle*, 4, Commander Francis Stirling, and the *Fly*, 4, Commander John Bruce, which went up the Perak River on the 8th with such few additional troops as by that time had been collected. From the China station were despatched the *Modeste*, 14, Captain Alexander Buller, the *Egeria*, 4, Commander Ralph Lancelot Turton, and the *Ringdove*, 3, Commander Uvedale Corbet Singleton, and, from the East India station, the *Philomel*, 3, Commander Edmund St. John Garforth. There being trouble in Sungei Ujong, a detachment from the *Thistle* was left in the Lingie and Lukut Rivers when the gun-vessel herself went to the northward. The *Ringdove*, upon her arrival, steamed up the Perak River to Durian S'batang, where she established a base; and a small Brigade from the *Thistle* and *Fly*, under Commander Stirling, pressing on with some troops, made such rapid progress that, on November 15th, the force was able to attack the stronghold of the chief in whose district Birch had been assassinated.

★★★★★★

Naval Brigade employed near Passir Sala on Nov. 14-16, 1875, under Commander Francis Stirling (*Thistle*): from *Thistle*, Lieut. Arthur Hill Ommanney Peter Lowe, Sub-Lieut. Thomas Francis Abbott, Boatswain Joseph Tyler, and twenty-five men: from *Fly*, Commander John Bruce, Lieut. William Codrington Carnegie Forsyth, Sub-Lieut. Duncan Munro Ross, Surgeon Edward Thomas Lloyd, Boatswain George Vosper, and twenty-five men; with one 7-pr., two 12-pr. howitzers, one coehorn mortar, and two 24-pr. rocket-tubes. Stirling to Ryder, Nov. 10, 1875.

★★★★★★

Four stockades and six guns were taken, without loss on the British side, the houses and villages of the offending people were destroyed, and the resident's papers and effects were recovered. (Dunlop to Jervois, Nov. 16, 1875. The Naval Brigade here employed was eighty-five strong.)

The trouble in Sungei Ujong was soon quelled. The insurgent Malays were badly defeated on December 7th by a purely military force, and on December 22nd were again attacked and dispersed by a detachment which included 32 officers and men from the *Thistle* under Commander Stirling. (Jervois to Carnarvon, Dec. 28, 1875.) The later operations in that state were carried out without much further help from the navy.

In the meantime the chiefs responsible for the Perak outrage, and for the political movements with which it was connected, had withdrawn to the district on the upper reaches of the Perak River; and it was decided to attack them simultaneously from two directions, *viz.*, by a force, under Major-General Sir Francis Colborne, moving up the Perak upon Blanja, and by another force under Brigadier-General J. Ross, disembarked at Telok Kartang, near the mouth of the Larut River, and moving overland thence eastward to Qualla Kangsa, on the Perak, afterwards, if necessary, advancing down the stream upon Blanja. While the movements were in preparation, the *Thistle* lay for a time in the Perak, near the point at which that river is joined by its northeast affluent, the Kinta; and the *Modeste, Fly,* and *Egeria* blockaded the Perak littoral from the mouth of the Bernam to that of the Krean. The *Egeria* also sent her boats up the Kurow River, and destroyed or carried off some guns, arms, and ammunition which might have been useful to the enemy. (Turton to Buller, Dec. 2, 1875.)

To Major-General Sir F. Colborne's advance up the Perak River from Durian S'batang and Banda Bahru was attached a Naval Brigade from the *Modeste, Ringdove,* and *Thistle,* consisting of 10 officers and 60 seamen. To Brig.-General Ross's advance across country from the mouth of the Larut to Qualla Kangsa was attached a Brigade from the *Philomel, Modeste,* and *Ringdove,* consisting of 7 officers and 98 seamen and marines.

★★★★★★

Naval officers employed with the Perak Field Force, Dec. 1875: from *Modeste,* Capt. Alexander Buller, senior naval officer. Straits' Division, Lieut. John Pakenham Pipon, Sub-Lieut. Walter Travers Warren, Gunner John Grant, Mids. Mansfield George Smith, Surgeon Charles Cane Godding, and Asst.-Paymaster William

Codgbrooke Gillies; from *Ringdove*, Com. Uvedale Corbet Singleton, Nav. Sub-Lieut. Valentine David Hughes, and Surgeon Anthony Gorham. Buller to Admlty., Dec. 19th and 29th, 1875. Naval officers employed with the Larut Field Force, Dec. 1875, Jan. 1876: from *Philomel*, Com. Edmund St. John Garforth, Lieut. Robert Thomas Wood, Sub-Lieut. Richard Poore, and Surgeon Robert William Williams; from *Modeste*, Lieut. Henry Townley Wright, Sub-Lieut. James Pipon Montgomery, and Mids. Thomas Philip Walker. Garforth to Ryder, Dec. 13, 1875.

★★★★★★

Buller records that the advance from Banda Bahru was begun on December 8th, and that Blanja was entered on the 13th, without opposition. The chiefs implicated in Mr. Birch's murder were reported to have fled eastward to Kinta, the capital. The Perak Field Force left 50 soldiers and 22 naval officers and men at Blanja, and started in pursuit on the 14th. Two miles out of Blanja opposition was met with, but the enemy was easily driven off. Later in the day a Malay stockade made a brief stand, but was evacuated upon a rocket-tube being brought into action. The Brigade halted for the night seven miles from Blanja, the advance having been intensely arduous, and, on the 15th moved forward six or seven miles further to Pappan. On the 16th the Brigade got within half a mile of Kinta, and, after some interchange of shot, entered it, the enemy fleeing up the Kinta River, and abandoning nine brass guns. The fugitive chiefs escaped into Lower Siam.

Garforth records that he landed his men at the mouth of the Larut River on December 11th and 13th, with a 24-pr. rocket-tube and a 7-pr. gun. He reached Qualla Kangsa without adventure.

Brig.-General Ross lay for some days at Qualla Kangsa, and on January 4th, 1876, proceeded thence with a force, which included 32 officers and men of Garforth's Brigade, to inflict punishment upon the village of Kotah Lamah, three miles further up the Perak River on the left bank.

A detachment of the troops were unexpectedly attacked by a concealed body of Malays, and, it was generally admitted, would have been cut to pieces, but for the extreme gallantry displayed by the seamen, who had been formed up as a guard for the Brig.-General. Lieutenant Wood, Sub-Lieutenant Poore, and seamen Henry Thompson, Henry Bonnet, and David Sloper gained special commendation for their bravery in this affair. (Jervois to Carnarvon, Jan. 14, 1876, with enclosures: Garforth to Ryder, Jan. 6.) The naval casualties were two killed or mortally wounded.

Stirling's share in the operations in Sungei Ujong was of a most creditable character, and his despatches single out for special mention Navigating Sub-Lieutenant Michael Stephens Beatty, and Assistant-Paymaster Thomas Foley Harrison, the latter of whom did duty as an executive officer. (Stirling to Buller, Dec. 21, 1875, and Jan. 7, 1876.)

These operations, and a punitive attack made on a village near Blanja by a small force which included a naval detachment under Lieutenant Henry Townley Wright, of the *Modeste*, practically brought the brief campaign to a satisfactory conclusion, though for some time afterwards much unrest prevailed on the Perak River. Ismail, the principal offending chief, surrendered at Penang on March 20th, 1876, and most of the other persons implicated also fell one by one into British hands. Garforth remained for some time in the neighbourhood of Qualla Kangsa, and, on February 4th, 1876, was slightly engaged at Enggar, but suffered no casualties.

Among the consequent rewards and promotions were the following:—

To be C.B.: Captain Alexander Buller, Mar. 25, 1876.

To be Captains: Commanders Francis Stirling, Mar. 9, and Edmund St. John Garforth, Aug. 18, 1876.

To be Commander: Lieutenant Henry Townley Wright, Mar. 9, 1876.

To be Lieutenants: Sub-Lieutenants Richard Poore, and Walter Travers Warren, Mar. 9, 1876.

Minor Operations, 1873–1876

In the autumn of 1875 a punitive expedition was once more sent up the River Congo. At the beginning of that year the trading schooner *Geraldine* had stranded while proceeding up the stream, and had been attacked and looted by native pirates, four of her people being killed while endeavouring to defend their ship.

It having been determined to punish the marauders, the paddle-sloop *Spiteful*, 6, entered the river early in August to reconnoitre the various creeks; and on August 30th, the vessels found in the list over the page proceeded up the Congo.

At 6 a.m. on August 31st the boats of the *Active, Encounter,* and *Spiteful* left their ships, and were towed to the entrance of Change Creek, four miles up which 150 marines, under Captain Bradshaw,

SHIPS.	GUNS.	COMMANDERS.
Active, scr. . .	10	Sir Wm. Nathan Wrighte Hewett, K.C.B., V.C., Commod. Com. Robert Lowther Byng.
Encounter, scr. .	14	Capt. Richard Bradshaw.
Spiteful, padd. .	6	Com. Mervyn Bradford Medlycott.
Merlin, scr. g.b. .	4	Lieut. Wollaston Comyns Karslake.
Foam, scr. g.b. .	4	Lieut. Henry Chapman Walker.
Ariel, scr. g.b. .	4	Lieut. Orford Churchill.
Supply, st. ship. .	2	Staff-Com. Frank Inglis.

were disembarked. The party destroyed three villages, and, though it sighted no enemy, was fired at from the dense jungle, but had no casualties. On September 2nd, the gunboats and the boats of the larger vessels bombarded several villages on the northern bank. A detachment which was landed discovered in the houses some relics of the plundered merchantman. There was again firing from the jungle, but only one man was wounded. All the villages on the north bank, as far as Melilla Creek, were destroyed. On the 3rd, other villages were bombarded; and a force which was landed, burnt yet other villages, and marched to the town of the chief, Armanzanga, who had been marked out for severe punishment.

In spite of dropping shots from the bush the place was taken and destroyed; and Captain Bradshaw, on his way back to the creek, burnt additional villages. On the 4th, the *Encounter* and *Spiteful* steamed further up the river and punished the natives in Luculla Creek; and the *Merlin* and other craft proceeded to Punta da Lenha, where Commodore Hewett summoned the local chief to give up the murderers of the *Geraldine's* people within forty-eight hours.

No reply being vouchsafed, the place was attacked by a landing party on the 7th; and, in spite of a brisk fire, it was taken and delivered to the flames. On the 8th, the boats returning down the north bank, a landing was effected under fire near Manoel Vacca's town, which was found to be deserted, and was razed to the ground. On the 10th, the smaller craft entered Sherwood creek, where two chiefs came off, and, visiting the commodore, were assured that people who had behaved themselves would not be interfered with.

On the 11th Commander Medlycott, with the *Spiteful's* boats and a detachment of bluejackets and marines, destroyed Polo Bolo, having one man wounded. On the 12th, the commodore, with the three gunboats, ascended the river to Emboma, seventy-three miles from the mouth, and there, on the 15th, had an interview with seven kings or chiefs, who expressed satisfaction with the work which had been done, and hoped that, since the pirates had been so severely punished, the peaceful trade in the river would increase. Sir William Hewett returned on the 17th, and a few days afterwards the ships separated. (Hewett's disps., and *St. Helena Guardian.*)

The labours of the expedition were most arduous, some of the creeks being literally overgrown with luxuriant vegetation which had to be cut away to admit of an advance, and the country generally being difficult to a degree. The entire loss by the enemy's fire, however, was only one killed (a Portuguese guide), and six wounded (including Engineer Robert Dixon, of the *Ariel*). Nor was there, at the time, much sickness. Later, however, the effects of the malarious climate showed themselves; and among those who perished from the results of the brief campaign were Navigating Lieutenant Edmond Carter Smith, and Paymaster William Alfred Brown, both of the *Encounter*. Numerous officers were mentioned as having rendered conspicuous service, the list including Captain Bradshaw, Commander Medlycott, (posted, Nov. 1, 1875), Lieutenant Karslake, (com., Nov. 1, 1875); Lieutenant Adolphus Brett Crosbie, R.M., Lieutenant Thomas Peere Williams Nesham, Lieutenant Ernest Neville Rolfe, Fleet-Surgeon Henry Fegan, C.B., Paymaster William Alfred Brown, and Sub-Lieutenants Arthur Charles Middlemass, (Lieut., Nov. 1, 1875), and Percy Moreton Scott, (Lieut., Nov. 1, 1875.)

In these years there was much unrest along the shores of the Gulf of Oman and the Persian Gulf. In 1873, Commander Robert Moore Gillson, of the *Rifleman*, 4, had to land a party, under Sub-Lieutenant Harry George Grey, for the protection of the Indo-European Company's telegraph station at Gwadur, Baluchistan; and in March, 1874, the fort of Masnaah, Gulf of Oman, was attacked and reduced by a naval force under Commander Edmund St. John Garforth, of the *Philomel*, 3, who was assisted by the *Nimble*, 5, Commander Henry Compton Best, and the *Hugh Rose*, of the Bombay Marine, the last named having on board a party from the *Rifleman* to work her guns. In August, 1875, intervention again became necessary in consequence of a disturbance at Muscat.

The reigning *Sultan*, Sayyid Turki, had occasion to visit Gwadur, which belonged to him, and, proceeding thither in the *Rifleman*, then commanded by Commander Francis Starkie Clayton, left Oman and Muscat in charge of his brother Abdul Ayuz. When, on August 25th, the *Daphne*, 5, Commander Charles Edward Foot, happened to call at

Muscat, the place was found to be in possession of the Bedouins. The presence of the man-of-war, however, which despatched four of her boats to police the coast, prevented the commission of any outrages; and, the situation having quieted down, trade was resumed.

On October 3rd, up to which time the *Daphne* remained off the town, news arrived that a former *Sultan*, Salim bin Thoweynee, who had been warned by the Indian Government not to enter Oman, was about to return and seize the throne. Commander Foot, in consequence, weighed and cruised to intercept him, and, after several disappointments, discovered the pretender on the 10th off the Suadi Islands. Boats were manned and armed, and he and his two *dhows* were captured without resistance. Two or three hours later he would have disembarked on the mainland, and would have been able to elude pursuit. (Muscat letter of Oct. 16 in *A. and N. Gaz.*, Nov. 20, 1875.)

A hostile collision between Great Britain and Egypt was within a little of taking place towards the end of 1875. Both Egypt and Zanzibar claimed the coastline north of the River Juba. It was occupied, however, by, and was eventually confirmed to, Zanzibar. Nevertheless, an Egyptian squadron, under M'Killop Pasha, had sailed down the coast, and substituted the Egyptian for the Zanzibari flag at Barawa. (Henry Fredk. M'Killop, a Capt. R.N. of 1862, who had retired in 1870.) Upon hearing of this Dr. John Kirk, British consul at Zanzibar, proceeded to the spot in the *Thetis*, 14, Captain Thomas Le Hunte Ward, in order to see how matters stood, and to look after the interests of the numerous Indian subjects of the queen who resided there.

Kirk and Ward landed, but other persons from the corvette were prevented from doing so, the Egyptians threatening to fire on them. Having returned on board, the consul demanded an apology, and the concession of the right of British officers to land without interference. Both demands were refused; and the *Thetis* had actually cleared for action and prepared to land bluejackets and marines ere the *commandant* on shore changed his mind, and hurriedly gave way. (Zanzibar corr. of *Western Morning News*.)

For some time afterwards, the *Thetis* was very active in the suppression of the slave trade off the east coast of Africa, capturing numerous *dhows* in the course of 1876-77.

The *Dido*, 8, Captain William Cox Chapman, which was paid off in the summer of 1876 after having been absent from Portsmouth for more than five years, served a singularly useful commission, owing largely to the tact and good temper of the officer in command. In the autumn of 1871 she was instrumental in settling without bloodshed a dispute among the kings of New Calabar, Bonny, and Ekrika, on the Niger, and in procuring safety for British trade in that river. In 1873 she was similarly successful in effecting a peaceful solution of difficulties which had arisen in Fiji between the native government and the white settlers. She also returned to their homes in the New Hebrides and other groups a number of South Sea islanders who had been kidnapped by a notorious brig named the *Carl*.

In 1874 she assisted the crew of the French man-of-war *Ermite*, which had been wrecked on Wallace Island, and was present at the formal transfer of the Fiji Islands to the British flag. On the death of Commodore Goodenough, Captain Chapman was appointed Commodore on the Australian station pending the arrival there of Captain Anthony Hiley Hoskins. A large proportion of the officers who left England with her in 1871 returned in her in 1876. The record of her commission, though unexciting, serves as a good example of the unostentatious but valuable work which is often done by British men-of-war of whose proceedings little or nothing is ever heard at home. (*A. and N. Gazette*, June 10, 1870.) It may be added that, on the occasion of one of her visits to Fiji, the *Dido* was so unfortunate as to introduce measles among the native population, and that lamentable loss of life followed. (Proc. of Ho. of Commons, Aug, 1, 1876.)

Samoa, 1868–1876

For many years, from 1868 onwards, a series of petty civil wars raged almost without intermission in the Navigators' Islands, better known as Samoa. At first nothing occurred to excuse active British interference, but in 1876 Captain Charles Edward Stevens, of the paddle-sloop *Barracouta*, 5, who was then at Apia, considered it to be his duty to intervene. It appears that an American named Steinberger had been appointed by the king to be prime minister for life, and that the king nevertheless desired to get rid of him. It was alleged that both the king and the American consul requested Stevens to take charge of Steinberger. The premier, therefore, was arrested, and conveyed on board the *Barracouta*.

This procedure was bitterly resented by the other ministers and the holders of offices, nearly all of whom owed their places to Steinberger; and they retaliated by seizing the king and transporting him to an outlying island. The *Barracouta* took on board Malietoa, the exiled monarch; and Stevens, landing with fifty seamen and marines at Apia, the capital, on March 13th, marched to the council-house, where the legislature was assembled, with a view to the restoration of His Majesty. The natives resisted; the marines were ordered to disarm them; a fight ensued; and two marines and one seaman were killed, and five marines and three seamen wounded. Only three natives fell in the struggle.

Stevens withdrew to the ship with his wounded, and then landed again with guns, and erected breastworks which he held for a fortnight. During that time, he was not re-attacked; and finally, he went back to the *Barracouta* on March 27th with three chiefs as hostages. Upon being relieved by the *Sapphire*, 14, Captain Elibank Harley Murray, the *Barracouta* transferred the native prisoners to her, and, with Steinberger on board, proceeded to Auckland by way of the Fiji Islands. (London newspapers of May 25, 1876; Stevens's disp. of Mar. 20: *A. and N. Gazette* of May 13 and 27, 1876.) This was the earliest of a number of interventions which would have been justifiable only if the home government had been consistently determined that British influence should be always paramount in Samoa. Seeing, however, that no steady policy was ever formed with regard to the islands, and that at length, in 1899, the group, with the assent of Great Britain, was divided between the United States and Germany, it is, perhaps, to be regretted that on several subsequent occasions, as in 1876, British life was sacrificed in support of causes which were in no adequate sense of imperial interest.

Stevens's interference was, there is no doubt, particularly unwise. He was a truculent and imperious officer, and, a little later, was tried, and dismissed the service, for tyrannical conduct. (C. M. of Ap. 11, 1877.) The action of the Samoans could not, however, be overlooked. The *Pearl* visited the islands to make enquiries; and eventually a claim for 6000 dollars, on account of the loss of life among the *Barracouta's* people, was lodged by the British Government. In the spring of 1878. the *Sapphire*, still commanded by Captain Murray, was sent to Apia to enforce the demand. As the natives declined to pay, preparations to bombard the town were made on March 18th. Happily, the Samoans gave way at the very last moment, and so saved further effusion of blood.

Niger & Dahomey, 1876–1877

In June, 1876, some native chiefs on the banks of the lower reaches of the River Niger took it into their heads to interfere with the navigation of the stream, and especially to endeavour to obstruct the outward passage of a British merchant steamer, the *Sultan of Sokoto*. As there had been previous outrages and unrest Commodore Sir William Nathan Wrighte Hewett, V.C., K.C.B., transferred his broad pennant from the *Active*, as being too large a ship for the work, to the *Sultan of Sokoto*, and directed the composite gunboats, *Cygnet*, 4, Lieutenant Robert Frederick Hammick, and *Ariel*, 4, Lieutenant Orford Churchill, to send their spare stores and their upper spars on board the corvette.

On July 29th, the two gunboats, being thus lightened, crossed the Nun bar and anchored in Akassa Creek; and, on the following day, in company with the *Sultan of Sokoto*, which had taken on board four guns and thirty marines from the *Active*, they moved up to a point half a mile above the village of Akado, where a party was landed, and three small guns were taken possession of without resistance.

On the 31st the ships weighed, and, after stopping at various places to communicate with the natives, anchored off Sabogrega at 5 p.m. The *Active's* steam launch was sent in to palaver with the people, who, however, made signs to Lieutenant Ernest Neville Rolfe, who was in charge, to keep off, and then opened fire. Sir William Hewett at once signalled to the gunboats to bombard the town, which was of considerable size and strongly defended with rifle-pits and stockades formed of trunks of trees. The natives replied in a spirited manner both with heavy guns and with small arms. At dark the shelling was discontinued, and preparations were made to assault the place on the following day.

At 5.30 a.m. on August 1st, accordingly, the bombardment was recommenced, and a landing-party of bluejackets and marines was assembled round the *Cygnet* in boats under the command of Commander James Andrew Thomas Bruce (*Active*). The rocket-party was under Lieutenant Thomas Peere Williams Nesham; the Royal Marines were under Lieutenant Adolphus Brett Crosbie, R.M.L.I.; the boats of the *Cygnet* were under Sub-Lieutenant Francis John Oldfield Thomas; and the boats of the *Ariel* were under Sub-Lieutenant Frederick Rigaud Gransmore. When everything was ready the boats dashed in under a galling musketry fire, dislodged the enemy, burnt the lower town, flung the heavy guns into the river, and blew up a quantity of powder. The force then re-embarked, and pulled up stream a quarter of a mile to the upper town.

Commander Bruce's gig, and the *Cygnet's* cutter, being in advance, did not wait for the main body, but landed at once, whereupon their people were set upon by an overwhelming force of the enemy, and somewhat roughly treated ere the other boats got up. The upper town was then destroyed, and the force, returning on board, moved up to Agberi, which, in the course of the afternoon, was burnt without much resistance. That day's work cost the squadron the loss of one marine killed, and of five officers and nine men wounded.

★★★★★★

Lieut. T. P. W. Nesham; Sub-Lieuts. F. J. O. Thomas, and John Casement (*Mallard*); Rev. Fras. Chas. Lang, Chaplain; and Paym. Hy. Cecil Wm. Gibson, Secretary. Nesham, Thomas, and Casement were promoted on Oct. 3, 1876. Sub-Lieuts. Harry Campbell Reynolds and Tom Bowden Triggs, both of the *Active*, were also promoted on Oct. 13.

★★★★★★

On August 2nd, 3rd, and 4th, the force proceeded steadily up the river, and on the 5th it reached Onitcha, about 170 miles above the Nun bar. Commodore Hewett there, on the 6th, had a satisfactory interview with the king, after which he returned, stopping, however, to burn Akado, at the point where the channel had been obstructed in June. The expedition re-anchored in Akassa Creek on the 10th, and, on the 11th, recrossed the bar, after having accomplished its objects in a most satisfactory manner. (Hewett's disps.; Madeira telegram of Sept. 5; Corr. of *Times*, Sept. 14.)

In order to carry out this Niger Expedition, Sir William Hewett was temporarily called away from troublesome business which occupied him elsewhere, and which, indeed, was his chief preoccupation during nearly the whole of the year 1876. Quite early in that year, Gelelé, King of Dahomey, who had succeeded his father Gezo in 1858, and who ever since had been intractable and anti-British, committed certain outrages on the persons of British subjects at Whydah. Hewett proceeded to the spot in February, and, having held an enquiry, sentenced the king to pay a heavy fine, and threatened that, unless the fine were paid within three months, the coast would be blockaded from June 1st onwards. (Hewett's letter to Brit. traders, dated off Lagos, Mar. 4, 1870.)

When the terms of this warning were conveyed to the Admiralty, their Lordships, for some not very obvious reason, directed that no blockade should be established until after June 30th, (*Gazette*, May 23, 1876), and so, it would appear, unwittingly encouraged Gelelé in his contumacy; for he showed no signs of any intention to hand over the 500 puncheons of palm oil demanded.

On and from July 1st, accordingly, a blockade was declared between 1° 30" and 2° 35" East, the *Spiteful*, 5, paddle, Commander Armand Temple Powlett, being stationed at Whydah, and the gunboat *Ariel*, Lieutenant Orford Churchill, being stationed at Little Popo to enforce it, and to protect British interests. (*A. and N. Gaz.* July 20, 1876.) Vessels already in the blockaded ports were, however, allowed thirty days wherein to load and depart. Gelelé retaliated by seizing some French subjects; and, as he held them practically as hostages, considerations for their safety thenceforth fettered Hewett to a very inconvenient extent. And so, the affair dragged on.

In the course of it, Captain Charles Pringle, of the *Sirius*, 12, one of the vessels engaged, succumbed to coast fever, and was ultimately succeeded by Captain George Lydiard Sulivan, who, towards the end of the blockade, was senior officer on the coast. Hewett, too, whose period of command expired in due course, was succeeded as Commodore by Captain Francis William Sullivan, C.B., who flew his broad pennant in the *Tourmaline*, 12, but who took little direct share in the dreary and unhealthy work. The most arduous part of the duty fell to the *Sirius, Seagull*, 3, Commander Frederick William Burgoyne Maxwell Heron, *Cygnet*, 4, Lieutenant Robert Frederick Hammick, *Contest*, 4, Lieutenant George Woronzow Allen, *Mallard*, 4, Lieutenant Alfred Wilmot Warry, *Avon*, 4, Commander Leicester Chantrey Keppel, *Pioneer*, 6, paddle, Lieutenant Edwin Hotham, *Spiteful, Ariel*, and *Supply*, 2, storeship, Staff-Commander Frank Inglis.

The whole conduct of the latter part of the blockade was left to Captain George Lydiard Sulivan, with the result that on May 4th 1877, Gelelé found it expedient to open negotiations with him at Whydah. On May 10th a preliminary instalment of 200 puncheons of oil was handed over; and two days later the blockade was formally raised. (*Times* corr. in *A. & N. Gaz.*, June 23, 1877.)

Sulivan received the approval of the government for the arrangements into which he entered.

Scarcely had affairs been settled with Dahomey ere, in consequence of the refusal of some of the Niger natives to release prisoners whom they had taken from the *Sultan of Sokoto*, it became necessary to undertake a fresh expedition into the lower reaches of that pestilential river. Accordingly, Captain John Child Purvis (2), of the *Danae*, 12, shifted his pennant to the *Pioneer*, 6, Lieutenant Edwin Hotham, and in her, with the *Avon*, 4, Commander Leicester Chantrey Keppel, and *Boxer*, 4, Commander Arthur Hildebrand Alington, in company, proceeded up the stream on August 15th, 1877. There had been previously transferred to the *Pioneer* from the *Danae* 6 officers, 42 seamen, and 17 marines. Two British consular officers were also with the expedition.

On the 17th the flotilla brought to off Emblana, and, after an unsatisfactory interview had been held with the head men, the people were ordered out of the village, which was promptly subjected to a fire of shell, case, and rockets. A landing party, under Lieutenant John Salwey Halifax, supported by another under Lieutenant Edward Henry Arden, then burnt the place, and a number of canoes. Off Osomari, on the evening of the 18th, the *Avon* piled up on a sandbank, delaying the advance for some hours. On the following day, Onitcha was reached, and on the 21st the local chief gave assurances of friendliness. The vessels next dropped down to Oko, on the other side of the river. The chief of that place, though contumacious and defiant, escaped punishment. On the 26th, when Emblana was repassed, the natives opened fire, whereupon a party landed, chastised them severely, and burnt more of their huts. A village on Stirling Island was subsequently destroyed, with but slight opposition. In these affairs the only loss suffered by the expedition was three men slightly wounded. The ships quitted the river on August 28th. (Desps., and corr. in *A. & N. Gaz.* of Oct. 6 and 13, 1877.)

At about the same period there was trouble of a similar character in the River Congo. On December 27th, 1876, when the *Avon*, 4, Commander Leicester Chantrey Keppel, lay at Loanda, the British steamer *Ethiopia* arrived there, having on board the master and crew of the American schooner *Joseph Nickerson*. These people, who had been picked up at Banana Creek, reported that their vessel had run on shore at Shark's Point, while endeavouring to enter the Congo, and had been plundered by natives, who had fought a serious skirmish with some Dutch settlers who endeavoured to interfere.

The *Avon* thereupon proceeded to the mouth of the river, and Keppel held a palaver on December 30th with the chiefs at Shark's Point, and demanded that the stolen goods should be returned. There being no sign of compliance, he landed six officers, forty men, and four guides on January 2nd, 1877, and burnt two villages. The party was fired at as it returned. The *Avon*, consequently proceeded higher up, burnt three more villages, and fired rockets into others. The effect was excellent, for quantities of the stolen goods were subsequently given up by the people. The *Avon* suffered no loss, and Keppel's action received the full approval of the government. (*A. & N. Gaz.*, Ap. 7, and June 23, 1877.)

Canada, 1877

On another occasion, at about the same time, did it fall to a British ship to avenge an outrage on the crew of an American vessel. In 1873 a steamer, the *George Wright*, while on her voyage to Alaska, had been lost in Queen Charlotte Sound, off the coast of British Columbia. About fifteen of her people had escaped to land, and had been brutally robbed, and then murdered by the Indians. Early in 1877 some of the belongings of these poor people were reported to be in possession of a tribe in Deane's Inlet, on the mainland. The gun-vessel *Rocket*, 4, Lieutenant Charles Reynold Harris, with an interpreter and a sergeant of police, sailed for the spot on March 14th from Vancouver, and soon discovered that men who had been implicated in the massacre were still in the neighbourhood. Harris seized some chiefs as hostages, and demanded that the culprits should be given up; but, this being in vain, he was ultimately obliged to shell and burn the village, ere he could secure compliance. Two of the culprits were thus taken. (Corr. of *Western Daily Mercury*, May, 1877.)

Peru, 1877-1878

In the course of a revolutionary movement which occurred in Peru in 1877, some adherents of the insurgent leader, Nicolas de Pierola, persuaded the officers of the Peruvian turret-ship *Huascar*, to rebel against the central government.

★★★★★★.

The *Huascar*, an iron single-turreted monitor of 1130 tons displacement, was built by Laird Brothers, of Birkenhead, in 1865, and fitted by them with simple jet condenser engines indicating 1200 horse-power, and working a single, four-bladed, non-raising screw. The dimensions were: length, 196 ft.; beam, 35 ft. 6 in.; depth of hold, 21 ft.; freeboard, 4 ft. 6 in.; draught, 15 ft. forward, 16 ft. aft. The hull was divided into five watertight compartments by four traverse 5/8-in. iron bulkheads with watertight doors. There was also a collision bulkhead forward; and on each side of the fire-room there was a longitudinal 5/8-in. iron bulkhead extending to the traverse bulkheads forward and aft, and leaving a space 3 ft. wide between it and the ship's side. The bottom was double. The turret, on Captain Coles's plan, was supported on rollers, and revolved by hand gearing. Its exterior diameter was 22 ft. The turret armour was 5½ in. thick, backed by 13 in. of teak set on end, and by a ½-in. iron inner skin, except around the two oval ports, where the armour was increased by 2-in. plates, and the backing proportionately reduced. The turret roof was of 2-in. plates, and slightly convex, and was provided with two bullet-proof sighting hoods. The side-armour, extending 3 ft. 6 in. below the load water-line, had a thickness of 4½ in. abreast of the turret-chamber and the fire and engine-rooms, and diminished to 2½ in. at the bow and stern. It was backed by 10 in. of teak, and a ½-in. inner iron skin.

The bow was strengthened and shaped for ramming. The deck was protected by 2-in. plates. Forward was a small top-gallant forecastle, 6 ft. high. Aft was an open poop. Abaft the turret was an hexagonal conning-tower 7 ft. 6 in. high and 8 ft. wide, by 5 ft. 2 in. long, carrying 3-in. armour in vertical slabs, backed by balks of teak 8 in. thick, placed on end. The summit of it supported a bridge. Abaft the conning-tower was an unarmoured funnel; and around this was the fire-room hatch, with a high wooden coaming, and no bomb-proof grating. Abaft the funnel was an iron mainmast with wire rigging set up to the rails without channels.

The foremast was a tripod of iron tubes, and the rig was that of a brig with movable bowsprit. The coal capacity was 300 tons; the turning period, through 180°, was 2 minutes 0.3 seconds; and the maximum speed was 11 knots. Her armament consisted of two 10-in. 12½-ton 300-pr. Armstrong R.M.L. mounted in the turret, and commanding 138° of the horizon, *i.e.*, from 10° on either side of the bow line to 32° on either side of the stern line; and two 40-pr. Armstrong R.M.L., placed one on each side of the quarter-deck.

★★★★★★

With the connivance of the officers, a number of the insurgents seized the vessel in the harbour of Callao, and, under cover of the darkness, put to sea, making for the southward. At Cobija, then a port of Bolivia, the *Huascar* took Pierola himself on board, and then returned to the northward with a view to effect a landing. Soon after the seizure of the turret-ship, Rear-Admiral Algernon Frederick Rous de Horsey, British Commander-in-Chief in the Pacific, arrived at Callao in his flagship, the *Shah*; and, being informed of what had occurred, and learning also that the *Huascar* had committed outrages against British subjects and British property, he made formal complaint to the Peruvian Government, which, in reply, disclaimed responsibility, declared the Huascar to be a pirate, and offered a reward for her capture.

★★★★★★

The *Shah*, an iron, wood and copper sheathed unarmoured frigate of 6250 tons displacement and 7480 indicated horse-power, was built at Portsmouth in 1873, and engined by Messrs. Ravenhill. At her official trials in April, 1876, her mean speed was 16.4: knots. Her armament at the time of the action consisted of two 9-in. 12-ton R.M.L., sixteen 7-in. 6½-ton R.M.L., and eight 64-pr. R.M.L., with Gatlings in the tops, and with three above-water torpedo ejectors. The complement was 602 officers and men. She was ship-rigged, with a single screw, and two funnels; and her dimensions were: length, 334 ft. 7 in.; beam, 52 ft.; mean draught, 26 ft. 5½ in. In 1892 the *Shah* was towed to Bermuda to serve as a hulk there. She was commanded at the time of this action by Captain Frederick George Denham Bedford.

★★★★★★

The rear-admiral determined, therefore, to proceed against the rebel vessel with his flagship and the corvette *Amethyst*.

★★★★★★

The *Amethyst*, a single-screw unarmoured wooden corvette, of 1970 tons displacement and 2140 indicated horse-power, carried fourteen 64-pr. R.M.L. guns, and had a complement of 226 officers and men. She was commanded on the occasion by Captain Alfred John Chatfield.

★★★★★★

The following brief account of the resultant proceedings is taken from *The War Ships and Navies of the World*, a valuable work by Chief-Engineer King, U.S.N:—

"Having put to sea for the purpose, the Rear-admiral sighted the *Huascar* off the town of Ilo on the afternoon of May 29th, and summoned her to surrender. This summons the commanding officer refused to entertain. The *Shah* then fired, first a blank cartridge, and then a shotted charge, but, the *Huascar* still refusing to surrender, a steady and well-sustained fire from both the *Shah* and *Amethyst* was directed against her. The fight was partly in chase and partly circular, the distance between the combatants being, for the greater part of the time, from 1500 to 2500 yards. the time employed in the engagement was about three hours, the fight being terminated by darkness coming on and the *Huascar* running close in shore where the *Shah* could not follow, consequent upon her greater draught.

Of the projectiles thrown from the English ships, it is reported that some seventy or eighty struck the ironclad, principally about the upper decks, bridge, masts, and boats. One projectile from a heavy gun pierced the side on the port quarter 2 feet above the water, where the armour was 2½ or 3 in. thick, and brought up against the opposite side, killing one man and wounding another. Two other projectiles dented in the side armour to the extent of 3 inches. The turret was struck once by a projectile from the heavy guns of the *Shah*. It was a direct blow, but penetrated 3 inches only. The hull showed that several 64-pr. shot had struck it, only leaving marks. When at close quarters—which the *Huascar* sought for the purpose of ramming—the Gatling gun in the *Shah's* fore-top drove the men from the quarter-deck guns of the former. On one of these occasions a Whitehead torpedo was launched at the ironclad, but, as she altered her course at about the same instant, the torpedo failed to strike its mark."

Neither British ship suffered any loss; neither, in fact, was struck about the hull. The action began at 3.6 p.m. and terminated at 5.45 p.m. The *Shah's* firing was telling and well-sustained, but the turret-ship, being a small and low target, and frequently end on, was a difficult object to hit, and the atmospheric conditions were not, it is reported, altogether favourable for good practice. The *Shah's* guns also were more than once ordered to cease firing, when, owing to the *Huascar* placing herself close under the town of Ilo, there was risk of injuring the buildings and property on shore. The *Amethyst's* fire was conducted with great precision; but, for the business in hand, her guns were, of course, useless.

The *Shah's* movements were impeded by the narrowness of the waters in which she was operating; by her great length; and by the danger of stopping in view of the possibility of being rammed. The *Huascar* lost one killed and three wounded. A boat expedition, despatched in the course of the following night under Lieutenant Charles Lindsay to attack the rebel ship, failed to find her, owing to darkness and fog. (*A. & N. Gazette*, July 14, and July 21, 1877. Desps., laid on table of House of Commons July 27, 1877). Lieutenant Thomas Francis Abbott, Sub-Lieutenants Hugh Talbot, and Scott William Alfred Hamilton Gray, Navigating Sub-Lieutenant Henry William Steele, Surgeons Marcus Allen, and Thomas Martyn Sibbald, and Assistant Engineer William Walter White volunteered for this service.

Two British officers who subsequently inspected the *Huascar* were of opinion that seventy or eighty projectiles, as mentioned by Mr. King, had struck her.

★★★★★★

The small effect produced by the *Shah's* 9-in. and 7-in. projectiles is very remarkable, seeing that theoretically their penetration of wrought iron, striking direct, should have been—

				At 1000 yds. in.	At 2000 yds. in.
9 in. .	.	.	.	9·6	8·4
7 in. .	.	.	.	6·5	5·6

The projectile of the 9-in. gun weighed 253 lb., and the powder-charge 50 lb. The projectile of the 7-in. gun weighed 112 lb., and the powder-charge 30 lb. The muzzle velocities should have been 1440 and 1525 foot-seconds respectively.

★★★★★★

Numbers of pieces of shell were sticking in the woodwork. One 9-inch common shell had struck the hull on the starboard side, about 2 feet from the water-line and 50 feet from the stern, in the foremost wardroom cabin. It had burst in the backing, the head splintering in all directions, and the base continuing its course until brought up against the inner skin on the opposite side. Don Manuel Carrasco, in his official report, stated that the explosion of this shell killed one seaman and wounded an officer and two men.

The plating at the spot where it struck was about 3½ in. thick. Two 64-pr. shells left indentations on the plating. One heavy shot, evidently a ricochet, hit the upper edge on the starboard side, scoring it to a depth of 3 in. after going through the bulwark. Another hit the plating 2 ft. from the water-line at an angle, making a dent 2 in. in depth and 18 in. in length. On the port side there was a shot similar to the ricochet. The hull showed that several 64-prs. had struck it, only leaving a mark. One shot struck the poop on the port quarter, and went out on the starboard side, splintering an iron beam. The funnel-casing and funnel had been hit about twelve times by shot and pierced

A Gatling gun

by the Gatling gun. The turret had only been struck once—by a 7-in. projectile hitting direct and penetrating 3 inches.

This account does not agree strictly with that given by Mr. King; but, no very important facts being at stake, it is not deemed necessary or worthwhile to endeavour to harmonise or explain the apparent differences.

The *Huascar* was afterwards surrendered to the Peruvian Government.

Minor Operations, 1877-1878

On the east coast of Africa, in 1877, the vessels there employed for the repression of the slave trade found plenty to do, the boats of the *London*, Captain Thomas Baker Martin Sulivan, continuing their activity and capturing numerous *dhows*. On one occasion Lieutenant William Rooke Creswell, when about to board one of these craft, had a narrow escape of his life. The slavers intended to allow him to board, and then to shoot him; but the officer was saved by the interpreter, who, catching sight of a half-hidden Arab, with his gun cocked and levelled, gave warning of the danger. Among other officers of the London whose names figure in the despatches of the time were Lieutenant Lloyd William Mathews, and Sub-Lieutenant Robert Maitland King. The *Lynx*, 4, Commander Francis Metcalfe Ommanney, which received permission to search vessels bearing the Portuguese flag, was another active cruiser on the station. The *Vulture*, 3, Commander Henry Holford Washington, also made herself useful on the same coast, and continued to do so, first under that officer, and then under Commander John Eliot Pringle, during great part of her commission, 1876-80. In the Persian Gulf, in 1878. Pringle's boats were engaged in an action of some importance.

The *Vulture* proceeded to Bahrein in October of that year in order to exact certain fines from the head men of the island for the infraction of a treaty which had been concluded in 1861. On arriving, she learnt that all communication with El Kateef. on the mainland, was suspended, and that that town was beleaguered by about 3000 Bedouins Pringle, in consequence, went on to El Kateef, and communicated with the governor, who informed him in the presence of a considerable piratical fleet of *dhows* near Ras Tinnorah. The *Vulture* steamed thither, and on October 10th found the *dhows* close in shore in shoal water.

Although it was blowing half a gale, Pringle manned and armed his boats, and led them to the attack. Six of the largest *dhows* made sail and stood out to engage, while the others, and many people on shore, opened a brisk fire. The British, however, pushed in, drove the Arabs from their vessels, and harassed their retreat with shrapnel and rockets. It was ascertained that the enemy lost no fewer than 34 killed and 85 wounded, while the attacking party escaped scot free. Twenty *dhows* were taken possession of, and, each in charge of a bluejacket, were navigated to El Kateef. The capture of the flotilla relieved the governor, who had long suffered from the depredations of the marauders and of their allies on shore. (*A. & N. Gaz.*, Jan. 11, 1879.)

The Dardanelles, 1878–1879

In 1875 Bosnia and Herzegovina revolted from Turkey. At that time the Ottoman Empire was bankrupt, misrule was general throughout the country, and Russian influence was all powerful at Constantinople. On May 30th, 1876, a palace conspiracy cost the Sultan Abdul Aziz his throne. His feeble, if not imbecile successor, Murad V., made way in three months for Abdul Hamid II., and, while these changes were going on, the Bosnian revolt extended to Bulgaria; and Servia and Montenegro also took up arms against the Porte. It was then, with a view to signifying to the revolted provinces and to their Russian instigators that she would not suffer Constantinople to become a prize to any of the *Sultan's* enemies, and with a view also to the protection of her own interests as a great eastern and Mahometan power, that Great Britain found it necessary to make a naval demonstration by dispatching her Mediterranean Fleet to Besika Bay, near the entrance to the Dardanelles. It assembled there in June, and the greater part of it remained there, or in the immediate neighbourhood, for many months.

There was then but one British flag-officer permanently employed afloat in the Mediterranean, but, as soon as the demonstration had been decided upon, Rear-Admiral Edward Bridges Rice, Superintendent of Malta Dockyard, shifted his flag from the guardship *Hibernia* to the armoured battleship *Triumph*, Captain George Henry Parkin, and joined the Commander-in-Chief, Vice-Admiral the Hon. Sir James Robert Drummond, K.C.B., who flew his flag in the armoured battleship *Hercules*, Captain Nathaniel Bowden-Smith. Rear-Admiral William Garnham Luard was also sent out as a temporary Superintendent to Malta.

The British Naval force in the Mediterranean in November, 1876, comprised ten ironclads, inclusive of the small and inefficient *Pallas*, corvette, and *Research*, sloop, among the number being the *Sultan*, then commanded by H.R.H. Captain the Duke of Edinburgh, K.G. It also comprised about a dozen unarmoured vessels, the only really valuable one of which, however, was the iron screw frigate *Raleigh*. Had the Mediterranean fleet of that year been obliged to undertake a campaign, it would have found itself even worse off for efficient cruisers and scouts than the same fleet was when Nelson most complained of its shortcomings in that direction. Happily, Drummond was not called upon to adopt active measures.

In the early spring of 1877 Drummond was succeeded in command by Vice-Admiral Geoffrey Thomas Phipps Hornby, an officer who, although he had not seen a shot fired in anger since 1840, had, at the age of fifty-two, established for himself a reputation scarcely second to that of any British naval officer then living. It is not astonishing. He was a great student of professional history; he had a wonderfully clear head, and a scientific mind; he was a natural diplomatist, and an unrivalled tactician: and, to a singular independence and uprightness of character, he added a mastery of technical detail, and a familiarity with contemporary thought and progress that were unusual in those days among officers of his standing. He might have derived no small additional advantage from the fact that he was a kinsman and close friend of the Earl of Derby, the Foreign Secretary with whom it became his duty to co-operate, so that his qualifications for the post were, upon the whole, greater probably than were possessed by any other man of the moment. Unfortunately, Lord Derby was one of the weakest Foreign Secretaries of his age.

Hornby hoisted his flag and went out in the battleship *Alexandra*, Captain Robert O'Brien FitzRoy, reaching Malta on March 17th. In July he took the fleet to Besika Bay, Russia having by that time declared war against Turkey, and crossed the Danube. Thenceforward, until December, Besika Bay remained the headquarters and usual anchorage of the fleet, which, in the interval, thanks to the energy and administrative ability of the Commander-in-Chief, was brought up to a very high degree of efficiency. As the Russians continued to advance, Rear-Admiral Sir John Edmund Commerell, V.C, was sent out in the *Agincourt*, Captain Richard Wells, as second in command.

On December 27th, the fleet weighed from Besika Bay, and proceeded to Vourla Bay, at the entrance to the Gulf of Smyrna, a place which Hornby had selected as a more suitable winter station; and, it then seeming improbable that the Russians could penetrate much further southward until the spring, the admiral quitted the fleet and went to Malta on January 4th. In consequence of a telegram which readied him there on the night of the 11th, he returned to Vourla Bay in the *Sultan*, Captain the Duke of Edinburgh, leaving in the hands of the dockyard authorities his own flagship the *Alexandra*, the *Achilles*, the *Devastation*, and the *Raleigh*, with orders to rejoin him as soon as possible.

At that time, and indeed for many months previous, he was most anxious to be supplied with troops from England to enable him, if necessary, to occupy the lines of Bulair, above Gallipoli, (across the narrow neck of the peninsula—a position easily defensible by troops supported by ships), and so to secure his own communications, and threaten those of the Russians, in case he should be required to undertake hostile action within the Dardanelles. As these troops were never sent to him, it is perhaps fortunate that, after all, he was not called upon to fight. He was also an importunate advocate for a more determined policy than found favour at Whitehall.

On January 18th, 1878, Mr. (afterwards Sir) Austen Henry Layard, British Ambassador to the Porte, telegraphed to the vice-admiral at Vourla:—

Russians advancing upon Adrianople, which they will probably occupy immediately. . . . Austria and England have remonstrated at St. Petersburg. Panic amongst ministers here.

On the 20th came a further telegram:—

Consul at Dardanelles reports that he thinks a further series of torpedoes have been laid at the entrance of the Straits between Castles Koum-Kali and Sed-ul-Bahr, and also at the northern extremity of the narrows between Forts Nagara and Bovali. The mid-channel at bottom of the places not believed to be obstructed. . . . About sixty heavy rifled guns are mounted now in the four principal forts in the narrows. The 50-ton Krupp gun at Sultanieh Fort may be called ready for service.

This was followed by:—

Admiralty, London, 6.40 p.m., Jan. 23, to Admiral, Vourla, 11.55 a.m., Jan. 24. Secret.
Sail immediately for Dardanelles; and proceed with the fleet now with you to Constantinople. Abstain from taking any part

in contest between Russia and Turkey, but waterway of Straits is to be kept open; and, in the event of tumult at Constantinople, protect life and property of British subjects. . . .

Thereupon Hornby, on the 24th, telegraphed to the ambassador:—

Have received orders to proceed to Constantinople with the fleet, and to keep Dardanelles open. I sail at 5 p.m. today. Request firman may be sent for the fleet to pass Tchernak, but orders do not permit me to wait for firman.

And to his wife he wrote:—

. . . . With a determined enemy in possession of the Gallipoli peninsula, this (the keeping open of the Dardanelles) is not possible for ships to guarantee. I fear from the vacillation our orders denote that we are not well commanded, (*i.e.,* not well directed from London), and I do not anticipate much credit will accrue to the country. . . .

When the fleet sailed, no one but the commander-in-chief, who led the starboard line in the dispatch-vessel *Salamis*, Commander Frederick Wilbraham Egerton, knew whither nor on what mission it was bound, though everyone guessed. By 8 a.m. on the 25th the fleet was off Besika. No fresh orders met it there, and it passed on. Close to the mouth of the Dardanelles, Hornby transferred his flag to the *Sultan*, and began to make such preparations for action as were possible without betraying a hostile purpose. The *Salamis* was sent in to Tchernak, (on the Asiatic shore at the mouth of the narrowest part of the Dardanelles), with the message:—

We came as friends, but I was bound to go on. It you fired at me I should be obliged to fire at you; and then we should only be playing the Russian game, which would be very disagreeable to me.

The *commandant* at Tchernak had the firman granting permission to pass, and handed it to Egerton, who was on the point of taking it off to the flagship, when a telegraph clerk ran after him with a message as follows:—

Admiralty, London, Jan. 24, 7.39 p.m., to Admiral, Tchernak, Jan. 25, .3.30 p.m.
Annul former orders. Anchor at Besika Bay and wait further

orders. Report arrival there.

This sudden reversal of policy was most annoying to the commander-in-chief, who feared not only that it would be prejudicial to British material interests, but also that it would be most injurious to British prestige throughout the East. He anticipated that it would encourage Russia, and would drive the *Sultan* into the hands of the *Czar*. The truth seems to be that the British Cabinet had been apprised in the interim of certain terms upon which Russia was willing to make peace, and regarded those terms as admissible. However, this may have been, a different view presently recommended itself to the Ministry, for, on February 9th Hornby, then in Besika Bay, received orders to proceed, if possible that afternoon, for Constantinople to protect the life and property of British subjects. He was informed that the Ambassador had been directed to obtain the necessary firman, to induce the Porte to send pacific orders to the forts, and to communicate the results to the vice-admiral.

Again, therefore, he proceeded for Tchernak, weighing at 6 p.m.; but at Tchernak there was neither firman nor message from Mr. Layard, and, to make matters worse, the *pasha* in command protested against the fleet entering the strait. After anchoring for some hours, Hornby returned to Besika Bay, and curtly telegraphed home to ask whether he was to go on and force a passage, or to wait for permission to pass. On the 10th he heard from the ambassador that permission had been asked for and had been refused, and next that the Russians had threatened to occupy Constantinople in case the ships should pass the Dardanelles.

On February 12th more definite and satisfactory instructions arrived from London. The vice-admiral was to proceed into the Sea of Marmora without waiting for a firman, and if he were fired upon and his ships were struck, was to return the fire, but not to wait to demolish the forts. (At the same time the Channel Squadron was ordered to Gibraltar, and, a day or two later, to Malta.) I take the following description of those works from Mrs. Fred Egerton's biography of her father, (*Admiral of the Fleet Sir G. T. Phipps Hornby*):—

> There were then only four formidable forts in the Dardanelles. The lowest of these was Fort Namasgbia, (below Kilid Bahr), in which were sixteen Krupp breechloading rifled guns, supposed to be about 26 centimetres, (*i.e.* of about 10.5-in. calibre), also one Krupp and two Armstrong 7-inch muzzle-loading

guns. Nearly opposite is the Sultanieh Fort, (near Tchernak), in which the monster 50-ton Krupp gun had been mounted to command the approaches to the Narrows. This was, however, the only formidable piece of ordnance in the fort. A mile above is the Medjidieh Fort, probably the strongest of all, having been reconstructed by a German officer, Blum. It had thirteen 6-inch breech-loading Krupp guns, seven of which enfiladed the channel. The fort of Nagara, (the ancient Abydos), two and a half miles further on, completed the defences, as the other forts were supplied only with obsolete guns, or the modern ones intended for them had not been mounted.

No mines were feared; for, although a number had been laid down, Hornby believed that recent gales, aiding the always strong current, had washed all of them into the Ægean Sea. Woods Pasha, who had to do with the laying and recovery of them, has since informed me that Hornby was mistaken.

The *Raleigh*, 22, Captain Charles Trelawny Jago, was detached to Dedegatch to embark fugitives; the *Salamis* was sent forward to communicate once more with the *pasha* commanding at Tchernak; and with the following six battleships, cleared for action and with their upper spars sent down, the vice-admiral, who had weighed at daylight, entered the mouth of the Dardanelles, a snowy gale blowing from the eastward:—

BATTLE-SHIPS.	HEAVY GUNS.	COMMANDERS.	ORDERS.
Alexandra	12	V.-Adm. G. T. P. Hornby, Capt. Robt. O'Brien FitzRoy, Com. Atwell Peregrine Macleod Lake.	To destroy the 50-ton gun.
Agincourt	17	R.-Adm. Sir J. E. Commerell, K.C.B., V.C., Com. Thomas Sturges Jackson.	To silence Namazghia.
Achilles	16	Capt. Sir Wm. Nathan Wrighte Hewett, K.C.B., V.C., Com Wm. Hargraves Mitchell Molyneux.	To silence Namazghia.
Swiftsure	14	Capt. Nowell Salmon, C.B., V.C. Com. Hilary Gustavus Andoe.	To attack Medjidieh Fort.
Téméraire	8	Capt. Michael Culme-Seymour, Com. Albert Baldwin Jenkings.	To attack Medjidieh Fort.
Sultan	12	Capt. H.R.H. the Duke of Edinburgh, K.G. Com. Richd. Fredk. Britten.	To destroy the 50-ton gun.

Note.—The *Hotspur*, 3, Capt. St. George Caulfield d'Arcy-Irvine, and *Ruby*, corvette, Capt. Robt. Hy. More Molyneux, which had quitted Besika Bay with the fleet, had been detached to assist the *Raleigh*, she having run ashore near Rabbit Island. Numerous other vessels were in the Mediterranean, but not then upon the spot.

As Egerton landed at Tchernak he noted that the tompion had not been taken out of the big gun. That was reassuring. The *pasha*, however, appears to have handed to Egerton a written protest, although he qualified it by saying, as he dismissed that officer, "Return to the admiral, and tell him that from motives of humanity I refrain from firing."

The flagship grounded on the edge of a shoal just below the narrowest part of the strait. Retaining the *Sultan* to assist the *Alexandra*, Hornby sent on the other four ships to Gallipoli. As soon as the *Alexandra* had been got off, she proceeded to Nagara Point, where she anchored for the night. On the 14th the commander-in-chief learnt that the Russians were within twelve miles of the Bulair lines. He therefore left the *Agincourt* and *Swiftsure* off Gallipoli, ordered forward the *Salamis* to communicate with Mr. Layard, and, with the *Alexandra, Achilles, Sultan*, and *Téméraire*, steamed leisurely across the Sea of Marmora, and appeared off Constantinople on the morning of February 15th. He anchored near Prince's Islands, within sight of the Russian and Turkish tents that faced each other close to San Stefano.

Hornby's opinion always was that, had the Turks tried to obstruct his passage, he could have silenced their batteries, and, with relatively small damage to himself, have reached Constantinople. Had the *Alexandra*, however, or any one of the ships grounded under fire, it might have been impossible to save her. He knew nothing of the mines. He believed, nevertheless, that if either the Turks or the Russians had determined seriously to hold the northern bank of the Dardanelles against the fleet, they could, with but little special preparation, have accomplished their purpose, or at least have prevented the passage of the Narrows by any vessels not armoured. His ships, he asserted, could have dealt with the existing guns, which were near the water level, but they could not have dealt with the guns which might have been quickly mounted on the cliffs above; and guns so mounted might have entirely prevented the upward passage of colliers, storeships and transports, and so have deprived the fleet off Constantinople of all resources.

It was for this reason that he ardently desired that he should be placed in a position to occupy the lines of Bulair and the peninsula of Gallipoli when ordered to pass the Dardanelles; and, as he was never placed in that position, it must be admitted that his situation in the Sea of Marmora was a most precarious one. his communications not being in any way secured. Fortunately, the Russians believed that the ships were crowded with troops. Fortunately, too, they remembered that their own long line of land communications northward to the Danube was a difficult one to protect, and that they had pushed southward with more hardihood than the rules of sound strategy warranted. Austria lay on the flank of the Russian advance, and was excessively irritated. And thus, although the grand duke had threatened to occupy Constantinople if Hornby should enter the Sea of Marmora, the very appearance of Hornby deterred him from risking so extreme a measure. Constantinople was saved.

The anchorage of the body of the fleet was presently removed to Touzla Bay, an inlet on the mainland, a little to the southward of Prince's Islands, Commerell, however, with the *Agincourt* and *Swiftsure*, remaining off Gallipoli to hearten the Turks there, and having orders to blow up the Dardanelles' forts rather than permit them to be occupied by the Russians, and to prevent any Russian force from embarking and crossing to the Asiatic shore. Having received news on March 4th that preliminaries of peace had been concluded on the previous day, Hornby, on the 9th, took his ships to pleasanter quarters off Ismid.

Before Easter Lord Derby resigned, and the home government, adopting a firmer policy, authorised the naval chiefs, if necessary, to take the Turkish troops at Bulair into British pay, and to land officers and men tor the defence of the lines. On the other hand, the Turkish Ministry became rather less anti-Russian and rather more anti-British than it had been; so that the prospects of peace did not immediately improve. In May, Lord Beaconsfield tellingly reminded both the late belligerents that he was prepared to interfere, with or without the Turkish alliance, if necessary; and his summoning of 10,000 Indian troops to Malta produced a powerful impression. At about the same time, the battleship *Devastation*, Captain Walter James Hunt-Grubbe. C.B., Commander Charles John Balfour, (2), took the place of the *Sultan* in the Sea of Marmora, the boilers of the latter ship being worn out. (The *Sultan* turned over her officers and crew to the *Black Prince*, of the Channel Squadron, at Malta on May 9.) Captain Algernon Charles Fieschi Heneage also superseded Captain Hewett in command of the *Achilles*. On June 18th, the squadron returned to the anchorage off Prince's Islands, the neighbourhood of Touzla Bay being reputed unhealthy in summer.

In the meanwhile, in order to strengthen the hands of the British representatives at the Congress which had been called at Berlin to arrange final terms of peace, the Channel Squadron, (the place of the Channel Squadron in home waters was taken by the Reserve Squadron, under Rear-Adm. Henry Boys), under Vice-Admiral Lord John Hay (3), C.B., in the *Minotaur*, Captain Harry Holdsworth Rawson, had been dispatched to the Mediterranean, anchored in Suda Bay, and placed under Vice-Admiral Hornby's orders. At the end of June, Hay was sent to Larnaca, in Cyprus, where presently the battleship *Invincible* and the cruiser *Raleigh* (both of the Mediterranean fleet) joined him.

Cyprus, 1878-1879

On July 8th the conditional cession of Cyprus to Great Britain was announced in Parliament, and, on the same day, Lord John Hay was directed to take possession of it. This and the decisions of the Congress marked the end of the period of extreme tension in the vicinity of the Dardanelles, although, on July 14th, the *Swiftsure's* steam-pinnace was fired upon by the Russians near Xeros, and two British officers were taken prisoners. General Todleben, the Russian commander-in-chief, offered, however, satisfactory explanations and regretful apologies.

On August 6th Hornby was deservedly rewarded with a K.C.B. Lord Charles Beresford wrote:

> How wonderfully complete your organisation must have been, as, if even a midshipman had lost his temper, he might have run the country into war.

The San Stefano lines were evacuated by the Russians on September 23rd, and, in accordance with an agreement which had been arrived at, the fleet moved to Artaki on the 28th. There it remained until January 1st, 1879, when it sailed for Ismid.

On January 2nd, while the battleship *Thunderer*, Captain Alfred John Chatfield, which had relieved the *Devastation* about two months earlier, was practising at quarters in the Gulf of Ismid, one of the 12-in. 38-ton Woolwich muzzle-loaders, supposed to be charged with 85 lb. of powder, and a common shell, burst in her fore-turret. (The full charge was 110 lb.; and a charge of that weight, with an empty Palliser shell, had, as was imagined, been fired a few minutes earlier.) The muzzle, from about two feet in front of the trunnions, was blown off, and terrible destruction was done. Two officers, Lieutenant Augustus Heyliger Coker, R.N., and Lieutenant Edward Daniel, R.M.A., with nine men, were killed, and thirty-five persons were injured.

Only one of those who were in the turret survived. The accident seems to have been due either to double loading or to a shifting forward of the projectile after it had been hydraulically rammed home in the depressed muzzle. The committee which reported upon the subject adopted the former theory. (Report issued Mar. 1, 1879. The correctness of the conclusion was to a great extent confirmed by experiments which were made with the sister gun at Woolwich in the following December and January.) Lord Charles Beresford, writing to the *Times*, said that:—

Any of the Woolwich pattern guns could burst, except under conditions unfair to the gun, I do not believe.

There was evidence, however, that flaws in the material might, in certain circumstances, cause an explosive burst, for on no other hypothesis can the bursting of a 9-in. 12-ton Woolwich gun in the turret ship *Wivern* in 1867 be explained. On that occasion, although about thirteen persons were inside the turret, and the breech of the gun, weighing about a ton, was blown off, there were happily no casualties. While the great balance of probability indicates that the *Thunderer's* gun had been doubly loaded by mistake, owing to a previous miss-fire during the discharge of an electric broadside not having been noticed, it cannot be said that the truth of this theory was ever demonstrated beyond all doubt.

Not until March 19th, when the Russians were withdrawing from Adrianople, did Sir Geoffrey Hornby repass the Dardanelles.

For many months Europe had been upon the verge of a general war. No individual, perhaps, did more to avert that catastrophe than the vice-admiral; yet certainly no Englishman was more determined than he to champion what he conceived to be British interests, and to fight for them if necessary. His fine performance affords a good example of the old truth that obvious readiness to strike more often saves than provokes a quarrel. How he would have fared, had he had to strike, is another question. His squadron, it is true, was small. On the other hand, he had under him, in Sir John Edmund Commerell, Sir W. N. W. Hewett, Captain Nowell Salmon, Captain Culme-Seymour, and many others, officers who, in their day, were among the very best in the navy, and who, almost without exception, believed in Hornby as, so more than one of them has told me, they believed in no other commander-in-chief of their time.

During the time of tension, Russia made numerous purchases, especially in America, of vessels suitable for service as privateers. Most of these were carefully watched by British cruisers. From the same period dates the formation of the Russian "Volunteer Fleet"—a flotilla consisting for the most part of large and fast craft which are chiefly used at ordinary times as transports and storeships, but which carry formidable armaments in their holds, and can mount them promptly in case of need.

It is not necessary to say much concerning the occupation of Cyprus. The ships concerned in it were the—

Ships.	Guns.	Commanders.	Remarks.
Minotaur, b.s.	17	V.-Adm. Lord John Hay (3), C.B. Capt. Harry Holdsworth Rawson. Com. John Fellowes.	Flagsh'p, Channel Squad.
Black Prince b.s.	28	Capt. H.R.H. Duke of Edinburgh, K.G. Com. Rich. Fredk. Britten.	Channel Squad.
Monarch, b.s.	7	Capt. Algernon McLennan Lyons. Com. Alan Brodrick Thomas.	Channel Squad.
Invincible, b.s.	14	Capt Lindesay Brine Com. Wm. Fredk. Stanley Mann.	Medit. Fleet.
Pallas, arm'd. corv.	8	Capt. Hy. Hamilton Beamish, C.B.	Medit. Fleet.
Raleigh, cr.	22	Capt. Chas. Trelawny Jago. Com. Day Hort Bosanquet.	Medit. Fleet.
Foxhound, g.b.	4	Lieut. Wm. Hy. Geo. Nowell.	Detained on way home from China.

These reached the neighbourhood of the island on July 7th, 1878, and, after the *Raleigh* had been sent in to take soundings, the squadron anchored in Larnaca Bay on the 8th. On the 10th the British dispatch-vessel *Salamis,* 2, Commander Frederick Wilbraham Egerton, arrived from Constantinople with the Pasha who had been empowered to transfer the island to British rule; and on the night of the 11th the flagship landed 53 marines, under Captain Henry Holdsworth Kelly, R.M.A., to take possession of the capital, Nicosia. Other detachments of Royal Marines, and a force of bluejackets, under Lieutenant Jasper Edmund Thomson Nicolls, were subsequently disembarked. The honour of having first hoisted the British flag in the island appears to be due to Lieutenant Horatio Fraser Kemble, first of the *Minotaur.* (*A. & N. Gaz.*, July 20, and Aug. 3, 1878.) Lord John Hay assumed the governorship of the place pending the arrival of Sir Garnet Wolseley, who had been appointed to the post, and who quickly assumed it.

Troops were soon sent to the island to relieve the bluejackets and marines on shore. An open beach was the only landing-place for them, but the navy improvised facilities. That the labour involved in doing so was very arduous may be gathered from the fact that the working hours for the ships' companies were from 3.15 a.m., to 9.30 p.m., with an interval of only one hour for rest, and that many of the men were up to their necks in water while engaged in pier-building.

Captain the Duke of Edinburgh personally superintended the landing of the whole of the men and stores. The following extract from a letter sent to the *Scotsman* by a non-commissioned officer of the 71st Highlanders gives an interesting glimpse of the energetic manner in which his Royal Highness threw himself into his work, and affords room for regret that this was one of the very few occasions when the lamented prince was able actively to exert himself in a service which he loved ardently to the day of his death, twenty-two years later:—

> The order was given for the regiment to disembark at 4 a.m. on the 24th, and so good were the arrangements (which were under the entire control of H.R.H. the Duke of Edinburgh) that at 4.20 a.m. there was not a 71st man left in the ship. We were taken on shore in large horse-boats, tugged by steam launches. As we came alongside the pier the first man I saw was the Duke of Edinburgh, who was helping the men out of the boats. As each of us carried our valise in one hand, and our rifle in the other, and as there was a swell on the water, you will understand that a man jumping out is apt, if he does not jump at the proper time, to find himself between the pier and the boat, with a very good chance of being drowned or crushed the next time the boat comes up.
>
> To prevent this, the duke, and others with him, caught each man by the arm as he jumped out; and so well was this attended to that not a single man, or rifle, or valise fell into the water. I can assure you that it will be a long time before we forget the cheery word and smile His Royal Highness had for each of us as he helped us on to the pier. Early as it was, the sun was blazing hot, and though we had our helmets on, he had only his navy cap, with a white cover on it. After we were all out of the boats, and when I was going to fall in with the regiment, I saw him amongst the baggage, directing and encouraging, all his anxiety being to get us out of the sun.

South Africa & the Zulu War, 1878-1879

What is remembered in South Africa as the Transkei, or "Old Colony" war, but which was, in fact, a number of small simultaneous campaigns against rebellious Galekas, Gaikas, Griquas, and other turbulent native tribes in 1877-78, was carried out mainly by the land forces; but the screw corvette *Active*, 10, Commodore Francis William Sullivan, C.B., (C. M. G. May 24, 1878), bore a certain share in the operations. Her boats having been unable to effect a landing through the surf at Bowker's Bay in presence of a large body of Galekas, she turned her guns on the natives, and, it was said at the time, impressed them so powerfully that, if only their responsible leaders had been on the spot at the time, peace might have been then and there concluded.

A little later, on January 14th, 1878, she landed a Naval Brigade of 196 officers, seamen, and marines at East London, under Commander Henry Townley Wright. This took part in the action at Quintana on February 7th, and rendered most useful service. Lieutenant William des Voeux Hamilton doing valuable work in command of the rocket party. (Norbury: *The Naval Brigade in S. Africa*; republished by Leonaur as *The Naval Brigade in South Africa During the Kafir and Zulu Wars 1877-79*) On July 3rd following the commodore and his officers received an address and vote of thanks from the House of Assembly of Cape Colony.

★★★★★★

The officers landed, besides those already mentioned, were Lieut. Robt. Wm. Craigie; Lieut. (R.M.) Townley Ward Dowding; Sub-Lieuts. Arth. Hy. Loring, Reg. Purves Cochran, and Lionel Aubrey Wallis Barnes-Lawrence; Staff-Surg. Hy. Fredk. Norbury; Gunner Hy. Bays; and Clerk Ralph Balsom Marwood.)

★★★★★★

These disturbances led incidentally to the annexation of Walfisch Bay, which was formally taken possession of on March 12th, 1878, by Staff-Commander Richard Cossantine Dyer, of the storeship *Industry*, 2. They also, no doubt, had some effect in encouraging the Zulus to become restless, and actively to prosecute their ancient feuds with their white neighbours.

★★★★★★

The Transvaal had been annexed to Great Britain on Apr. 12, 1877, by Sir Theophilus Shepstone, who continued to administer it until Mar., 1879. Great Britain, however, inherited the Boer feuds both with Cetewayo, of Zululand, and with Sikukuni, chief of the Bapidi tribe of the Bechuanas.

★★★★★★

Before the actual outbreak of the Zulu war, the *Active* again landed a Brigade. The detachment disembarked at Durban on November 19th, 1878, and proceeded to the neighbourhood of the Zululand boundary line, there to garrison Fort Pearson and other posts on the Lower Tugela with a view to preventing incursions into Natal.

The Zulu question as it then stood may be thus summarised.

Cetewayo, the king, had had a dispute of long standing with the South African Republic concerning some land between the Buffalo

The R.N. in the Zulu War

and the Pongola which had been occupied as Transvaal territory. After the annexation of the Transvaal by Great Britain, Cetewayo had built military *kraals* on that territory, and had given its inhabitants notice to quit. Attempts had been made to arrange the difficulty, with the result that a commission had been appointed, and had reported in June, 1878; but the final award had been left for the consideration of Sir Bartle Frere, High Commissioner for South Africa.

Frere proceeded to Natal in September, 1878, and, in dealing with the situation, took account not only of the boundary question, but also of the general relations of Cetewayo with his neighbours. After making a careful survey of those relations, (Frere's Mem. of Jan., 1879), which was very unsatisfactory, he decided that the award on the boundary question should be made known to Cetewayo simultaneously with certain demands, the concession of which was regarded as necessary for the welfare as well of the Zulus as of the inhabitants of Natal and the Transvaal.

The award, which was favourable to the Zulu claims, and the demands, were delivered to Cetewayo's representatives on December 11th, 1878; and twenty days were allowed the king for compliance with the most pressing requirements of the ultimatum. When those twenty days had expired without any sign of submission on the part of the Zulus, Sir Bartle Frere transferred the further conduct of the affair to Lieutenant-General Lord Chelmsford.

For some months before the delivery of the ultimatum preparations for a struggle had been made by both the parties concerned. The Imperial authorities had landed troops and munitions of war at Durban, had called out the mounted volunteers of Natal, had formed three regiments of Natal natives, and had massed all their forces on the Zululand border, in three columns. The first of these, at the mouth of the Tugela, was under Colonel Pearson, and included the Naval Brigade from the *Active*. The second, or main column, under Colonel Glyn, had its headquarters at Helpmakaar; the third, under Colonel Evelyn Wood, V.C, had Utrecht as its base, and lay in territory the ownership of which was in dispute.

Colonel Wood crossed the Blood River into Zululand on January 6th, 1879, and, on the 17th, moved towards the sources of the White Umfolosi, and thence to Kambula, where he entrenched himself. Colonel Glyn crossed the Buffalo at Rorke's Drift on January 11th, gained a facile and delusive success over the Zulus at Usirayo's stronghold on the 12th, and then moved tediously towards Isandhlwana, a mountain at the base of which he encamped on the 20th. On the 22nd. Lord Chelmsford and Colonel Glyn moved out of camp to reinforce Major Dartnell, who had proceeded with a patrol in the direction of Matyana's stronghold; and, during their absence, the rest of the column, under Colonels Pulleine and Durnford, about 1100 strong, was surprised, overwhelmed, and practically annihilated.

★★★★★★

The only representative of the navy present at Isandhlwana was William Aynsley, a signalman belonging to the *Active*. He was seen, "his back against a waggon-wheel, keeping the Zulus at bay with his cutlass; but a Zulu crept up behind him, and stabbed him through the spokes." Hallam Parr: *Sketch of the Kaffir and Zulu Wars*; (also published by Leonaur). Lieut. A. B. Milne, R.N., was at the time with Lord Chelmsford.

★★★★★★

The little commissariat and hospital post at Rorke's Drift, ten miles to the rear, was afterwards attacked by the victorious Zulus, but was heroically defended by Lieutenants Chard, R.E., and Bromhead (24th Regiment), until the enemy was beaten off, leaving 350 dead behind him. Lord Chelmsford did not learn what had befallen his camp until comparatively late in the day. On the 23rd, after having passed an anxious night in the devastated camp, he moved back to Rorke's Drift.

Colonel Wood, from his post at Kambula, harried the enemy very successfully, though not without some reverses. Colonel Pearson crossed the Tugela River near its mouth on January 22nd, and on the same day was attacked by, and defeated, a Zulu force at the Inyezane River. He then resumed his march, and next day reached Ekowe. (Or Etshowe.) He had intended to move upon Cetewayo's *kraal* at Ulundi, but, upon hearing of the disaster at Isandhlwana, he decided to hold Ekowe fort, sending, however, his mounted troops back to the border. He retained about 1,300 men, inclusive of the Naval Brigade, and plenty of ammunition; and he held his position until his relief on April 3rd. He was never attacked.

After Isandhlwana and Rorke's Drift, Lord Chelmsford evacuated Zululand, and awaited reinforcements. At the beginning of April, he advanced to relieve Ekowe, and, on the 2nd, defeated the enemy at Ginginhlovo, six miles south of the Inyezane River. Pearson, freed on the 3rd, returned to the Tugela. From that time forward no considerable action was fought until July 4th, just after the arrival in South Africa of Sir Garnet Wolseley to take over the supreme command. On

The Naval Brigade from the Active in the Zulu War

that day Lord Chelmsford signally defeated the Zulus at Ulundi, and virtually ended the war; and on August 28th Cetewayo was captured in the Ingome Forest by Major Richard Marter, of the King's Dragoon Guards. The Zulu king was sent to Port Durnford, where, embarking in the transport *Natal*, under the charge of Lieutenant Crawford Caffin, he was escorted to Cape Town by the gunboat *Forester*, 4, Lieutenant Sidney Glenton Smith.

The general course of the war having been thus briefly summarised, the share taken in it by the Royal Navy may be followed in somewhat greater detail.

It has been mentioned that the *Active* disembarked a detachment at Durban on November 19th, 1878, and that Commodore Francis William Sullivan sent it to the neighbouring Zululand boundary line. (Sullivan, Rear-Adm. Dec. 31, 1878. Soon afterwards Commod. Fredk. Win. Richards arrived in the *Boadicea*, Sullivan, however, remaining on the station for some little time, and surrendering the command only on Mar. 24.) This detachment garrisoned Fort Pearson, on the Natal side of the mouth of the Tugela, and established and worked a pontoon, by which eventually Pearson's column crossed into Zululand. The naval force consisted of 174 blue-jackets, 42 marines, about 14 West African *Kroomen*, two 12-prs., one 10-barrelled Gatling gun, and two rocket tubes, under Commander Henry John Fletcher Campbell (acting Captain); Lieutenants Robert William Craigie, and William des Voeux Hamilton; Sub-Lieutenant Thomas Guthrie Fraser; Navigating Sub-Lieutenant John George Heugh; Staff-Surgeon Henry Frederick Norbury; Surgeon William Thompson; Lieutenant (R.M.) Townley Ward Dowding; Midshipman Lewis Cadwallader Coker, (died in Ekowe); and Boatswain John Cotter. Lieutenant Archibald Berkeley Milne, who was also landed from the *Active*, was attached as naval *aide-de-camp* to Lord Chelmsford's staff.

On December 20th, 1878, the *Tenedos*, 12, Captain Edward Stanley Adeane, arrived at Durban; and on January 1st, 1879, she also landed a Naval Brigade of 3 officers and 58 men, under Lieutenant Anthony Kingscote, who took them to the Zulu side of the mouth of the Tugela, and there built and garrisoned Fort Tenedos.

When Colonel Pearson advanced into Zululand, he was accompanied by the *Active's* Brigade, of the behaviour of which at the action of the Inyezane River on January 22nd, Commander Campbell wrote, (Report to R.-Ad. Sullivan):—

All were remarkably steady under fire. Those employed on the ridge were exposed to a cross fire for nearly two hours, after which they responded to my call for the final assault with alacrity, and led the rush till success was secured. I particularly recommend Lieutenant Hamilton, whose company was in front during the action. Sub-Lieutenant Fraser also did good service in command of the reserve, being under fire the whole time. Boatswain Cotter was most successful with the rockets I placed in his charge. Lieutenant Craigie . . . rendered valuable services as acting-adjutant. . . . I beg to recommend to your notice E. White, P. O. First Class, who continued to fight after having been struck by a ball; E. Futcher, P. O. First Class, who took a leading part in the movements; Thomas Harding, ordinary, who was the first unmounted man in enemy's position.

The Brigade had seven men wounded.

In the meantime, the disaster of Isandhlwana had struck Natal with panic, and had caused the Colony to fear an immediate Zulu invasion. When the *Boadicea*, 16, Commodore Frederick William Richards, which had gone from England to relieve the *Active*, reached the Cape, smallpox had broken out in her, so that it was impossible for her to land a Brigade as promptly as she would otherwise have landed one. There was also small-pox in the *Flora*, guardship at Simon's Bay, so that people could not be drawn from her. Chelmsford's column was shattered; Pearson's was shut up; Wood's was fighting in the enemy's country; the cry was for steady fighting men. It was unexpectedly answered from the sea.

The screw iron frigate *Shah*, 26, Captain Richard Bradshaw, on her way home from the Pacific, called at St. Helena, the governor of which island, having heard of Isandhlwana, allowed him to take on board all the available troops, 200 in number. With them Bradshaw sailed for Simon's Bay on February 12th, arriving on February 23rd. He acted on his own responsibility, and was rewarded with the full approval of the Admiralty and the country. From Simon's Bay he was ordered up to Durban, where, on March 7th, he disembarked 16 officers and 378 men, under Commander John William Brackenbury, thus at once doubling the strength of the naval detachments in, and on the borders of, Natal.

On March 18th the *Boadicea* also was able to land a Brigade of 10 officers and 218 men, under Commander Francis Romilly. These two detachments, together with the one from the *Tenedos*, joined the force which presently proceeded to the relief of Ekowe, where the *Active's* contingent remained shut up with Pearson. They had a conspicuous share, consequently, in the battle of Ginginhlovo on April 2nd, 1879, when Brackenbury was in command of the united Brigades, Commodore Richards, however, being present. (Richards's disps. of Apr. 11, and Sept. 13, 1879. The Royal Marines were commanded in the battle by Capt. Joseph Philips, R. M.L.I.) The navy held the corners of the British square, and its guns rendered excellent service. The naval casualties that day were one officer (Staff-Surgeon William Digby Longfield) and 6 men wounded.

On April 4th, the day after the relief of Ekowe, Acting-Captain Campbell, of the *Active*, was placed by the commodore in command of the entire Brigade, then numbering upwards of 800 officers and men; and he retained that position until the *Active's* and *Shah's* contingents re-embarked on July 21st; but, up to the time of the general forward movement in June, Commander Brackenbury commanded that part of the Brigade which remained with the advanced force on the Inyezane River. The *Tenedos's* contingent had by that time been withdrawn, having re-embarked on May 8th. Says Commodore Richards:—

> During the occupation of Fort Chelmsford, several reconnaissances were made for the examination of the different drifts for the passage of the Emlalazi River; in which Commanders Brackenbury and Romilly, and Sub-Lieutenants (James) Startin, and (Arthur Hale) Smith-Dorrien took part. These reconnaissances were made under fire. The division encamped on the Emlalazi plain on the coast, at the position known as Port Durnford; and, on the arrival of the *Forester* with the surf-boats, and of storeships, for the purpose of opening communications with the shore at that place, the services of the Brigade were immediately put in requisition for this operation; and so well was the work done that in three weeks' time over 2000 tons of commissariat and ordnance stores had been landed on the open beach, to the entire relief of the land transport.

The last naval contingent to re-embark was that from the *Boadicea*, which returned to its ship on July 31st. The only other vessel which had any of her people serving ashore during the war was the *Flora*, which sent two officers to the front on April 20th; but it may be mentioned that two members of the Royal Naval Artillery Volunteers went up country at their own expense, and joined the *Active's* Brigade, and that some others attached themselves to other commands. A Royal Marine battalion sent out from England was so unfortunate as to land in Africa too late to participate in the final actions of the campaign. It was also a matter of great disappointment to both the Royal Navy and the Royal Marines that they were not represented at the Battle of Ulundi, save by Lieutenant A. B. Milne, who still served as Lord Chelmsford's *aide-de-camp*, and who was wounded; but they had the satisfaction, previous to their re-embarkation, of being inspected by Sir Garnet Wolseley, who, in his General Order, declared:—

> The conduct of the men has been admirable, and their bearing in action in every way worthy of the service to which they belong, while they have worked hard and cheerfully in their laborious duties, which constitute so important a part of all military operations.

The *Forester*, 4, Lieutenant Sidney Glenton Smith, made herself indispensable in surveying the coast with a view to finding suitable landing-places for troops and supplies; and she enabled Port Durnford to be utilised as a base. Her second visit to that neighbourhood was made on April 22nd. On the 24th, when the gunboat was lying off Port Durnford, and two of her boats were sounding close in shore, a large body of Zulus suddenly appeared and opened fire from the beach. The boats retired, firing as they went; and the *Forester* then shelled the coast and bush, killing a number of cattle, and probably causing other casualties. (*Natal Mercury.*)

The transport service during the war was managed mainly by Captain Guy Ouchterlony Twiss, Commander Edward Henry Meggs Davis, Lieutenants Crawford Caffin, and Frederick Streatfield Pelly, Staff-Surgeon James Hamilton Martin, and Paymaster William Besley Ramsey (all borne in the *Boadicea*), and by Lieutenant Alexander Milne Gardiner, of the *Shah*. Among the numerous officers whose names were mentioned in the dispatches, the following were rewarded with honours or promotion:—

To be K.C.B.: Rear-Admiral Francis William Sullivan, Nov. 27, 1879.

To be C.B.: Captains Frederick William Richards, Richard Bradshaw, Henry John Fletcher Campbell, and Fleet-Surgeon

Henry Frederick Norbury, Nov. 27, 1879.

To be C.M.G.: Captains Edward Stanley Adeane, and John William Brackenbury, Dec. 19, 1879.

To be Captain: Commander Henry John Fletcher Campbell, July 3, 1879.

To be Commanders: Lieutenants Crawford Caffin, and Anthony Kingscote, July 3, 1879, and Frederick Ralph Carr, (gazetted, but subsequently cancelled), and Robert William Craigie, Nov. 6, 1879.

To be Lieutenants: Sub-Lieutenants James Startin, and Thomas Guthrie Fraser, and Navigating Sub-Lieutenant John George Heugh, Nov. 6, 1879.

To be Chief-Boatswain: Boatswain John Cotter, Nov. 6, 1879.

To be Major, R.M.: Captain Joseph Philips, R.M., Nov. 9, 1879.

To be Captain, R.M.: Lieutenant Townley Ward Dowding, R.M., Nov. 15, 1879.

To be Fleet-Surgeons: Staff-Surgeons Henry Frederick Norbury, and William Digby Longfield, July 3, 1879.

Minor Operations, 1878–1881

In 1878 much needless importance was given, in Parliament and elsewhere, to an incident which had occurred at Tanna, in the New Hebrides, in September, 1877. The schooner *Beagle*, 1, Lieutenant Crawford Caffin, had proceeded thither in order to make inquiries with respect to the murder of a white man named W. Easterbrook; had demanded the murderer from the head men of the village of Numukur; had been refused; and, in concert with the commander of the schooner *Renard*, 1, Lieutenant Horace John Moore Pugh, had seized a number of hostages. As a result, one Nokwai, a younger brother and accomplice of the actual murderer, had been surrendered, though the chief criminal, Yuhmaga, had not been given up. Nokwai had thereupon been sentenced to death, and on September 25th had been hanged at the fore yard-arm of the *Beagle*. Before dying the prisoner had admitted his guilt. (Caffin to Hoskins, Sept. 26, 1877.)

In his comments to the Admiralty on the case, Commodore Anthony Hiley Hoskins, while expressing the opinion that Caffin's proceedings deserved general approval, had added that:—

It would have been more satisfactory had the man executed

been the actual murderer, Yuhmaga, and had it been clearly established that Easterbrook was free from all imputation of having given provocation. I also think that it would have been better in any case that the execution should have taken place on shore—if possible, on the scene of the murder: and I purpose so informing Lieut. Caffin.

Upon these facts certain well-meaning people based an agitation which lasted for five or six months. Eventually it was decided that Lieutenant Caffin was not deserving of censure, but that, upon the whole, it was undesirable that executions of the kind which had taken place should be carried out onboard H.M. ships. (Procs. of Ho. of Com., Aug. 5, 1878.)

The *London*, store ship at Zanzibar, to which Captain Hamilton Edward George Earle was appointed in the summer of 1878, continued to be invaluable as a centre of operations against the slave trade. Her boats were unceasingly active, and on several occasions her officers and men were under fire. A petty officer named Cornelius Duggan specially distinguished himself. In a dinghy, with one seaman, William Clark, only, he was stationed one night to watch a channel between an outlying island and Pemba, with a view to noting whether slaves were being removed from the former. In the small hours, two canoes full of people suddenly quitted the small island.

Although his possible opponents were at least thirty or forty in number, (about half seem to have been slaves, and half Arab dealers and their men), Duggan instantly gave chase. The Arabs opened fire, and several bullets struck the dinghy, while one passed through Duggan's clothes. The pursuit was, however, most pluckily persisted in, until one of the dinghy's oars broke; whereupon Duggan and his companion had to content themselves with emptying their revolvers after the fugitives. (Corr. in *A. and N. Gazette*, Dec. 14 and Dee. 28, 1878.) At about the same time Sub-Lieutenant Neville Edmund Cornwall Legh behaved with great gallantry in an affair at Uzi, and also made numerous captures of slaves at Pemba.

Early in 1879 the white inhabitants of Sitka, in the United States' territory of Alaska, had reason to fear that their Indian neighbours were about to rise and massacre them, and, having in vain petitioned their own government for assistance, sent an urgent appeal for help to the senior British naval officer at Esquimalt, the result being that in February the *Osprey*, 6, Commander the Hon. Henry Holmes à

Court, was ordered to the threatened spot, where she remained until the arrival on the scene of a United States' corvette.

During the *Osprey's* presence off the coast, her commander was boastingly informed by the Indians that, whenever they might choose to do so, they could make themselves masters of the little United States' revenue steamer *Oliver Wolcott* which lay there. To prevent the possibility of anything of the sort, à Court, by permission of the American naval officer in charge of the feeble craft, put a body of British bluejackets and a Gatling gun on board of her to supplement her crew; and with these the *Oliver Wolcott* undertook an expedition to intercept some war canoes belonging to the turbulent chiefs. (*A. and N. Gazette*, Mar. 22 and Apr. 12, 1879: Corr. of *Times* and *Hampshire Telegraph*.)

In the Pacific several small punitive expeditions were undertaken by Her Majesty's ships in the course of 1879. A boat's crew belonging to the British trader *Mystery* had been massacred by the natives of Aoba, or Lepers' Island, in the New Hebrides, and there had been other murders of white men in the Louisiade Archipelago and elsewhere. The vessels employed were the *Cormorant*, 6, Commander James Andrew Thomas Bruce, which visited, among other places, Brooker Island, New Guinea, and Brother Island, shelling and burning villages at each; the *Wolverene*, 17, Commodore John Crawford Wilson; *Conflict*, 1, schooner. Lieutenant John George Musters; and *Beagle*, 1, schooner, Lieutenant Thomas de Hoghton, which proceeded to Aoba, Marau Sound, and the Louisiades; and the *Danae*, 12, Captain John Child Purvis (2), which also went to Marau Sound, in the Solomon Islands.

Wilson spared the Marau natives, understanding that they had already been sufficiently dealt with by traders, but inflicted severe punishment at Ferguson Island, and in the Louisiades. Purvis, being subsequently despatched to Marau Sound, where, after all, the people had not been taught a sufficiently instructive lesson, destroyed some villages and canoes, but suffered a loss of one killed and two wounded. (*A. and N. Gazette*, Mar. 29, Apr. 19, May 24, Aug. 16 and 30, Sept. 6, and Dec. 6, 1879.)

Elsewhere some useful police work was done in the same year by the *Boxer*, 4, Commander Arthur Hildebrand Alington, first on the west coast of Africa, where the gun-vessel was employed to lodge a protest against the French occupation of the island of Matacong, was engaged in the delimitation of the Liberian boundary, and hoisted the British flag on the Scarcies River; and subsequently off the coast of

Haiti, where, in the summer, a revolution was in progress. At Port-au-Prince, besides protecting British interests, she embarked a number of refugees, including a rebel leader who had sought shelter in the British consulate; and more than once, while lying there, she was threatened with attack from the shore.

Unhappily, owing to the insanitary condition of the town and of the people whom she saved from it, yellow fever attacked her officers and crew, and carried off, among others, Lieutenant Edward Henry *Arden*, and Paymaster James King Bell. The *Decoy*, 4, Lieutenant Victor Edward John Brenton von Donop, in the earlier half of 1879, rendered useful police service in the Coanza River, where the negroes had risen and murdered two white people and several natives.

More serious business fell to the lot of another vessel of the West African command, the *Pioneer*, 6, paddle. Lieutenant John Leslie Burr. In April, 1879, she proceeded into the Scarcies River with a force under Governor Rowe, of Sierra Leone, in order to re-hoist the British flag, which had been hoisted there in March by the *Boxer* in face of some opposition, and which had afterwards been hauled down by the natives.

The island of Kikoukeh, which was the chief point annexed, was occupied as a set-off to Matacong, which, a short time before, had been annexed by the French. Lieutenant Burr had some trouble with the natives, who resented the seizure of their territory; but he managed the affair with singular success.

A little later he took his ship about 700 miles up the River Niger, carrying presents from the imperial and colonial governments for the Emir of Nupi. On his return he attacked and destroyed the village of Onitsha, the inhabitants of which, not for the first time, had murdered British traders and committed other outrages; and, making a short overland expedition, he burnt another town about three miles from the river. The effect of his action was excellent, and earned him the thanks of the African Company, which also presented him with a piece of plate. (Disps., and *A. and N. Gazette*, June 7, Dec. 6, Dec. 20, 1879.)

The African slave-trade languished, though a few captures of *dhows* were made upon the east coast, especially by the *Spartan*, 12, Captain Richard Edward Tracey, by the *Vestal*, 9, Commander Dashwood Goldie Tandy, and by the boats of the *London*, Captain Hamilton Edward George Earle. In the Malay Archipelago, however, the kidnapping piratical tribes, the Balinini and Illanuns, were so active in seizing fishermen whom they subsequently sold as slaves along the east coast of Borneo, that, at the desire of Governor Treacher, of Labuan, the *Kestrel*, 4, Commander Frederick Edwards, proceeded against them in August, 1879.

Having traced certain outrages to the inhabitants of the Balinini village of Tarrebas, Edwards invited the local chief to pay him a visit on board the gun-vessel. The man made excuses, and declined to appear; whereupon, after due notice had been given, Tarrebas, and about fifteen piratical craft, many of which had bullet-proof bulwarks of iron-wood, were burnt. (*Straits Times* in *A. and N. Gazette*, Nov. 8, 1879.) Shortly afterwards, with the *Encounter*, 14, Captain the Hon. Albert Denison Somerville Denison, the *Kestrel* took part in a demonstration in the Larut River, on the west coast of the Malay peninsula, with a view to overawing the natives who threatened disturbances.

Early in 1880 the Royal Navy sustained a disaster somewhat similar to the loss of the *Eurydice* in 1878. (See Appendix of Ships Lost.) The sixth-rate *Atalanta*, employed on training service, sailed from Bermuda for England on February 1st and was never heard of again. On June 29th a reward was offered by the Admiralty for information concerning her, but it was never claimed. There were lost in the ship Captain Francis Stirling, the crew of 113 officers and men, and 170 ordinary seamen who were under training.

A committee which was appointed to inquire into the vessel's efficiency reported, (Sessional Papers, 1881, Report of Atalanta Committee), to the effect that: the *Atalanta* was sound when she left England for the West Indies in November, 1879; she was on the whole a very stable ship, save at large angles of keel; Captain Stirling was most able and experienced; the other officers had been carefully chosen; and nothing could be more satisfactory than the character of the crew. All that is known and that bears on her fate is that storms of exceptional violence raged at that time in the part of the Atlantic which she would have had to cross.

Just before her last cruise the ship had been very thoroughly repaired in the dockyards. The original estimate had been £11,000, but it had grown to £28,000. As the *Atalanta* had been built in 1844, and as it was estimated that a new ship of the class could be had for £36,000, it was naturally argued at the time that she was not worth so large an expenditure.

From a comparison of her dimensions with those of the *Eurydice*—

Ship.	Length between Perpendicular.	Length for Tonnage.	Beam.	Depth.	Builder's Measurement.
	Ft. In.	Ft. In.	Ft. In.	Ft. In.	Tons.
Atalanta . . .	131 0	107 2	40 3	10 10	923
Eurydice . . .	141 3	117 10	38 4	8 9	921

It will be seen that the *Atalanta* should have had considerable advantage in point of stability. (Brassey, *British Fleet*, iv.)

In the same year the Eastern question once more, necessitated action on the part of the great Powers. It had been decided at the Berlin Conference that Turkey should hand over Dulcigno to Montenegro; but, although the resources of diplomacy had been exhausted, the Porte still refused to carry that decision into effect. England, therefore, proposed, and France, Russia, Austria, and Italy agreed, that a combined naval demonstration should be made off the Albanian coast, there being an understanding that no troops were to be landed. It was further agreed to regard as commander-in-chief the senior flag-officer present, (*Times*, Sept. 13, 1880, etc.), and thus Vice-Admiral Sir Frederick Beauchamp Seymour, then in command of the British Mediterranean fleet, assumed command of the allied squadrons at Ragusa on September 20th, 1880.

The ships of the Royal Navy present were the *Alexandra* and *Téméraire*, ironclads, with the *Condor*, gun-vessel, and the despatch-boat *Helicon*. The display was enough. Negotiations followed, and on November 26th Dulcigno was handed over to Montenegro. Consequent on this it was determined that the squadrons should part company after communicating their respective destinations; and on December 5th the force dispersed.

Early in 1881 the sloop *Wild Swan*, 6, Commander Seymour Henry Pelham Dacres, was ordered to cooperate with the Portuguese authorities, who were making efforts to suppress the slave trade which had long been carried on by the Makuas of the Mozambique coast. With that object she left Zanzibar on January 22nd, and proceeded down the coast to Chuluwan, subsequently moving, in company with some Portuguese gunboats, to Conducia Bay, where she arrived on February 12th. A Portuguese landing-party, which was presently disembarked, was accompanied by Commander Dacres, Sub-Lieutenant Arthur Henry Stuart Elwes, Clerk Warwick Arthur Green, and three men from the sloop; but the only important work done by the British was accomplished by the *Wild Swan's* guns, and by that vessel's rocket apparatus in her steam cutter. (*A. & N. Gaz.*, Feb. 26, Mar. 12 and 26, 1881; Letters of Offrs.) The behaviour of the Portuguese on shore was not good; and, had it not been for the support afforded by the ships, the landed force would have met with serious disaster.

The First Boer War, 1880–1881

On December 16th, 1880, the Boers of the Transvaal, after a brief experience of British rule, (consequent upon the annexation by Sir Theophilus Shepstone, who, in 1877, had been sent into the country, and who saw no other way of protecting the settlers against the natives), had re-proclaimed the South African Republic, and then, without delay, had laid siege to nearly all the British military posts in the country.

General Sir George Pomeroy Colley who, at the time, was governor and commander-in-chief in Natal, and high commissioner for South-East Africa, began immediate preparations, though on a very inadequate scale, for the relief of the threatened towns and the suppression of rebellion, and, while collecting such military forces as were within reach, appealed for help from the navy. The appeal reached Commodore Frederick William Richards, C.B., of the *Boadicea*, 16, a few hours after that vessel's arrival off Durban, on January 5th, 1881, and was instantly and loyally responded to.

On the following day Commander Francis Romilly, of the *Boadicea*, with whom were Lieutenants Cornwallis Jasper Trower, and Reginald Purves Cochran, and Sub-Lieutenant Augustus Lennox Scott, accompanied by Surgeon Edward Elphinstone Mahon, of the *Flora*, guardship at Simon's Bay, landed with 124 petty officers and men, two Gatling machine-guns, and a couple of rocket-tubes, and proceeded to Pietermaritzburg, there to place himself under Colley's orders. (Parl. Papers, 1881. Vol. LXVII. contains three Blue Books on S. Afr.)

The morning of January 28th, 1881, found the combined force encamped at Mount Prospect, inside a spur of the Draakensberg, opposite, and about four miles distant from, the pass of Laing's Nek, where the Boers were known to be in force and to have erected defences. At 6 a.m. camp was struck: two companies of infantry, and Lieutenant Cochran, with 40 *Boadicea's* and the two Gatlings, were left behind to hold three entrenched positions for the defence of the *laager*; and at 6.10 a.m., Colley, with the remaining 1211 officers and men, (besides 196 horses and 9 guns), moved forward to the attack. The *Boadicea's* 4 officers and 84 men, with their rocket-tubes, were in the centre of the column.

At 9 a.m. Colley, with whom was the Commodore, placed his guns on an undulating ridge facing the *nek*, and 2200 yards from it, and ordered Romilly and his detachment to take up a station in advance. Behind knolls above and to the right, and about 1700 yards off, bodies of Boers could be seen. Only on the left was the position assailable. A mealie field and the garden of a farm house enabled the Naval Brigade finally to bring its rocket-tubes within about 1500 yards from the pass, and to post a covering party in skirmishing order along a stone wall where, to the right, the line was continued by a company of the 60th Rifles. Half an hour later, when these dispositions had been completed, the guns and rocket-tubes opened upon the enemy; and, as soon as it was supposed that the bombardment had shaken the Boers, the British infantry and mounted troops charged up a grassy spur on the right of the *nek* to assault the left of the hostile entrenchments.

For a time, success seemed possible; yet the Boers fired so well and so heavily that soon the troops were driven down again with serious loss, nearly all the mounted officers falling. The enemy not only followed up, but also appeared on the British right. The Naval Brigade sent rockets in the latter direction, and presently found itself engaged on both flanks as well as in front. But for the stone wall, it must have lost heavily. As a matter of fact, it had only two killed, (including Gunner's Mate Henry Ransome, who was mentioned in desps), ere it was ordered to fall back on the guns.

After the retirement had been effected, a flag of truce was sent out, and the dead and wounded were brought in. At 4 p.m., the force returned to camp, and learnt from Lieutenant Cochran that, during its absence, a body of 400 Boers had reconnoitred the laager, but had moved away without attacking. Colley, in his despatch, expressed his indebtedness to Commodore Richards and the Brigade, and made special laudatory mention of Surgeon Mahon, Lieutenant Trower, and Sub-Lieutenant Scott. (Colley to Sec. for War, Feb. 1, 1881.)

The general decided to remain at Mount Prospect until reinforcements, which were on their way in the transports *Euphrates, Crocodile,* and *Tamar,* could reach the front; and, in the meantime, at his request. Commodore Richards caused an additional 50 men, with two field-guns, to disembark from the *Boadicea* and the *Dido,* (Captain Compton Edward Domvile), under Lieutenant Henry Asgill Ogle, of the latter vessel. (Richards to Admlty., Feb. 7, 1881.) These men, however, did not join until after February 8th, when Colley fought the Battle of

Ingogo with the object of keeping open his communications with Newcastle. In that unfortunate action the Naval Brigade had no share.

The Boers made no important advance, but concentrated most of their energies upon the strengthening of the works in the pass leading from Natal into the Transvaal. Dominating the western extremity of their lines was the flat-topped hill of Majuba, which, nevertheless, they made no attempt to hold. Colley, reinforced during the second and third weeks of February, came to the conclusion that Majuba was the key to the enemy's position, and, in an evil hour, decided to occupy it with a detachment which proved utterly inadequate to the end in view.

At 10 p.m., therefore, on February 26th, the general in person moved from Mount Prospect with 554 officers and men only, including 64 petty officers and men of the navy under Commander Romilly, Lieutenant Trower, Sub-Lieutenant Scott, and Surgeon Mahon. Neither guns nor rocket-tubes were taken. Small though the original detachment was, three companies which had left camp with it were dropped at various points to guard the line of communications, so that but four companies and the little Naval Brigade reached the front.

The top of the hill was reached by a very precipitous route; but all the men were at their assigned stations by 4 a.m. on Sunday, the 27th, there having been no opposition whatsoever. A section of the Brigade, under Lieutenant Trower, remained near that end of the mountain where the ascent had been made. The rest of the force was placed in a hollow at the end closest to the Boer lines; and at dawn the enemy's *laagers* could be seen below. The summit was not entrenched, in spite of the fact that its conformation was such that the people holding it could not properly command the exterior slopes without dangerously exposing themselves; and an extraordinary degree of overconfidence seems to have prevailed.

Soon after daylight the Boers showed some signs of activity about the base of Majuba, and steady firing followed; but for a time, it did not look as if any serious object had occurred to the enemy, who, on the other hand, was deemed to be throwing away his ammunition. Sub-Lieutenant Scott, with the second section of the Naval Brigade, was presently sent to line the edge of the mountain top in the rear, and, a little later, part of the 58th Regiment was withdrawn from the left, where its post was taken by portions of the first and second sections. The men lay down under good cover, seeing very little of the Boers, most of whom appeared to be out of range, and firing seldom.

Trower and Scott were with them.

So also, was Romilly during great part of the morning; but at about 11 a.m. a dozen men were ordered to be sent from the left to the front, and Romilly went across to fetch them. In returning, the gallant commander was shot through the body, and fell close to the general. Mahon attended to the mortally wounded officer, who presently was carried into the hollow, out of reach of gun-fire. At about that time, Scott, with six men, was stationed by Trower on a ledge about twenty feet below the summit on the right side of the mountain, near the track by which the ascent had been made.

During the whole of the morning, and more especially during the half hour or so after noon, the people on the top of Majuba had their attention held by the general firing, and failed to see that a small force of Boers was working its way stealthily up the mountain, covered by the much larger force below. Shortly before 1 p.m., the firing increased greatly. Hearing that the enemy was close at hand, Scott ventured to take his men from the ledge, and lead them to the point which appeared to be most threatened. He found the 92nd Highlanders and part of the 58th Regiment firing on the foe, who was then nearing the top, but he was at once ordered back by the general. A few moments later the Boers gained the summit, and the British began a retreat which soon became a rout.

Colley, until he fell, shot through the head, and his officers, did all that lay in their power to stem the panic; but the frightened troops were not to be stayed. Many rushed at break-neck speed down the almost precipitous sides of the mountain, exposed to a terrible fire from the Boers, and, for the most part, losing their arms in the descent. Seeing how few in number were the assailants, the flight is one of the most extraordinary in history. It can be explained only by the completeness of the surprise, and by the men's sudden realisation of the fact that no due precautions had been taken by their own leaders.

Earlier in the day a hospital had been established behind a ridge of rocks near the centre of the plateau. The enemy crowned the rocks, and fired upon all indiscriminately, (Mahon to Richards, Mar. 4), shooting down a doctor while he was caring for the wounded. Perceiving how things had gone, Surgeon Mahon, who but lately had quitted Romilly in order to cross to the hospital, returned to his commander's side, and, to save further slaughter of the wounded and non-combatants, hoisted a white flag. All the fugitives, however, were not then clear of the top, and firing continued on the summit. To avoid the bullets,

Mahon, and Assistant Sick-Berth Attendant Bevis, who was with him, lay down till the plateau was clear of their flying friends, and until the enemy was within a few paces from them. When they rose, they were not molested, and were suffered to carry poor Romilly to the hospital from the point where he had lain sheltered on the south-west front.

Throughout that afternoon and the following night Mahon remained on the mountain, seeking out and attending to the wounded, and receiving much kindly help from the enemy. He took upon himself to send four blue-jacket prisoners to carry Romilly back to camp; but, soon after they had started, they were ordered back by the enemy, the result being that the unfortunate commander had to lie in the open during the whole of the wet, dark, and chilly night of the 27th. At 6 a.m. on the 28th, Lieutenant Cochran came up from camp with a burial party, and with stretchers and medical comforts.

Of the fifty-three men who were buried on the summit, ten belonged to the Naval Brigade. But these were not the whole of the naval casualties. The *Boadicea* lost Lieutenant Trower, (lieut., Apr. 28, 1876), and 10 men killed, and Commander Romilly and 5 men mortally wounded. The *Dido* lost 3 men killed. In addition, 10 *Boadicea's* and 3 *Dido's* were wounded; so that of the total naval force engaged, 33 (being practically 50 *per cent.*) were put out of action. (Admlty. to Col. Off., May 2, enclosing Richards to Admlty. of Mar. 14, covering Ogle to Richards, Mar. 3, and Scott to Ogle, Mar. 1, 1881.)

Trower's body was found on the extreme ridge, and, being taken back to camp, was buried there. Romilly, (com., Apr. 11, 1877), died on March 2nd. A Boer *commandant* pointed out to Cochran the bodies of two men who had most bravely stood their ground and perished there. They were those of George Hammond and Samuel Witheridge, quarter-masters, R.N. Mahon, who reached camp at 5 p.m. on the 28th, with five ambulances full of wounded, behaved throughout with magnificent devotion and gallantry, and was specially promoted, (Staff-Surgeon, July 18, 1881.) In the opinion of all those who were left on the fatal hill, he deserved the Victoria Cross.

Upon the death of General Colley, the command of the troops devolved temporarily upon General Sir Evelyn Wood; and on March 4th, Captain Compton Edward Domvile, of the *Dido*, went up from Durban to take charge of the remnant of the Naval Brigade. On the same day a detachment of 50 seamen, who had been sent out in the *Danube*, (Merchant steamer), to fill vacancies, left for the front under Lieutenants George Morris Henderson, and Andrew Henry Farrell

Duncan. Sir Evelyn Wood went from Newcastle back to Pietermaritz-burg, where he assumed for the nonce the functions of governor of Natal; but ere the new permanent governor and commander-in-chief, General Sir Frederick Sleigh Roberts, arrived on the scene. Wood had held a prolonged conference with the Boer general, Piet Joubert, and had concluded an armistice, which resulted, on March 24th, in a peace.

This is not the place in which to enter into any wide criticism either of the tactics pursued by the British leaders in the field, or of the policy directed by Mr. Gladstone's government at home. Col-ley paid for his negligence and his contempt for the enemy with his life: Mr. Gladstone, who was animated by motives some at least of which were doubtless excellent, but who was congenitally incapable of understanding the Boer character, patched up an unsatisfactory ar-rangement which, it was generally felt, could not be lasting. In spite of what had happened at Laing's Nek, Majuba, and elsewhere, the Boers might have been brought to reason with comparative ease in March. They did not realise that fact, and they mistook British generosity and quixotism for pusillanimity. Less than twenty years later, both parties had to pay a frightful price for their misapprehensions. Yet in 1881, as in the subsequent struggle, the navy, happily, had nothing with which to reproach itself. (Among naval officers who did good service in Natal in connection with transport work were Capt. Hilary Gustavus Andoe and Lieut. Edward Chichester.)

The *Doterel*, 6-gun sloop of 1,137 tons, while at anchor off Sandy Point, Straits of Magellan, was destroyed by an explosion on April 26th, 1881. Commander Richard Evans, Lieutenant John Martin Stokes, three other officers, and seven men were saved, but the rest of the crew of 156 perished. The ship was a new one, being then on passage to the Pacific station for her maiden commission. Commander Evans reported that the explosion had been so sudden and destructive that there was no possibility of lowering boats to save life. He, with the surviving officers and men, was acquitted of all blame by the finding of the court-martial, September 3rd, 1881. (*Times*, Aug. 27 and Sept. 5, 1881.) It was decided that the destruction of the ship had been due to an explosion of gas given off by coal in the bunkers, and that this had communicated with the fore magazine, causing that also to explode. It was never proved how the explosions had originated, but it was sug-gested that, as the ship had been about to complete with coal, a light may have been introduced into one of the bunkers. Another theory was that the disaster had originated with a spontaneous explosion of xerotine siccative, a material which, on November 23rd of the same year, undoubtedly brought about an explosion in the *Triumph*, off Co-quimbo, and caused the loss of three lives.